Painting Nature with Clare

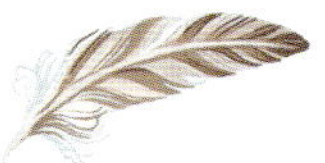

Create Beautiful Gouache Motifs of the Garden, Countryside, Sea, River and Forest

Clare Therese Gray

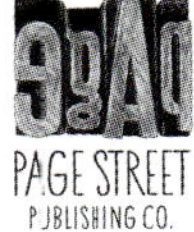
PAGE STREET PUBLISHING CO.

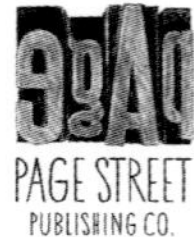

First published in 2021 by
Page Street Publishing Co.
27 Congress Street, Suite 105
Salem, MA 01970
www.pagestreetpublishing.com

Distributed by Macmillan, sales in Canada by The Canadian Manda Group.

25 24 23 22 21 1 2 3 4 5

ISBN-13: 9781645673705
ISBN-10: 1645673707

Library of Congress Control Number: 2021931353

Design by Melia Parsloe

Printed and bound in China

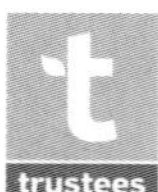

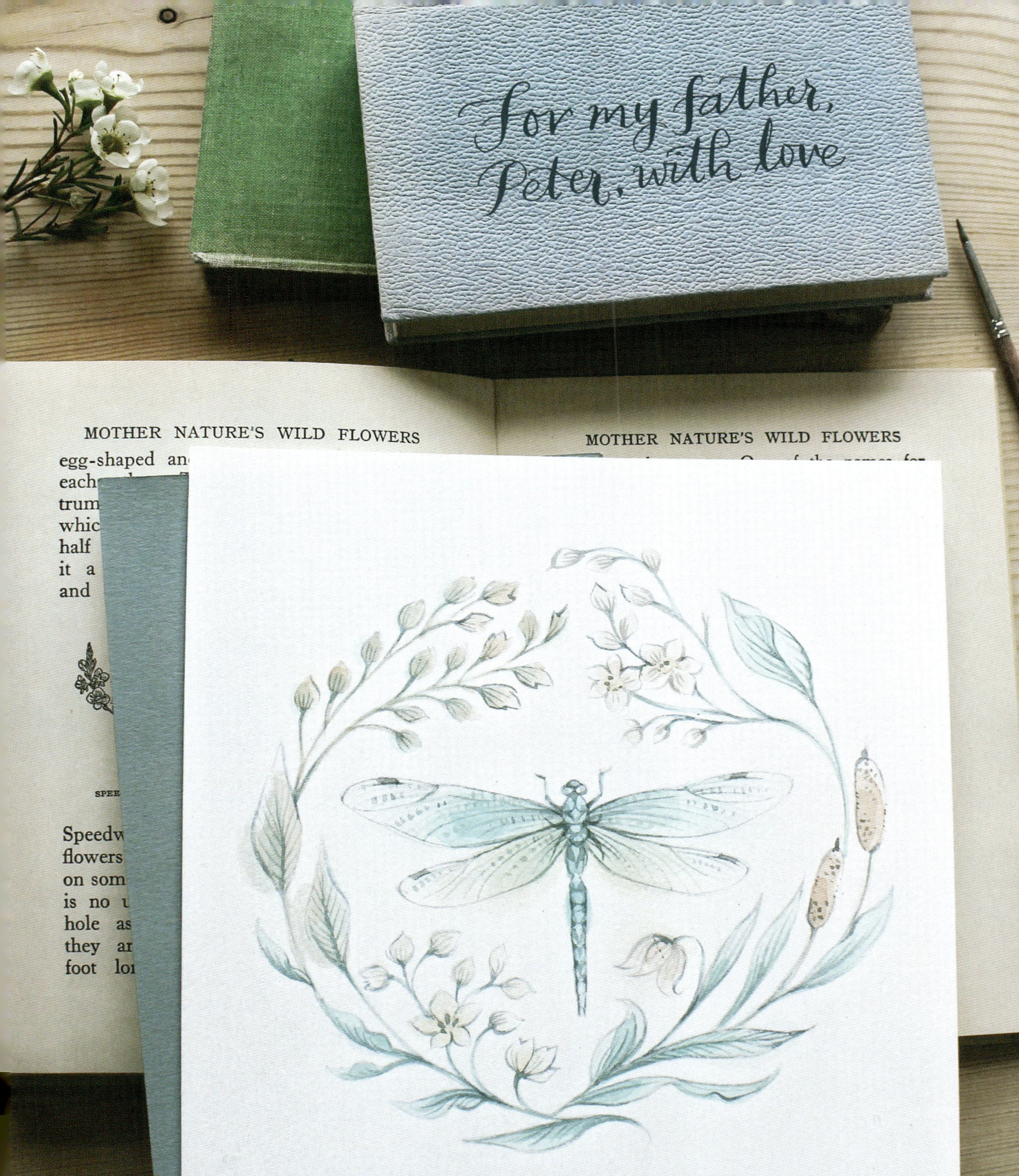
For my father,
Peter, with love
MOTHER NATURE'S WILD FLOWERS
MOTHER NATURE'S WILD FLOWERS

Table of Contents

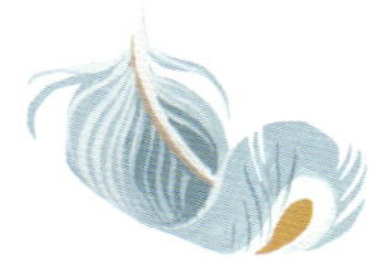

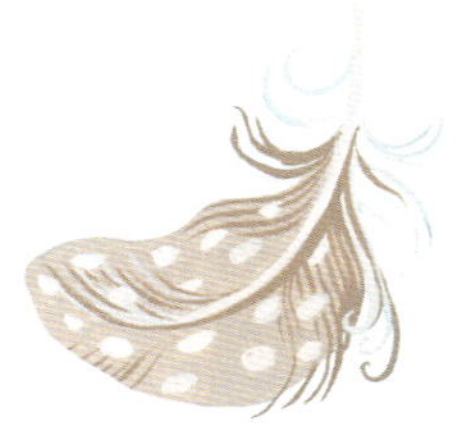

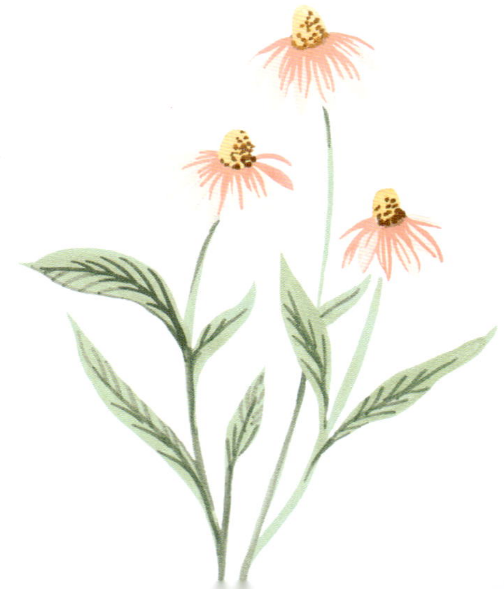

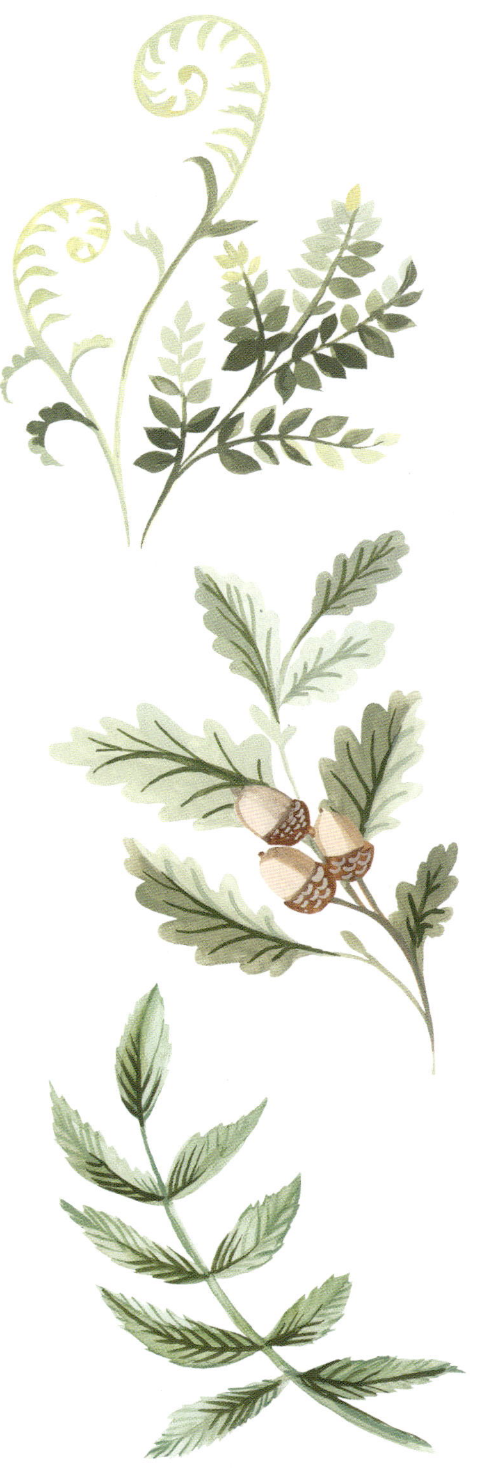

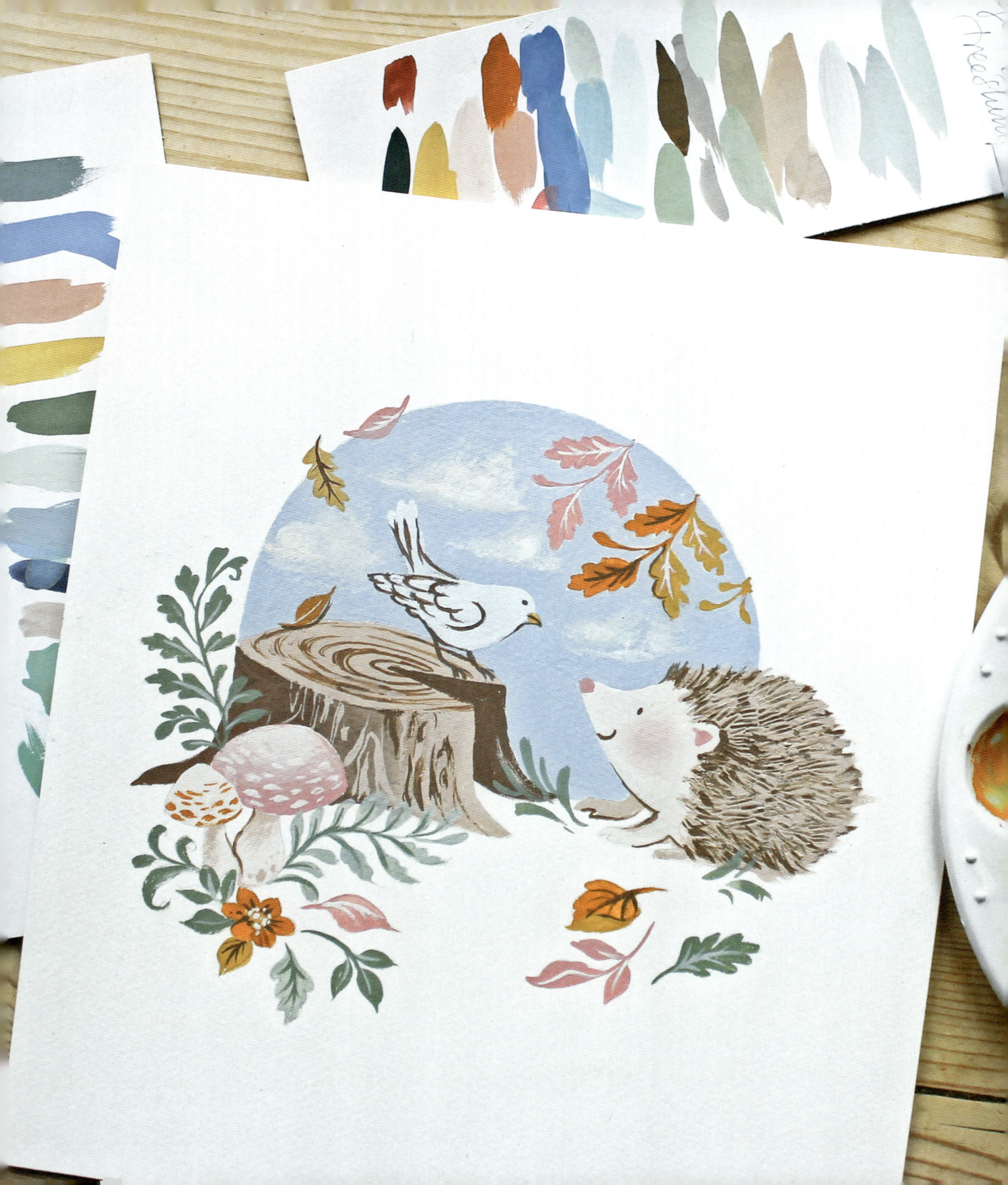

Introduction

Nature gouache has grown from two of my real passions—painting and the natural world.

In this practical, project-based book, I invite you on a journey through day and night, summer and winter, from close to home in your garden or local park, out into the countryside and forest, along rivers and down to the sea. We will create a spectrum of elements, scenes and patterns inspired by the flora, fauna and landscapes we find along the way.

I first stumbled across gouache painting when starting out as a freelance pattern designer. Its fast-drying nature appealed to me as it meant I could layer paint quickly and create a vibrant matte finish. I quickly realized I could replicate the effects I was familiar with in watercolor painting, but with the bonus of being able to mix with opaque white to create a rich range of pastel shades. This makes gouache ideal for digitalizing into print and great for photographing and posting on social media. Most of the projects in this book have been drawn from familiar subjects that I paint day to day in both my personal and professional work.

This book explores the potential of gouache to create a great variety of techniques. It is primarily a painting book, but as drawing is an integral part of the process, I begin each project by instructing you on how to compose the scene. I use darker guidelines to help with the basic composition of some projects and to break down elements into simple shapes. The introductory chapter is a handy reference and walks you through the basics of choosing and mixing colors as well as practical paint handling.

All the projects in the book are designed to be accessible to beginners, but with enough scope to engage and satisfy the more experienced amateur artist. Each chapter progresses from relatively simple pieces to slightly more complicated ones so you can challenge yourself, try new techniques and grow your skillset. However, you can also dip into the book wherever you fancy. It is certainly not necessary to work through it sequentially.

There are plenty of things you can do to nurture your own sources of inspiration. I would say the most important thing to do is draw. Draw from your imagination, but also refresh yourself by carving out some time to draw from life. It doesn't take much—just keep a small sketchbook and pencil that you can pop in your bag or coat pocket and have a play with leaves and flowers you might find in the garden, hedge or supermarket.

Wherever you are, I hope this book will help you find inspiration in the natural world and will give you the confidence to turn that inspiration into beautiful, original artwork of your own—designs, cards, invitations, even all-over patterns!

I would love to see how you get on! Find me on Instagram @claretheresegray and please do share your nature gouache painting journey using the hashtag #paintwithclare.

Clare

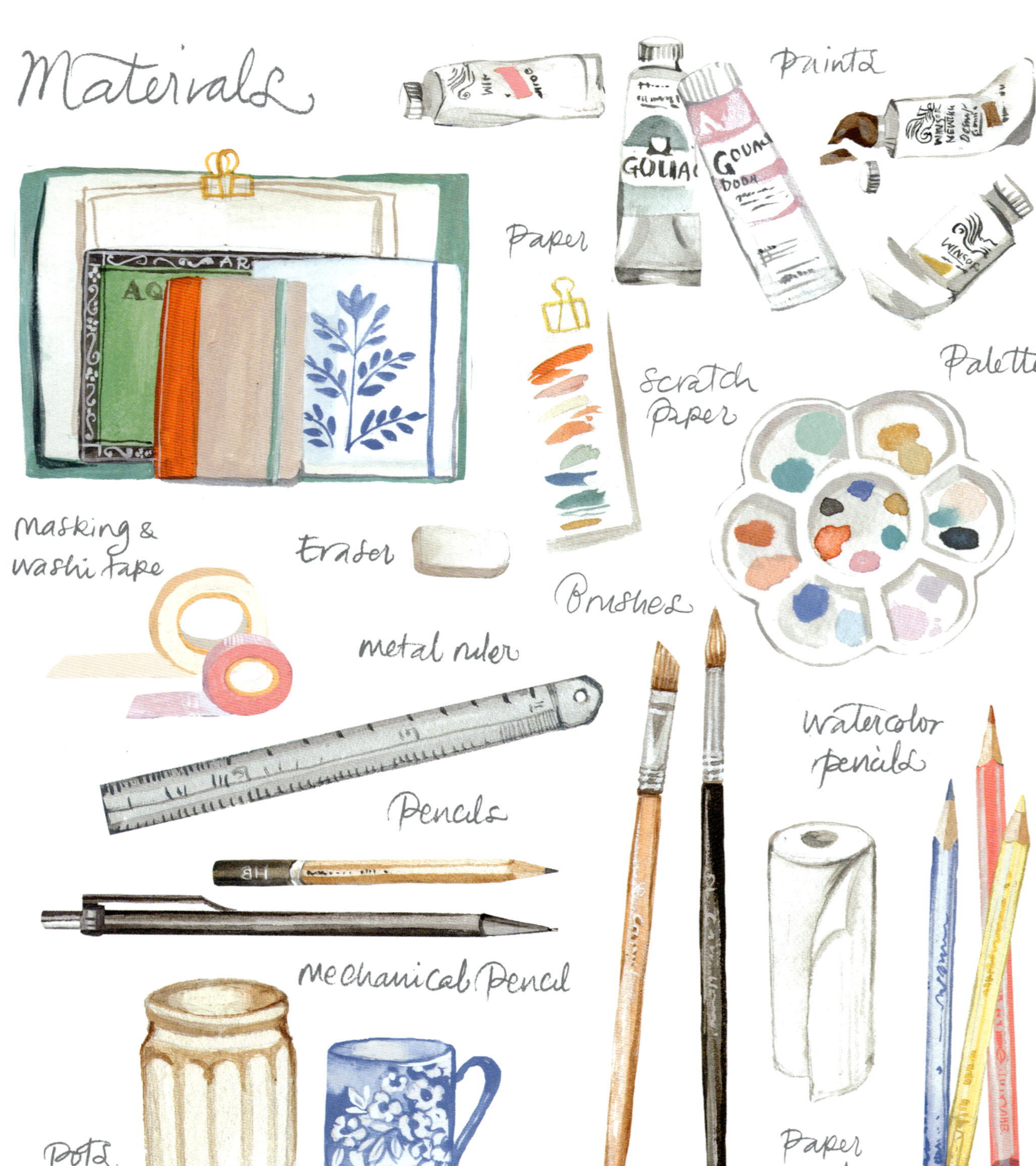
Materials
Paints
Paper
Scratch Paper
Palette
Masking & washi tape
Eraser
Brushes
metal ruler
Pencils
Watercolor pencils
Mechanical Pencil
Paper towels
Pots

Materials

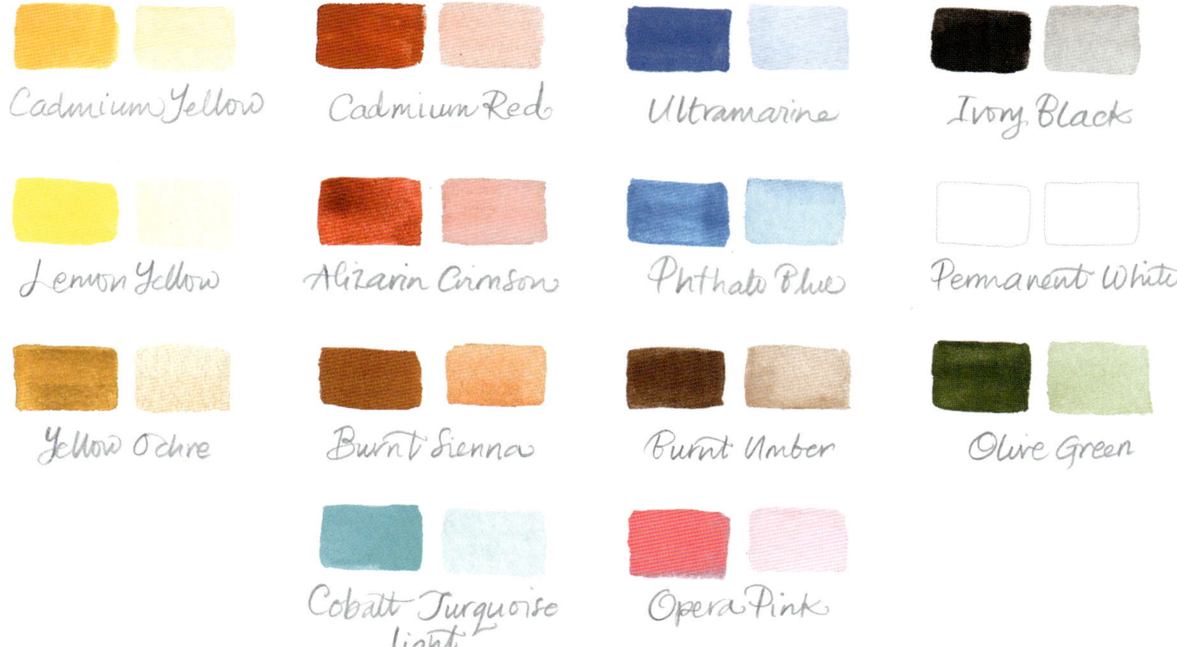

PAINT

I'm told that the correct way to pronounce gouache is *gwash*, but whenever I say it like that, no one seems to understand me so I'm going to stick with *goo-ash*!

To get started with gouache painting, you will need a carefully selected range of colors. Traditional artist sets will include one cool and one warm shade of each primary color. I personally find this very helpful. A limited palette with a few premixed colors offers a real breadth of color-mixing possibilities.

The main colors I use in this book are Cadmium Yellow, Lemon Yellow, Ultramarine, Phthalo Blue, Cadmium Red and Alizarin Crimson. I also use four very versatile earth colors: Yellow Ochre, Burnt Umber, Burnt Sienna and Olive Green; and then Ivory Black and Permanent White. I have chosen two additional premixed brights: Cobalt Turquoise Light and Opera Pink, which are not strictly necessary, but create extraordinary vibrancy and are a joyful addition to any set.

If you are starting out, I would recommend getting your hands on the paints I have listed. Each project requires a different set of colors, so you could always invest gradually. Bear in mind that if you do go for a starter set, you may not end up using all the colors, so purchasing them individually may end up reducing waste.

Don't worry if you already have a nice set of gouache paints with slightly different color names. Many can be easily substituted and a quick online search will give you a ready list. An example of a color I have used is Phthalo Blue, but Winsor Blue, Monastral Blue, Prussian Blue or Indanthrene Blue would all make fine substitutes, and will give you a very similar result in your painting.

My preferred brand of paint is Designers Gouache by Winsor & Newton, and I have used it for all the projects in this book. I find it to be of great quality, as well as affordable and easily available online and in plenty of art stores. There is no right or wrong brand to use and several other great quality ones are available such as Holbein, Schmincke, Horadam™, Caran D'Ache™ and Royal Talens. These have similarly named paints and colors. For example, Ultramarine or Yellow Ochre will be very similar across brands and which brand you go for is entirely up to you.

BRUSHES

I tend to use four different shapes of synthetic brushes in a variety of sizes. Brush brands are also very much subject to your personal preference. In these projects I use a variety of brushes from Winsor & Newton, Pro Arte and Arteza. The key is to have a range and not to be at all put off if you don't have the exact one I describe—just use the closest thing you have on hand.

Round: An all-purpose round head with a pointed tip is great for lines of varying thicknesses. Small ones are useful for when precision is key, and spot brushes have shorter bristles for extra control.

Flat: Square-ended heads are good for crisp, straight edges, stripes, fine lines, washes and broad deposits of even color.

Angled: This is a flat brush with an angled edge. The point can be used to create fine flowing lines and for getting into corners. The wide head can create curved or straight wedges.

Filbert: A filbert is simply a flat with a semi-oval or a semi-circular shaped end. It is halfway between a round and flat brush and can be used for both details and covering flat areas. A filbert brush is great for blending, painting round or angular objects and creating rounded edges for things like flower petals or leaves.

I have not been specific with brush sizes in the projects because your designs will probably not be exactly the same size as mine. However, for those who would like to specifically use the exact brushes I paint with, you can go by my descriptions below. Bear in mind that the projects are designed for the exact scale and size of this book.

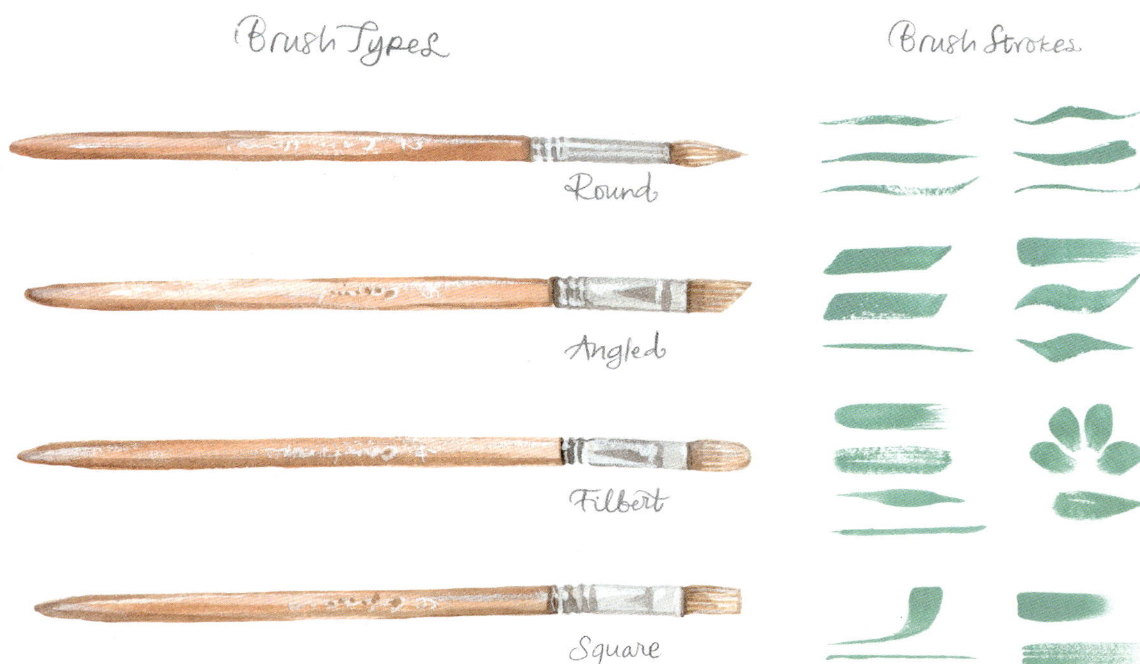

ROUND
3/0 or 4/0—very fine or finest round

2/0—fine round

1—small round

2—smallish round

spot—I generally use a size 3/0

FLAT
2—small flat

ANGLED
¼—medium angled

½—large angled

FILBERT
Size 4—medium filbert

Size 8—large filbert

PENCILS

Almost all of my designs begin with some sort of drawing. When using graphite, I generally go for a 0.7 mm Derwent mechanical pencil, but for design work, any kind of HB pencil will work. For plein air observational drawing, I prefer a softer 3–5B pencil so I can easily create texture and shading.

I often choose to draw out my painting with watercolor pencils because I like the way they blend into the artwork as I go along. Artist grade pencils are noticeably better quality with higher pigment and can be sharpened to a fine point. I usually have a selection on hand in white, black, indigo, umber, Burnt Sienna or chestnut and one gray or greenish color such as Derwent's Juniper Green.

PAPER

I like to use smooth, hot press watercolor or heavy cartridge paper that is between 135 lbs (220 gsm) and 140 lbs (300 gsm) in weight. Paper comes in pads or large sheets that you can cut down. Gummed pads are useful and have all four edges of the paper glued into a block so that you can apply plenty of water without it warping, leave it to dry and then cut it off when you have finished. Sometimes with drier designs, I like to work on heavy bright white card because fewer gray areas appear when scanning and digitally editing. Heavyweight colored paper and cardstock are also great to experiment on.

SCRATCH PAPER

I like to keep a large stash of scratch paper on hand, which I save from when I cut down designs. I use this for testing the colors I am mixing before committing them to the final paintings. It's also great for loosening up your linework before starting a layered piece. I find that doing a couple of strokes on scratch paper warms me up and gives me the confidence to make decisive lines. These little swatches are also a great addition when creating flat lays for social media images.

PALETTE

I use a basic round plastic palette with ten small wells around a larger central one, which you can easily find in any art supplies store or online. However, I often run out of clean ones and use anything from plates to pencil tins as palettes, which wash just as nicely and store well.

USEFUL MATERIALS

Paper Towels: It is a good idea to have a stash of these readily available to blot rogue blobs of water and color, especially when working with wet techniques. They are also very useful after cleaning brushes—a quick dab onto the paper towel will reveal any residual color that has not been properly removed and may warrant another quick swill or water change.

Eraser: I always have a good quality eraser on hand to remove graphite pencil and watercolor pencil lines. Be aware that vigorous rubbing can actually remove or smudge gouache, so work gently with a clean eraser.

Tape: Low tack masking tape is less sticky than regular masking tape and is useful for taping artwork to a table or board when working with wet techniques. This will allow the paper to dry flat instead of curling or warping. *Washi tape* is also great for taping the border of a painting in progress and will ensure clean crisp edges after it is removed.

Other Essential Tools: A metal ruler is useful for drawing out grids and artwork dimensions. You can also use it with a cutting mat and Stanley knife for crisp paper edges. A knife or sharpener are also essential to keep your pencils pointy.

All About the Color

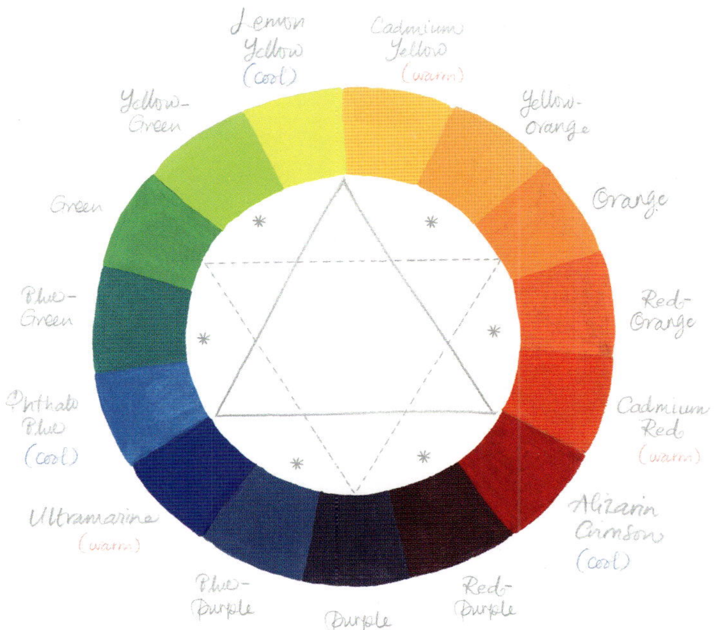

The term *color theory* can be a little daunting if you're not very familiar with using or mixing color. Color wheels are a helpful visual aid to understanding color harmony. This wheel shows some of the basic colors that can be mixed with both warm and cool versions of the three primary colors. The color wheel is made up of the following:

The *primary colors* are red, yellow and blue. You cannot make these three colors by mixing.

Secondary colors are created by mixing two primary colors together. For example, red and yellow make orange, blue and red make purple and blue and yellow make green.

Tertiary colors are created by mixing a primary and a secondary color together and are shown on the wheel.

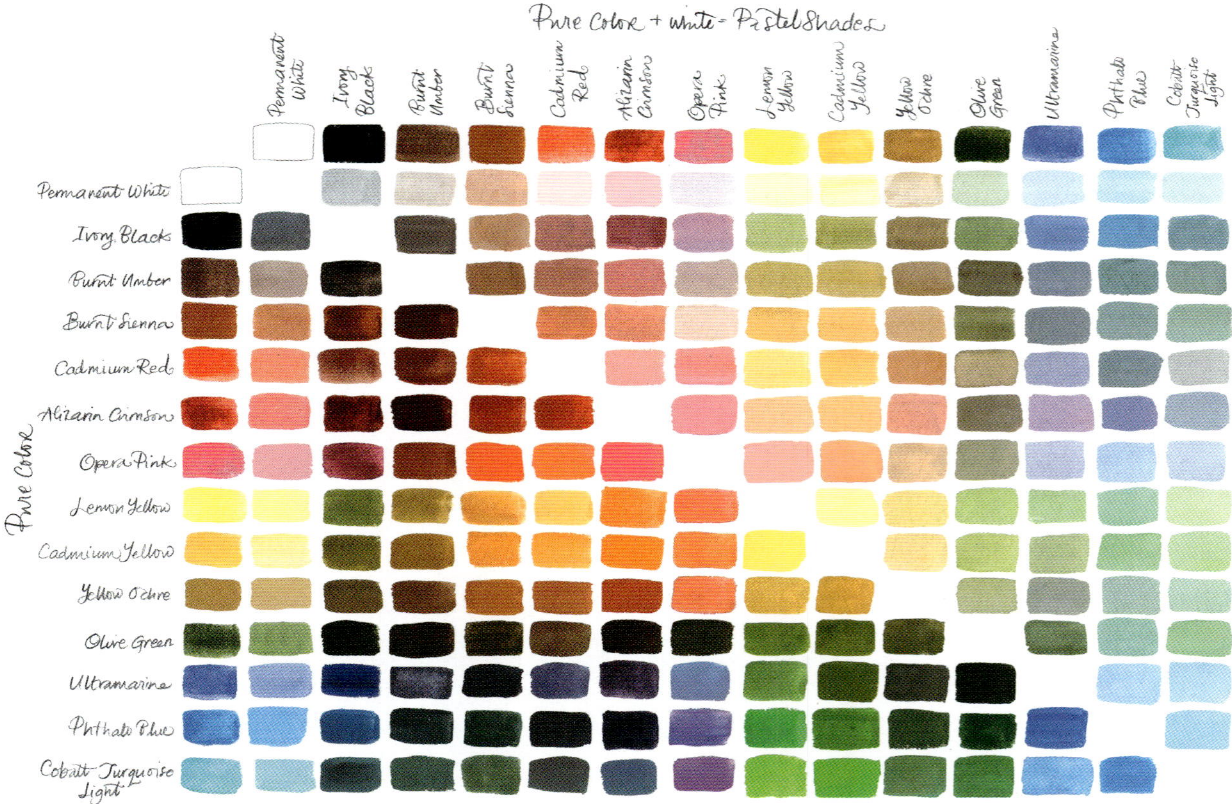

This detailed color chart includes all the colors in your set and has been painted to show the range of color you can mix. To use, choose one color on the top and one on the side and the swatch where the two lines meet is the color you will create when they are mixed!

I tend to use a lot of white when mixing my palettes, so the top right half of this chart has been painted with the addition of white to show some of the pastel shades you can achieve. The chart is simple to use and you could even try making your own.

Complementary colors are colors that sit directly opposite each other on the color wheel such as red and green or orange and blue.

Analogous colors are groups of three colors that sit next to each other on the color wheel and are generally thought to be harmonious, calm pairings that are easy on the eye. An example might be three different shades of blue.

Triadic colors are colors that are evenly spaced around the color wheel that are often vibrant and contrasting. These are fun to play with, particularly when adding tints and shades of these three. Some of my favorite color palettes are made up of triadic colors such as the ones on the next page.

TINTS & SHADES

You'll see me mention these quite a lot in the book and the theory is very simple. *Tints* are colors mixed with white to lighten and *shades* are colors mixed with black to darken. A *tone* is produced by tinting or shading colors or by adding gray. The term *shade* can also refer to any variety of one particular color you have mixed.

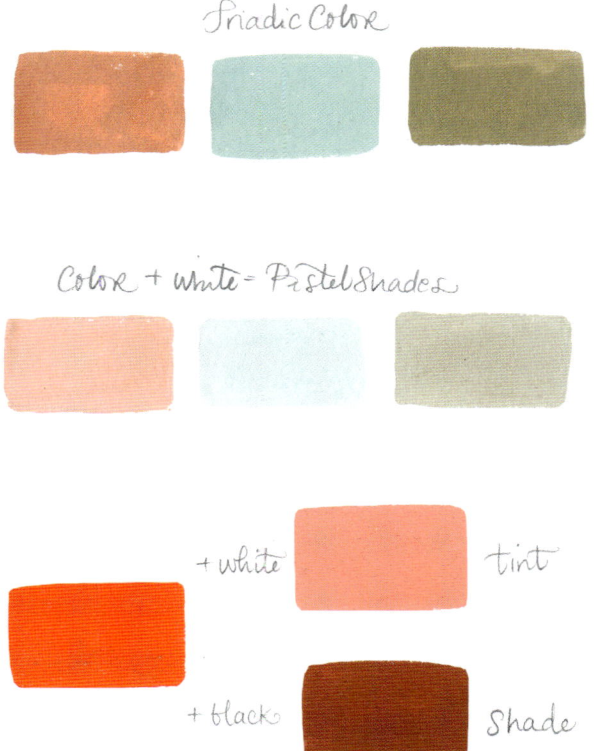

WARM & COOL COLORS

The *temperature* refers to the coolness or warmth of a color. Generally speaking, red, yellow and orange are referred to as warm and greens and blues as cool. This isn't entirely helpful however, as all primary colors have the potential to be warm or cool and you should have one of each in your set to create a full and varied spectrum of colors.

Very briefly, talking about the *bias* of a color is a way to describe which hues are influencing a primary color.

WARM

Cadmium Yellow—red bias

Ultramarine—red bias

Cadmium Red—yellow bias

COOL

Lemon Yellow—green bias

Phthalo Blue—green bias

Alizarin Crimson—blue bias

EARTH COLORS

These are warm colors that contain some brown pigment and inherently emulate natural colors. I find these extremely useful and often use Burnt Umber to darken colors instead of black.

CHOOSING & MIXING HARMONIOUS PALETTES

I get asked all the time how I come up with new palettes and if the truth be told, it is often completely by trial and error! It never ceases to delight me when new or unexpected pairings come alive in my palette. Here are a few tips that might be worth bearing in mind when mixing your own colors.

Limited color palettes can be remarkably striking—just look at how relief printmakers layer two or three colors. One light and dark shade of the same color would be a good place to start, or three complementary colors such as Ultramarine, Burnt Umber and white.

Alternatively, I would suggest you begin with a few analogous colors that you know will work well together such as several shades of blue with a pop of orange for contrast or a range of greens with a contrasting pop of pink.

An obvious suggestion would be to look at the work of other artists, illustrators and designers for inspiration. For example, something as random as the colors in an advertisement may inspire me to create a palette for a painting of a vase of flowers—that is a valid approach to take too!

It is worth bearing in mind that you can create two entirely different pieces with the same palette by varying the techniques, opacity and balance of the colors you use as shown in the illustration above. You may have leftover paint in your palette after completing a project, but the potential for creating unique artworks is never exhausted. Try another design with a different balance of color!

A lot of illustrators, designers and painters will return to palettes they are familiar with time after time. Some palettes become immediately recognizable as belonging to the style of an artist and the more you paint, the more you will come to know and favor particular palettes yourself.

Getting Started

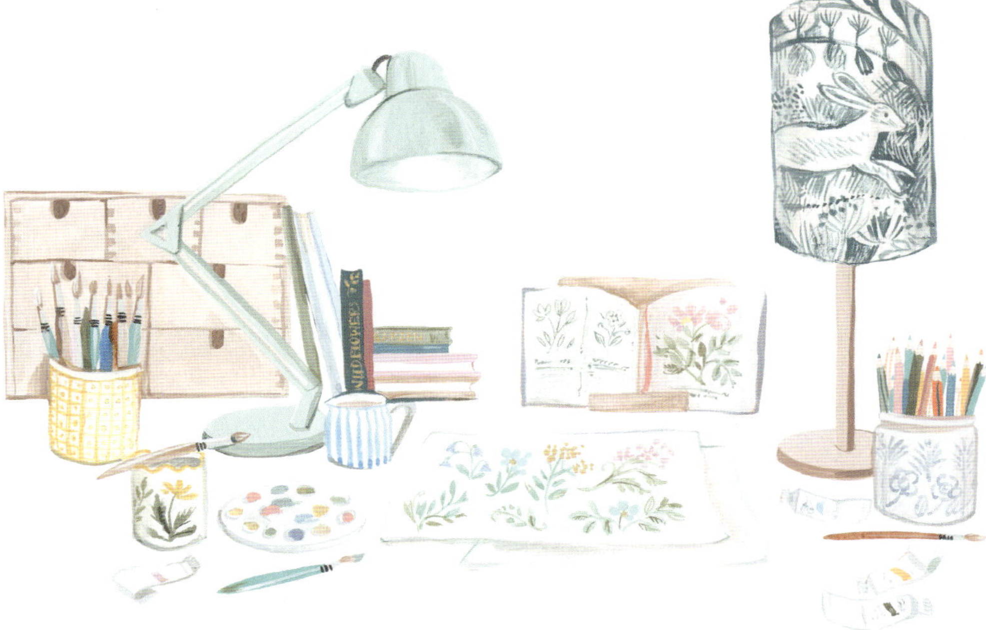

MIXING YOUR PAINT

If you read any section of this introduction thoroughly, make sure it's this bit!

Firstly, I recommend always having your materials laid out and ready on hand. This ensures more painting and less faffing. You'll need space for your paper pad, a palette, a pot of water and, if possible, somewhere to perch this book for reference.

Each project starts with a guide for mixing your entire palette of colors before beginning to paint. This will hopefully be helpful in a number of ways. Firstly, it gives you the opportunity to see all the colors in the design before you begin and helps you understand how they are being spread across the piece. It also allows you to dip into them more fluently for tiny details without having to stop to mix.

When choosing a color palette for a design, I often find myself unintentionally mixing colors I am familiar with and know work well together. Premixing the colors helps me stick to the planned color scheme and results in a more original design.

Bear in mind that color mixing is not an exact science. My guides are an approximation so do not be afraid to tweak proportions if need be. You will begin to naturally understand your paints as your experience grows. Testing swatches of color and leaving them to dry is a helpful way to check that they are exactly what you want.

I will use a few descriptive phrases throughout the book that may need a little explanation before we begin. If you are unsure, you can always refer back to the next page. I tend to use a small size 2 flat head brush to mix colors.

Use this guide to better understand my proportions.

Speck: Dip the very tip of the brush into the color to extract a minute amount.

Dot: This is a slightly larger dip of paint on the end of your brush but much smaller than a dab!

Dab: This is about a lentil-sized amount. Try generously dabbing half the end of the brush tip into a blob of pure color and use what is on the brush.

Small Blob: This is about the size of a pea and is a very small squeeze of paint.

Blob: Squeeze a small amount about the size of your middle fingernail.

Large Blob: Squeeze a fair-sized amount of color about one and a half times the size of a blob.

There is no right or wrong way of mixing, but this is how I like to create my palette. Squeeze a blob of each color, except for white, around the inside edge of the central well. As I mix each individual color, I dab a little bit of paint on my brush and add it to an adjacent well. I tend to go through a heck of a lot of white, so I squeeze it directly into one of the small wells. Be sure to combine all colors evenly and thoroughly or your painting may end up with streaks.

ADDING WATER

You will have to add water pretty much every time you paint with gouache. The consistency of the paint straight out of a tube is thick and gloopy. Whenever your paint feels too dry, dipping your brush in clean water will help loosen the paint when mixing.

Once I have created the perfect color in my palette well, I tend to mix a little on the edge with some water so that it is the perfect consistency for applying it to paper. This may sound confusing now, but by the end of one project you'll get the hang of it and before long, it will be second nature!

Thick Opaque Layers: Only add the merest touch of water or none at all! This will be quite textured so that some of the paper or layers may be partially visible beneath.

Fluid Yet Opaque Layers: This is the consistency I refer to most often. Use a wet brush to ever so slightly thin the paint so that it is still creamy but covers opaquely without the need for more water. Any drawing lines should be just about covered up.

Semi-Opaque Layers: Add a dab of color on the side of your well and mix lightly with a couple dabs of water. To test, draw a few pencil lines and then paint a swatch over the top. You should still be able to see the lines through the paint.

Watery Layers: This will be unique to individual pieces, but as a rule, add a dab of your mixed color to a clean well and add water as required. As with watercolor, you'll be able to clearly see any drawing beneath the paint.

Something you will notice as you go along is that when dry, dark colors tend to lighten and light values tend to darken. To mix the perfect color, it helps to have scratch paper on hand so you can paint a test swatch as you work. This will dry within minutes, so you'll be able to work with accurate colors rather than finding they are darker than you like once you have painted your design. This will save you from having to re-mix and add another layer.

One thing that's worth bearing in mind is that the paint can dry almost instantly on a hot, dry day! This can be remedied by spritzing the paint with a little water, particularly on any unmixed blobs to keep them fluid.

Paint Mixing & Sizing

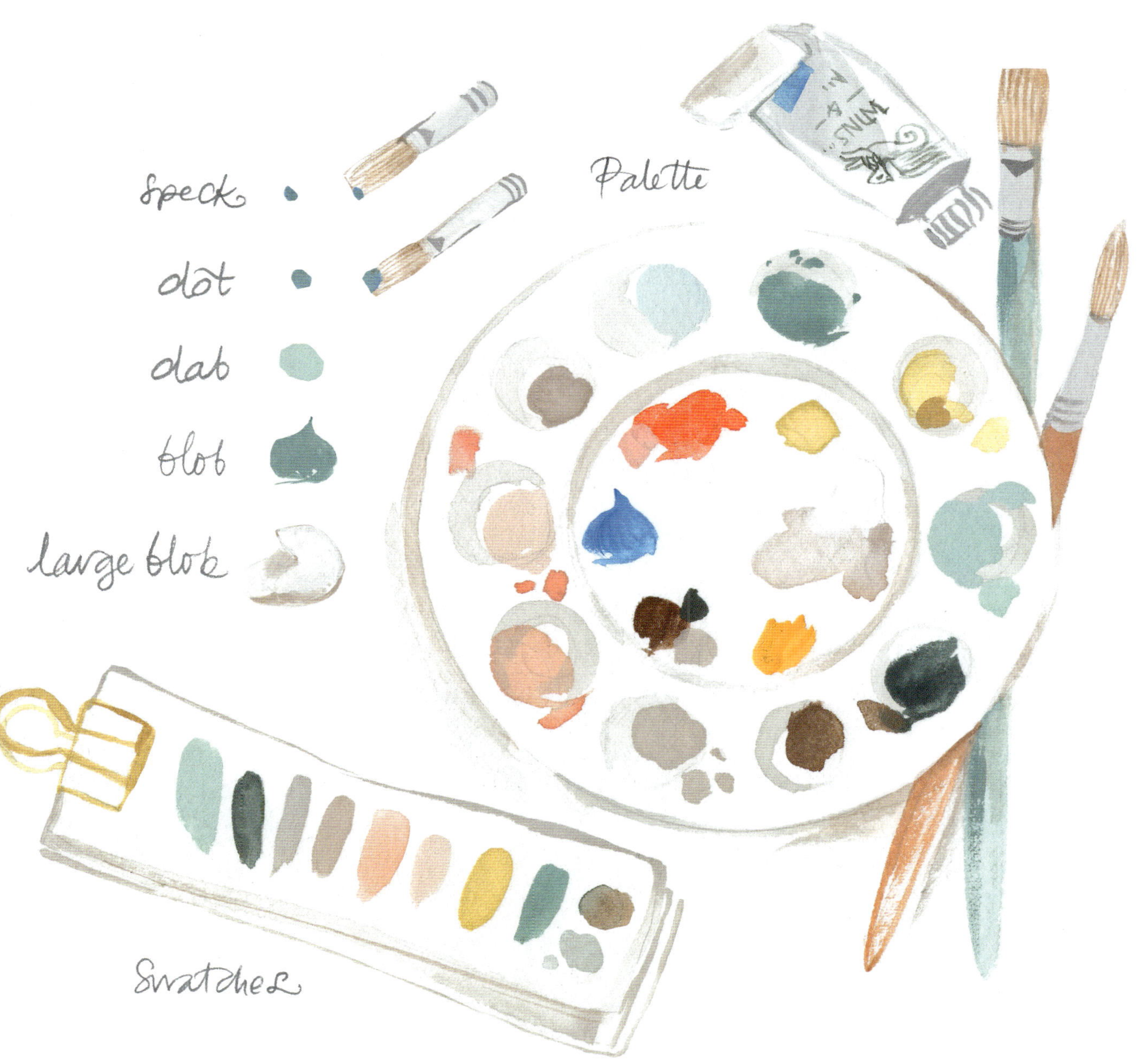

TAKING CARE OF YOUR EQUIPMENT

Take good care of your materials and they will last. Store your paints together carefully and always keep your lids screwed on tight. If you find a hard old tube lurking, you can reactivate it by slicing it open and adding a little water to it, but you'll struggle to recreate the lovely creamy consistency of a fresh tube. Similarly, tubes left open and partially dried will reactivate after leaving the opening in water for a little while before screwing the cap back on.

Store brushes in a pot with the bristles facing upward, preferably clean and definitely not festering in your used water pot. Leaving your brushes in water can cause the bristle tips to become permanently bent and weakens the glue holding them in, eventually causing them to fall out.

Wasting paint is a strong consideration for many when mixing color. Often, you only need to mix a little touch for small areas but remember to be generous when mixing to cover large areas such as backgrounds, so that you can create even coverage. You can store mixed and dried palettes for a later date and reactivate them with a little water.

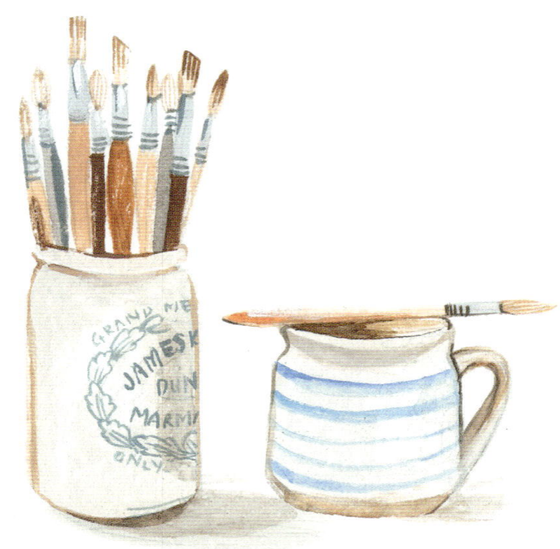

TAPING EDGES

This is a handy way to create a piece with sharp edges. Mark out your square with a ruler and pencil and then neatly tape all four outside edges. Leave the tape on until the design is complete and dry and then gently peel it off so that you don't damage or remove any of the paper underneath. The resultant edges should be neat and crisp.

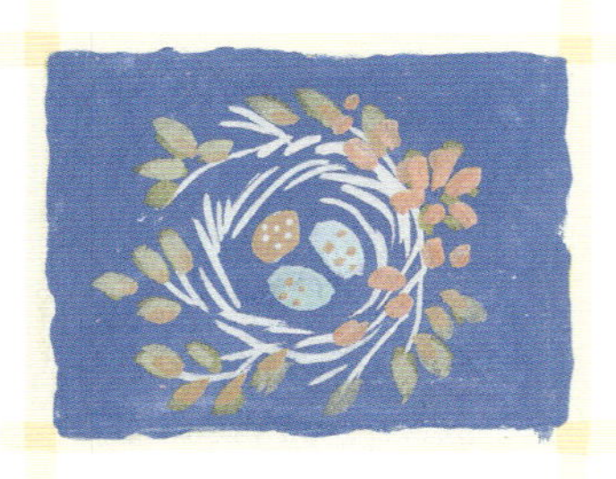

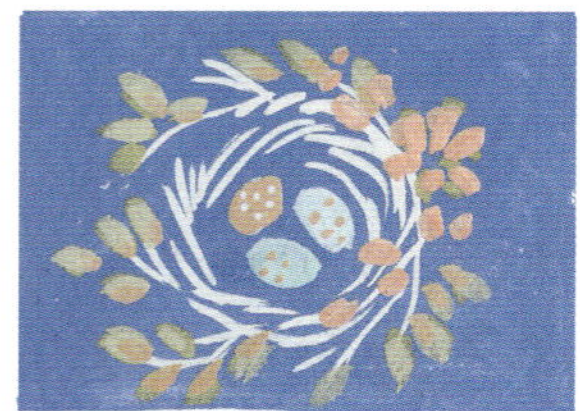

Basic Painting Techniques

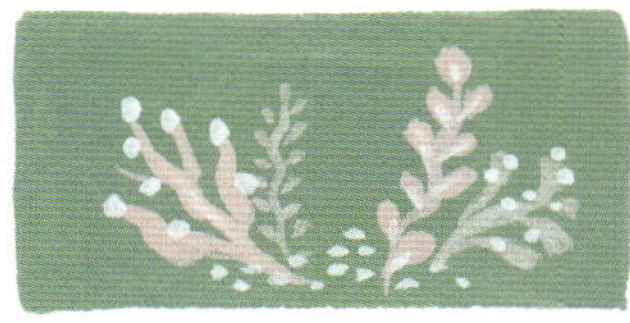

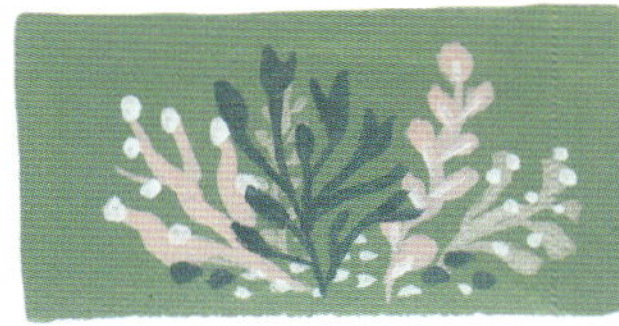

Examples of Layering

Most of these techniques will be covered within the different book projects, but if you need a little refresher as you go along, pop back to this page for reference!

WET-ON-DRY

LAYERING

Gouache is known for being wonderful for layering, no matter the consistency of the paint underneath. It is generally best to build up from light to dark. However, unlike watercolor, you can also add light layers on top of dark ones. It's worth bearing in mind that gouache will reactivate when you add another wet layer so it may get mixed with the layer beneath. Furthermore, it can crack when applied too thickly.

As gouache dries very fast, it's great for building up thin layers on top of one another. This technique is called glazing and is essentially creating shadow effects with a variety of transparencies.

INTRICATE LINEWORK & ADDING DETAILS

This is one of my favorite things about gouache, as I like to draw a lot with the paint to create fine details and add contrast with smaller loose marks. Dark gouache and a fine tipped brush can create details in their own right, or as a contrast to blocked areas of flat color.

Mix a little dab of color into your palette with a small amount of water to create a consistency that is similar to light cream. Use slightly more water if you are trying to create lighter color and then paint with the tip of the brush to make fine, fluid lines.

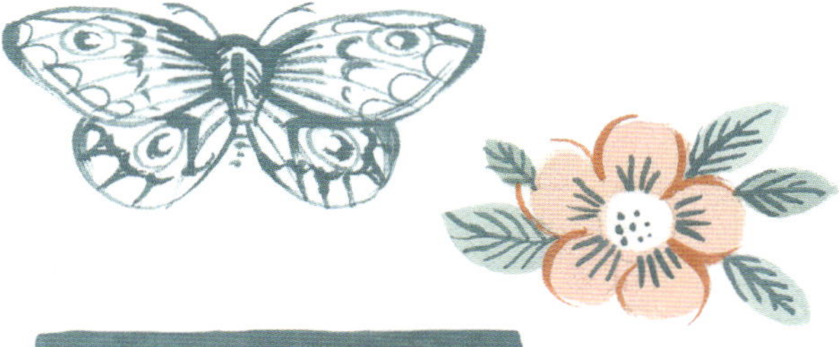
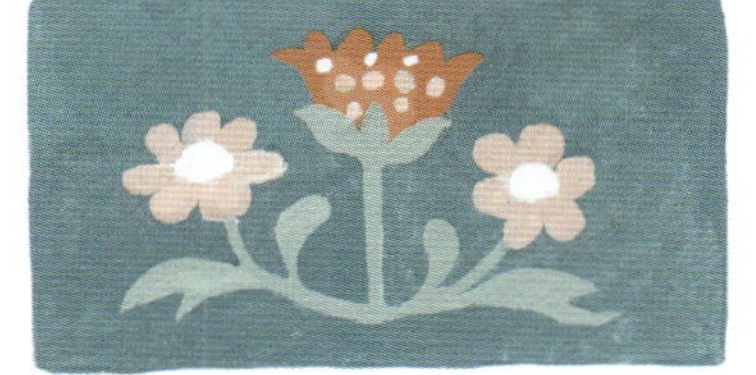

Examples of fine detailing

DRY-BRUSH & CREATING TEXTURE

The dry-brush technique is a way of creating texture and depth in your designs. It is essentially using gouache with little to no added water. This is a great way to loosen up as the effect is somewhat spontaneous and keeps you from being too controlling.

To practice, apply a little wet mixed paint to a dry brush without adding any water. Remove excess paint on a piece of scratch paper or a kitchen towel and you're ready to experiment with a range of brush strokes on some dry paper. This technique can be used for anything from detailed animal fur to filling in large areas of background and creating soft edges.

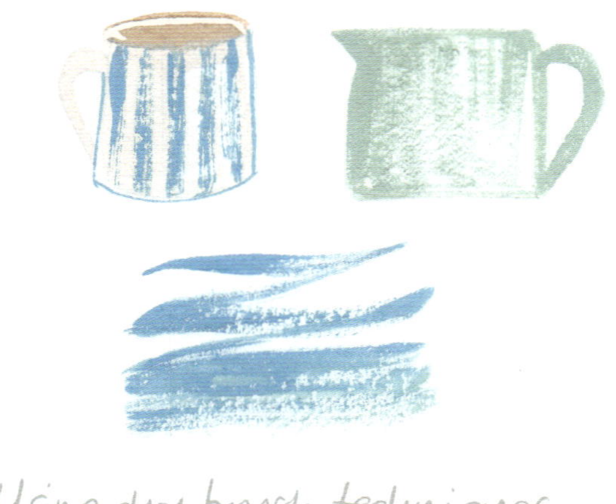

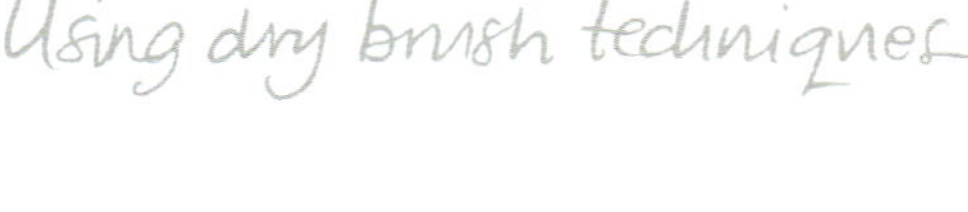

Using dry brush techniques

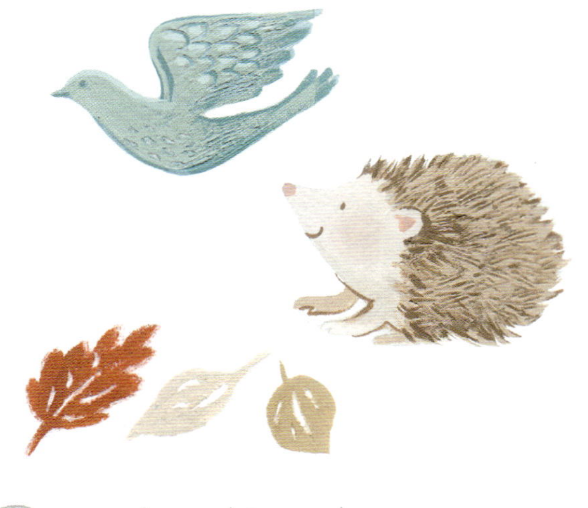

Examples of scraping

SCRAPING

Scraping is the method of using a pointed instrument to scrape away either wet or dry paint to expose the paper or color below. Be aware that thick gouache can crack, so make sure you keep your finished piece flat—that is, don't roll it!

Try painting a thick area of color and then scratching a variety of marks into the paint while it's still wet to expose the paper below. Wipe any excess paint onto paper towels as you go.

You may also try painting a normal opaque layer of gouache and blowing away the removed flakes of paint when completely dry.

REWORKING: BLENDING DRY COLOR & SOFTENING EDGES

As gouache reactivates when wet, you can rework and blend two dry layers. To do this, first paint two solid rectangular areas very slightly apart and leave to dry. Using a lightly wetted brush, dampen the edge of each. As the paint rehydrates, it will become liquid again and you will be able to blend the two colors together.

You can soften dry painted edges in the same way very easily. Use your lightly wetted fine brush to carefully reactivate the color and merge a little in to the white of the paper. The less water you use, the more control you will have over the paint.

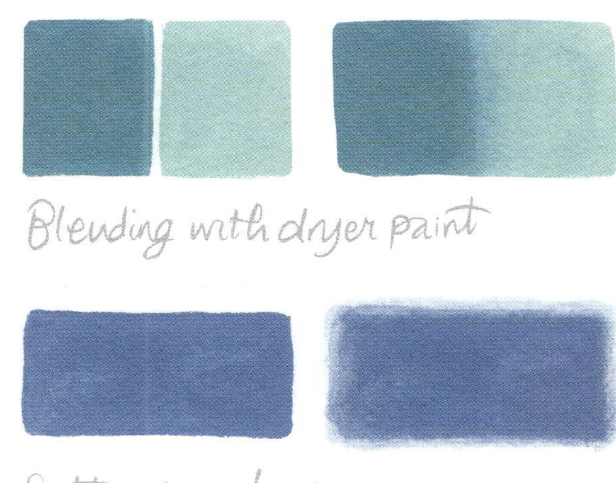

Blending with watery paint

WET-ON-WET

BLENDING & OMBRÉS

Paint can also be blended with two wet colors painted directly onto your piece, which can be helpful when trying to create subtle color variations. To do this, paint two colors with a fluid consistency side by side and then paint over the top where they meet, merging them together with light strokes. When two painted watery areas meet, both colors will automatically start seeping into one another. The dryer the paint, the less they will interact.

Ombré is the French word for shaded and means blending two colors or, more often than not, shading from light to dark with tints and shades or vice versa. To create an ombré effect, repeat as above but extend the shading more carefully outward into the two different colors, aiming to create a seamless gradient of color.

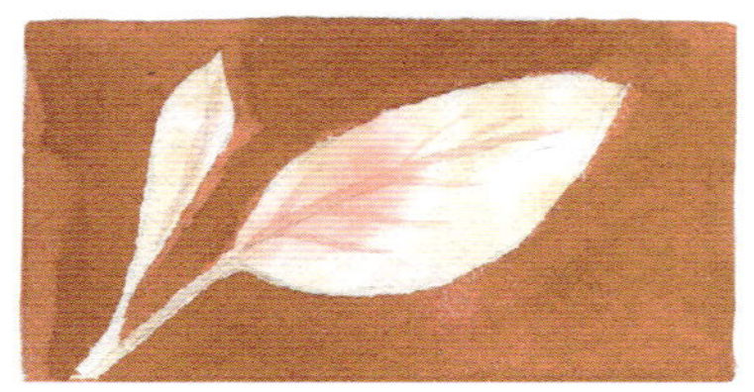

BLOOMING

Blooming is deliberately adding specks of color to beads of water in a defined space so they randomly disperse and bleed, creating spontaneous *blooming* patterns when dried. Unpredictable flows of paint can be called blossoms or even cauliflowers, which I think is rather nice.

To manipulate your blooms of color, you can tilt the page if you have it taped to a board, or even move the swirls of color a little with the tip of a clean dry brush.

I like to create organic blooming patterns within precise shapes. To do this, I use watercolor paper and first draw out the shape, which I will fill with water. Next, using a clean brush and water, I paint in the shape carefully. Then, working quickly while it is still wet, I paint dots that spread over the damp paper.

Examples of blooming

STAINING, REPLICATING WATERCOLOR & CREATING COLORED GROUNDS

Staining is painting a large area of color with very watered-down gouache as you might with watercolor. It's a great basis for layering as it can add a texture to build on top of. It's usually a good idea to tape your paper down on all four sides so that you can get a neat edge and the paper dries flat.

Using a large filbert or angled brush, take a dab of mixed color and add to a fresh well with a couple dabs of clean water and mix evenly. The more water you add, the lighter the shade will be. On your paper, paint in wide sweeping strokes to cover your area and then leave it for some time to dry thoroughly.

Examples of Staining & replicating watercolor

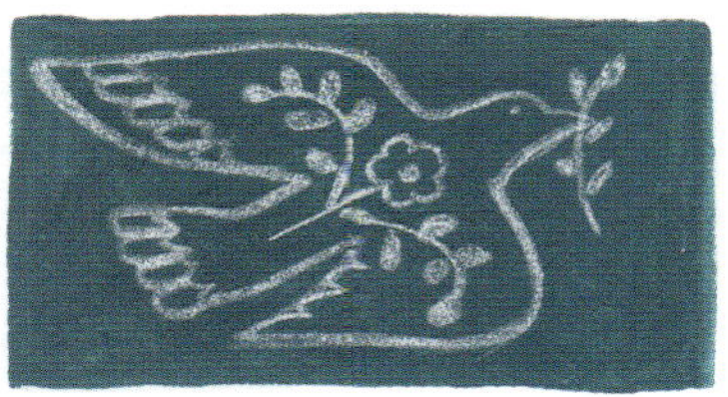

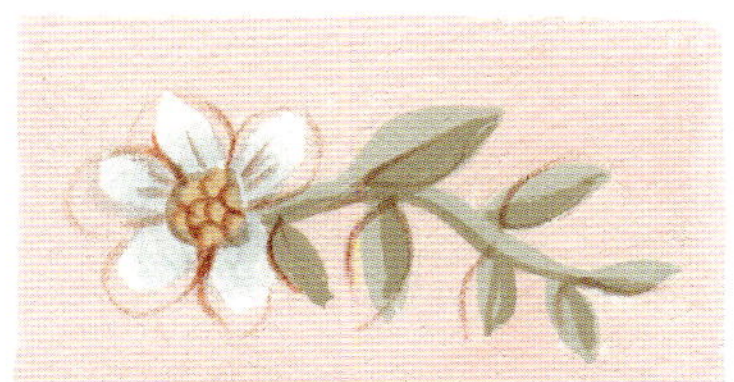

ADDING MIXED MEDIA

I have touched on using a watercolor pencil for drawing designs and then blending with them as part of the design, but don't have space to explore the possibilities of combining other media with gouache. However, gouache and watercolor can be freely intermixed—just try to keep them on separate palettes.

In my experience, gouache is a wonderful medium on which to add others, particularly pencil. Rough lines can add textured contrast to blocked areas of flat color. Drawing with a light pencil on top of a dark layer can be helpful as it allows us to draw out designs before adding another layer, or it can simply be used as a striking variation.

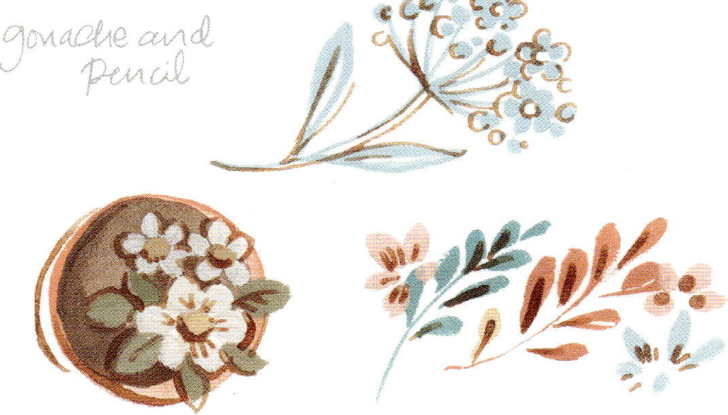

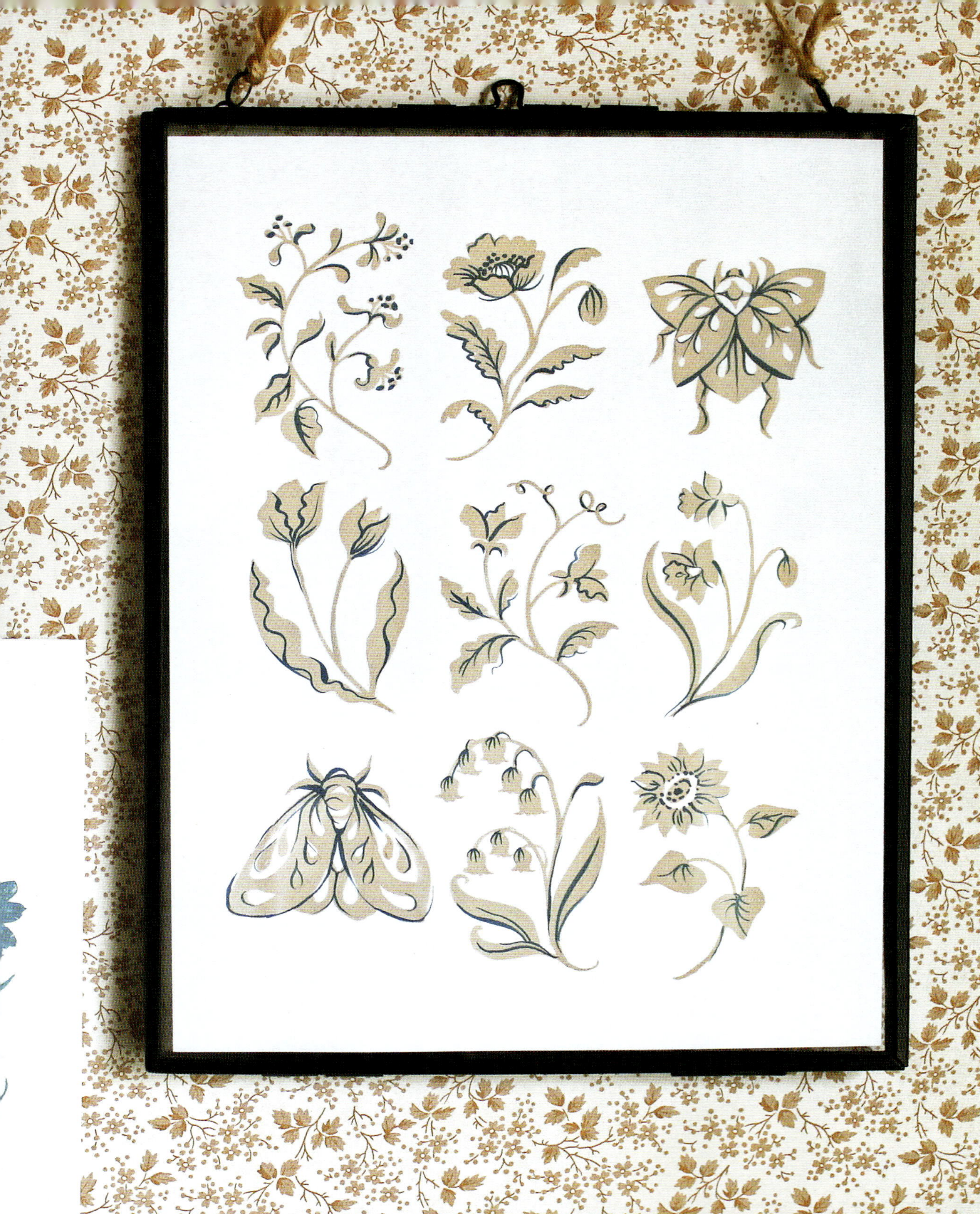

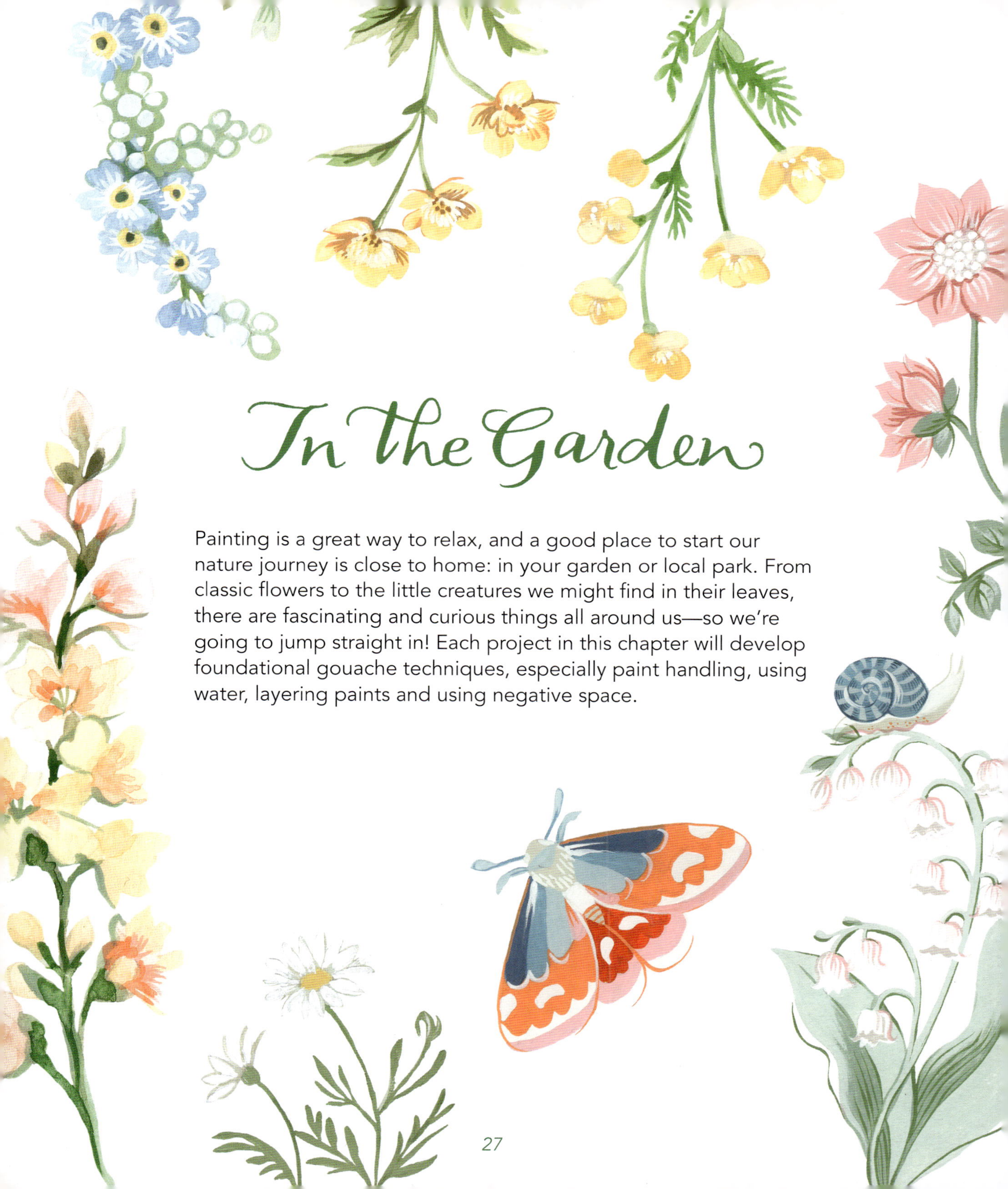

In the Garden

Painting is a great way to relax, and a good place to start our nature journey is close to home: in your garden or local park. From classic flowers to the little creatures we might find in their leaves, there are fascinating and curious things all around us—so we're going to jump straight in! Each project in this chapter will develop foundational gouache techniques, especially paint handling, using water, layering paints and using negative space.

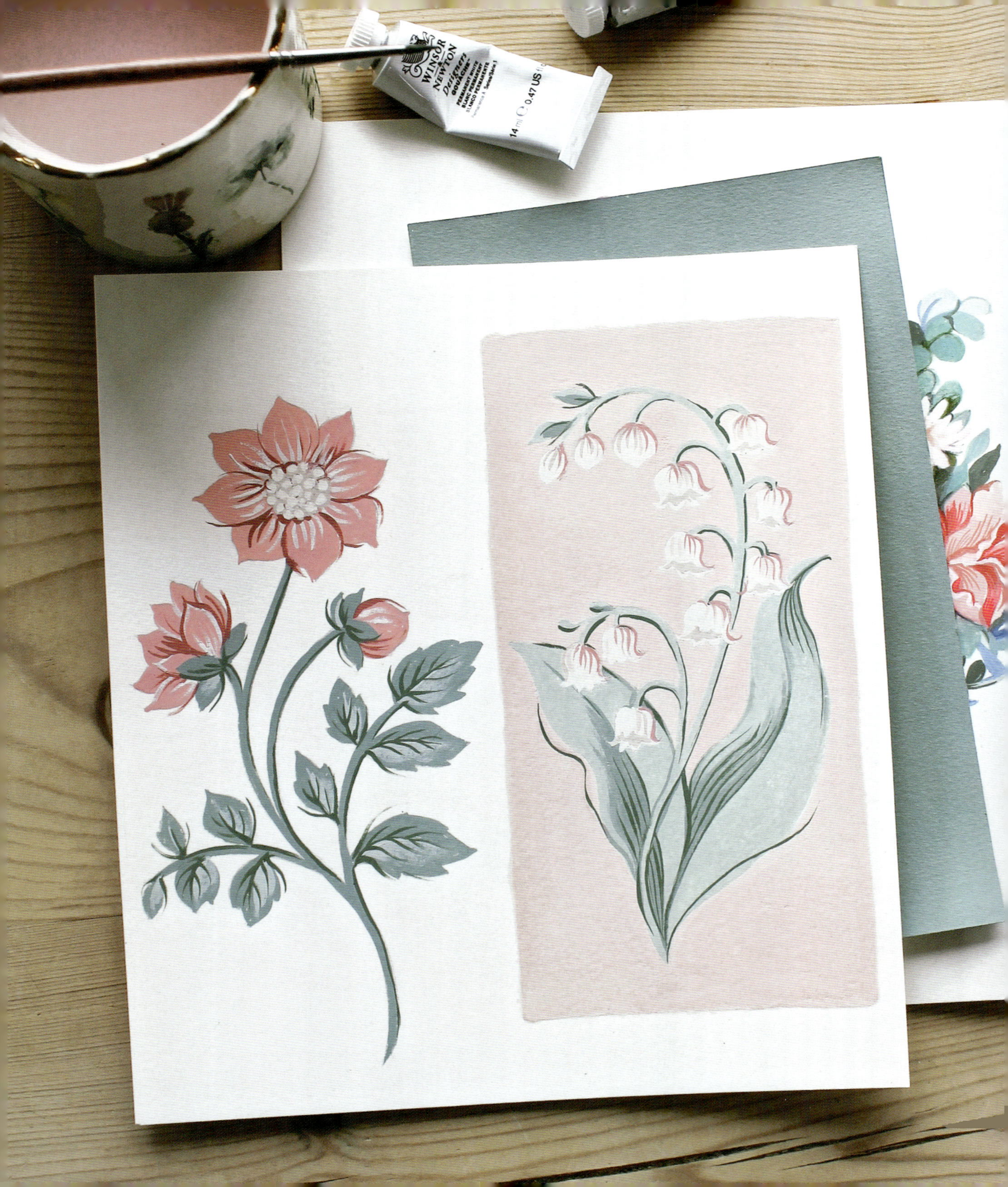
WINSOR
NEWTON
Designers
GOUACHE

Flower Portraits

In this first project, we dive straight in with three techniques I find essential to working with gouache: using negative space on a painted ground, basic layering and detailed linework. We also start with some simple color mixing and the use of *tints* and *shades*. I have chosen two classic flowers, a single headed dahlia and a lily of the valley, to create a striking botanical portrait. Any flower with a limited palette of two fundamental colors will work well as a substitute for this project.

COLOR MIXING

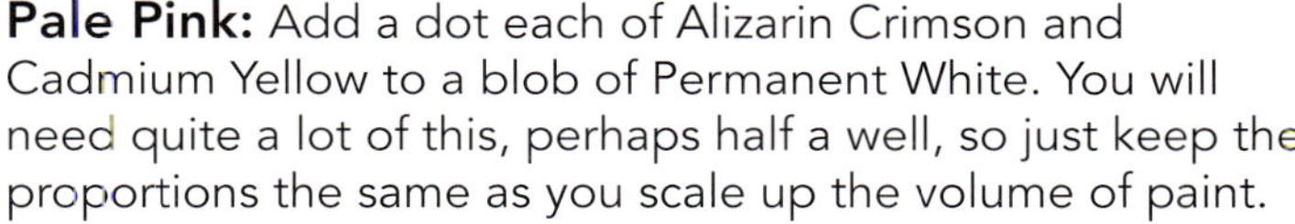

Pale Pink: Add a dot each of Alizarin Crimson and Cadmium Yellow to a blob of Permanent White. You will need quite a lot of this, perhaps half a well, so just keep the proportions the same as you scale up the volume of paint.

Medium Pink: Add two dabs of Alizarin Crimson and one dab of Cadmium Yellow to a small blob of Permanent White.

Off-White: Add a dot of Cadmium Yellow and the tiniest speck of Ivory Black to a blob of Permanent White. Mix until you have an even color and check on some scratch paper to see how it looks. It is very easy to make a shade too dark, so if need be, add more white to lighten.

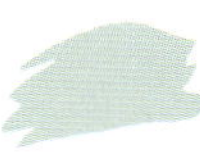

Medium Sage Green: Add a dab of Cadmium Yellow, a slightly larger blob of Phthalo Blue and two spots of Ivory Black to a large blob of Permanent White.

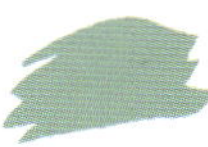

Dark Sage: Take a few dabs of the mixed medium sage green and add a dab each of Phthalo Blue, Cadmium Yellow and Ivory Black, mixing thoroughly.

Grayish Pink: Add the tiniest speck each of Ivory Black, Cadmium Yellow and Alizarin Crimson to a blob of Permanent White. It should look hardly darker than the off-white when mixed in the palette, but will be very noticeable when painting.

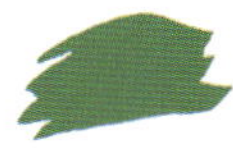

Mossy Green: Add a dab each of Ivory Black and Phthalo Blue and mix with two dabs each of Cadmium Yellow and Permanent White.

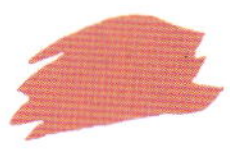

Dark Pink: Add a dab each of Alizarin Crimson and Cadmium Yellow to two dabs of Permanent White and a spot of Ivory Black.

SUPPLIES

Brushes: Medium angled, smallish round, small round, fine round

Paint Colors: Alizarin Crimson, Cadmium Yellow, Ivory Black, Permanent White, Phthalo Blue

Other Supplies: Pencil and eraser, scratch paper

1

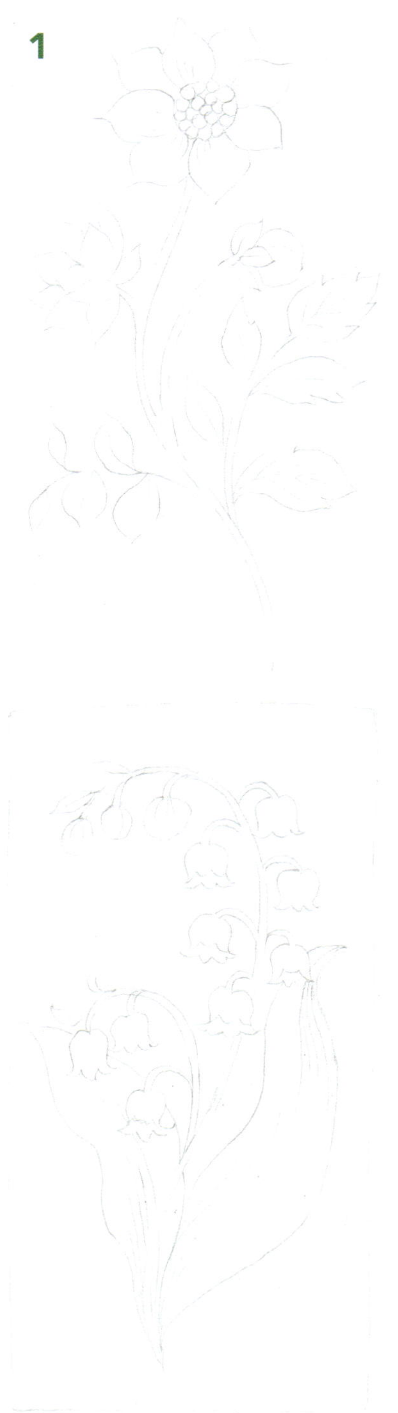

Step 1: Drawing the Flowers

Begin by lightly sketching out the flowers. We want to imagine them at their prettiest and perkiest, with petals and leaves blooming up and out in a way that they might not in nature. It is a piece of two parts, so begin by dividing the page down the middle with a faint line. On the right, draw in a large portrait rectangle, which will house the lily of the valley flower.

We will draw the dahlia first, on the left of the page. Begin with a circle for the flower head about a quarter of the way down the page and fill it with tiny circles. Draw in four large teardrop-shaped petals with pointy tips, then another four petals poking out from behind these. A long curved stem extends right to the bottom of the page, with four stems of varying length poking out, two on each side. On the top right stem, draw in a rounded, closed bud and on the top left stem, draw a small side-facing flower head.

On the bottom two stems, draw in leaves on both sides of the stalk. The leaves may look complex but can be broken down into a few easy steps. I'd suggest lightly drawing each one as a basic pointed almond shape. Split the leaf down the middle with a slightly curved line to immediately create movement. Lastly, choose how to define your leaf edges. In this case they are not smooth, so draw over your almond guide with some uneven jagged points. Vary the scale and embrace irregularity!

Start the lily flower by drawing one long sweeping curved stem, with another smaller one branching to the left. At the bottom of the stem and behind it, draw in the large curved leaves, one on either side. Use the same premise as before for drawing these in—they are essentially still pointy almond shapes but the edges are elongated and wavier this time. Divide the leaves in half with a curved line on the left leaf and a wavy line on the right leaf.

Draw the tiny stems on both sides of each stalk for the flower heads. The flowers at the top are teeny rounded buds and the flowers resemble little bells with frilly edges.

2

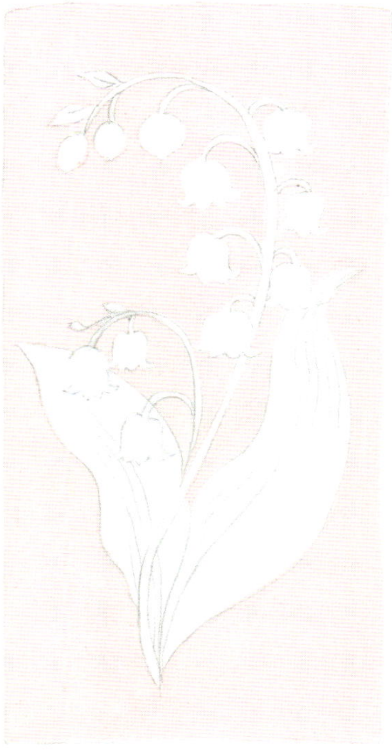

Step 2: Painting the Lily Background & Flower Heads

We will use the pale pink for the background behind the lily. Using a small round brush, carefully paint around the flower shape and then fill in the rest of the square with the medium angled brush. Load your brush with plenty of paint and use only a touch of water so that you create opaque, even coverage. Don't worry too much about getting a perfectly crisp line when you reach the edge of the rectangle.

TIP: *Light-colored gouache tends to dry darker than it appears in the palette and it helps to have some spare scratch paper on hand to check the color. Paint a little swatch and then leave it to dry and compare with the book image. If the color appears too dark, add a little more white.*

Using your medium pink, paint in the dahlia petals one by one, as well as the lower flower and the bud.

TIP: *Don't forget to clean your brush between mixing and be sure to blot the tip on some paper towels to dry.*

The base color for the lily of the valley flower heads is off-white. Using a semi-opaque consistency, paint these in, followed by the round dotty circles in the center of the dahlia flower.

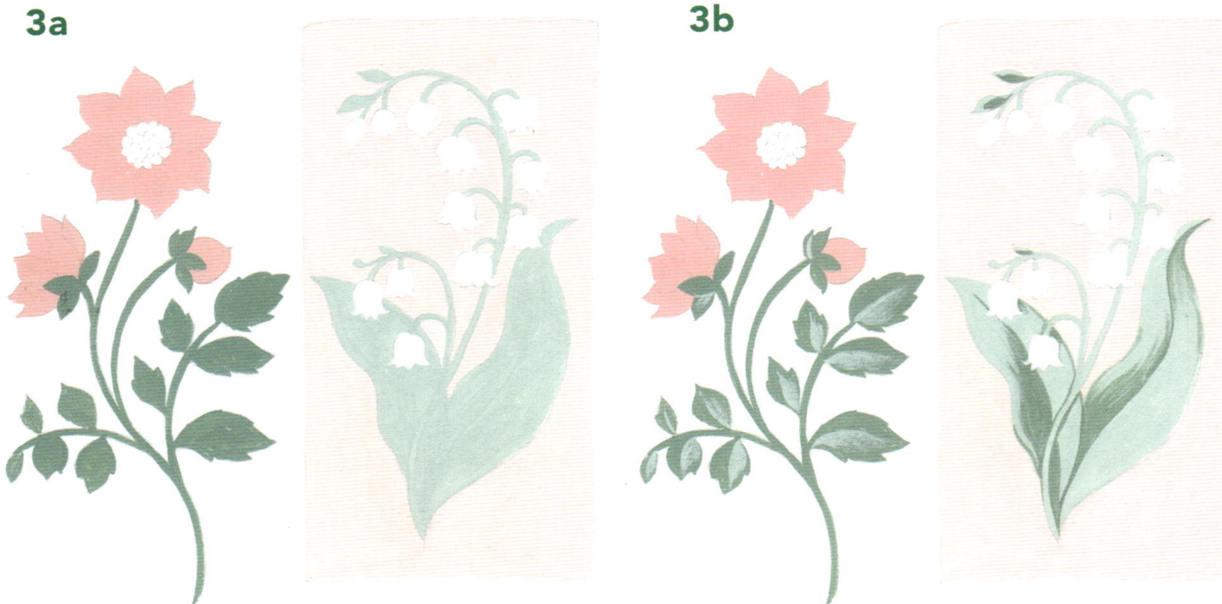

Step 3: Leaves & Stems

For the lily of the valley greenery, I've chosen a medium sage green as a complementary color to the light pink. For more control, use a fine round brush to carefully paint in the stem of the lily of the valley and, if you like, a slightly larger small round brush for both the leaves, being careful not to paint over the petals.

Turning to the dahlia, we will use the dark sage shade to paint in the stem and leaves with a fine round brush.

Next, we will add some light and shade on one half of each of our leaves to make them look three-dimensional. I tend to think of the leaf in two parts with a line down the center and shade one half. A few simple lines on top can give your plants the feeling of being alive.

Using a semi-opaque watered-down dark sage, paint fine dividing lines between the two lily leaves so you can see where the left overlaps the right. Divide the right-hand leaf in two with a fine wavy line and paint a little shadow on the bottom left, as well as top right of the leaf. On the left-hand leaf, outline the edges of the stem and divide the leaf in two. Paint loose strokes on the left side to create a subtle shadow.

With a dryish small round brush, use some of the medium sage green to paint highlights on one half of each of the darker dahlia leaves. We will add the fine details a little later.

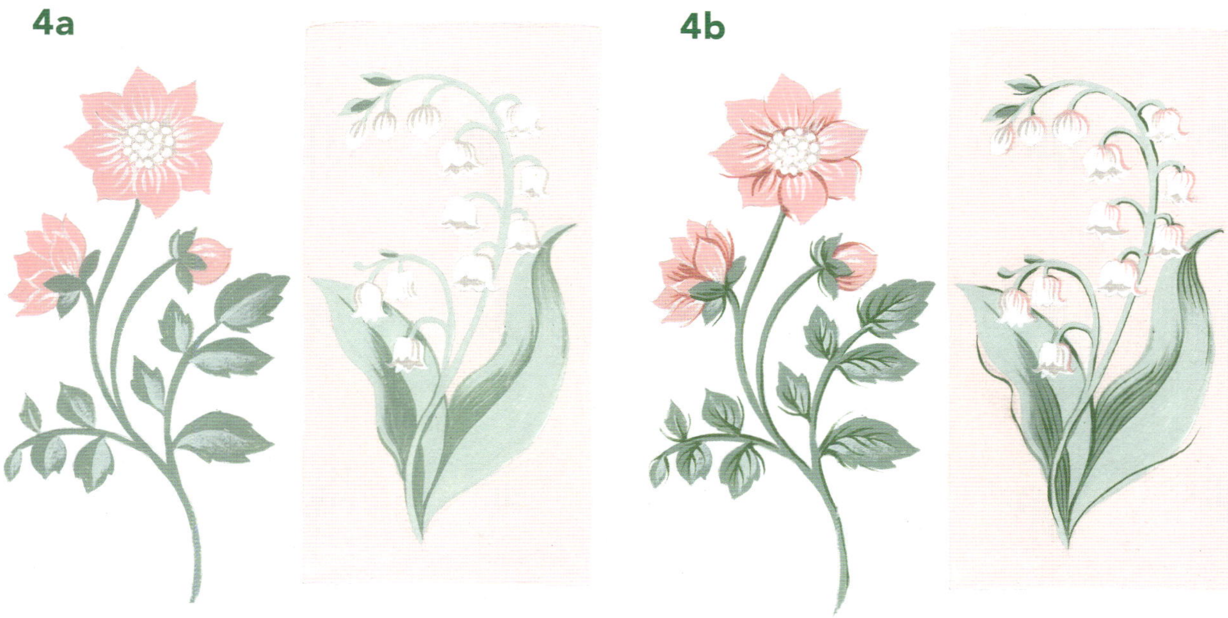

Step 4: Detailed Linework

Next, we add loose yet detailed linework to the flowers by using a fine round brush. It's your chance to draw freely with your brush and I would encourage you to overlap your lines outside the edges of your shapes.

Beginning with the dahlia, use the off-white to add detail. Follow the curve of the petal edges with small light strokes, being careful not to simply outline the flower petals—less is more in this case! With your light grayish pink color, outline the tiny circles on the flower head.

Now for the lily of the valley: Continue using the grayish pink to add shadowed detail to the inside of the flower heads and shade the outside of petals to give the sense of three-dimensionality. Use a tiny amount of the pale pink to add some line detail on the lily heads.

Now, with our finest brush, we add structured lines to the leaves and stems. If you are right-handed, start on the left side of the page so you don't smudge the lines as you work across the page and vice versa if you are left-handed. Retaining looseness in your brush marks, use the mossy green color to start outlining the right side of the dahlia stems. Divide each leaf in two and then paint curved parallel lines to indicate the veins. I like to flick outside of the shape edges so that the design doesn't look too neat and tidy! Using my design as reference, outline the lily stems—not always on both sides—and paint the narrow wavy veins on top of the shaded areas of the lily leaves.

Lastly, with your dark pink color, add a few lines here and there on both of the flower heads to define the flower petals and slightly break up the block color and background.

TIP: *One of the great things about gouache is that it's easy to paint over mistakes! Don't stress if your line is wonky or your hand slips. You will have mixed the colors already in your palette and when your mistake is dry, you can just paint over those areas with a fine dryish brush.*

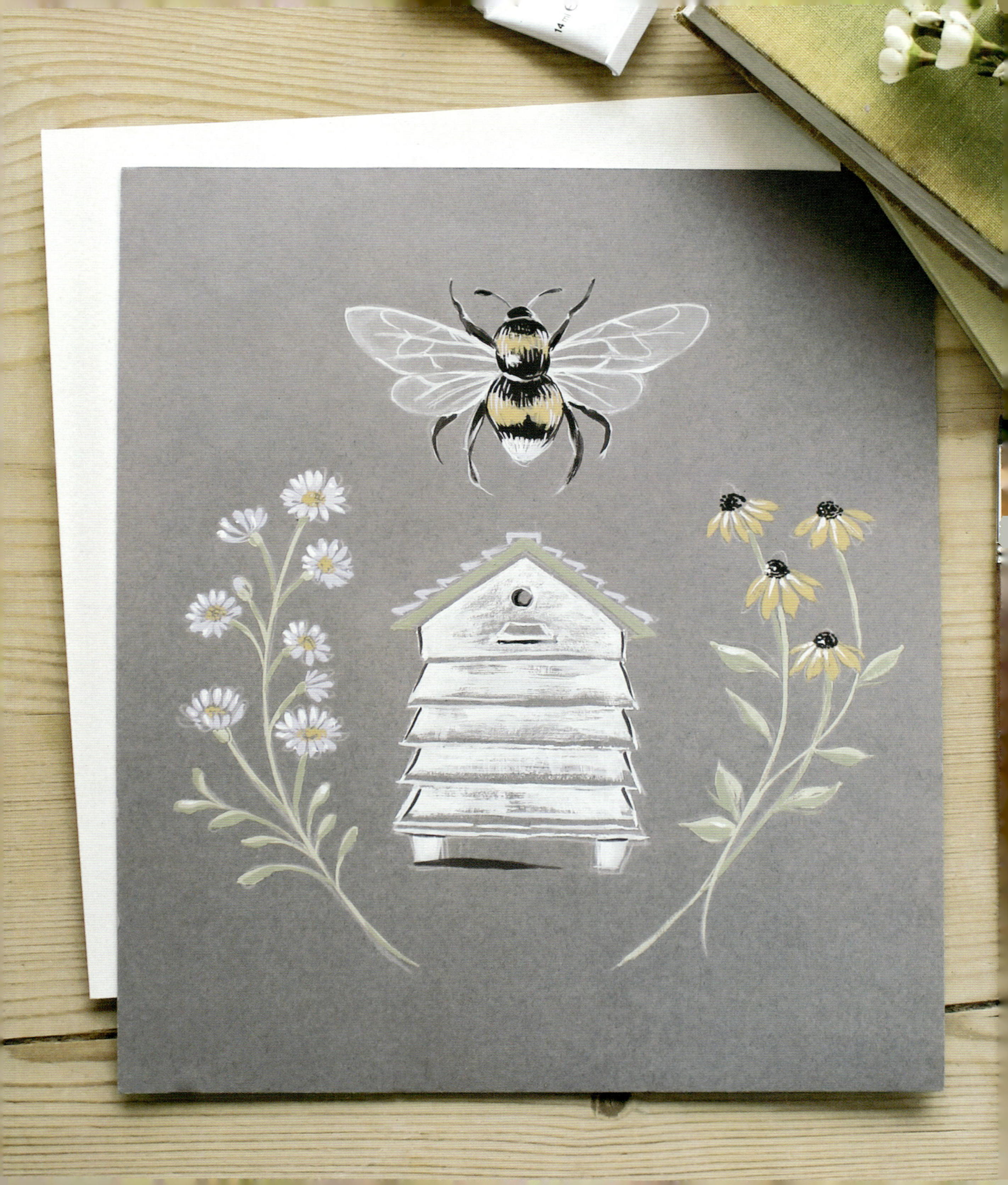

Beehive & Bee

This project develops three important skills, the first of which is painting with a light color on a dark ground. I have chosen a medium gray for the background to really emphasize the white of the wooden hives, the fresh purple of the flowers and the complementary yellow of the bumblebee. This technique gives you scope to use the negative space of the paper to suggest shadow without painting it in. Secondly, we will think about creating narrative to draw the viewer into the piece. This design tells a little story about a bee, a hive and bee-attracting flowers. Thirdly, we will be practicing our brush control using angled and fine round brushes as well as different paint consistencies to create a variety of strokes and textures.

COLOR MIXING

Pure White: Permanent White, straight out of the tube, no funny business.

Dark Gray: Add a speck of Permanent White to a very small dab of Ivory Black.

Yellow: Add a tiny dot each of Alizarin Crimson and Ivory Black to a small blob of Cadmium Yellow. Mix and then add a small dab of Permanent White to lighten.

Pale Purple: Mix a tiny dot of Alizarin Crimson and Phthalo Blue with a small blob of Permanent White.

Pale Green: Add a dab of yellow and a just slightly larger dab of Phthalo Blue to a small blob of Permanent White. Mix in a speck each of Ivory Black and Alizarin Crimson to darken slightly.

Dark Green: Set aside half of the pale green and add dots of Ivory Black, Cadmium Yellow and Phthalo Blue, mixing thoroughly.

SUPPLIES

Brushes: Very fine round, fine round, small round, medium angled, small flat

Paint Colors: Alizarin Crimson, Cadmium Yellow, Ivory Black, Permanent White, Phthalo Blue

Other Supplies: Ruler, pencil and eraser, white watercolor pencil, extra gray scratch paper

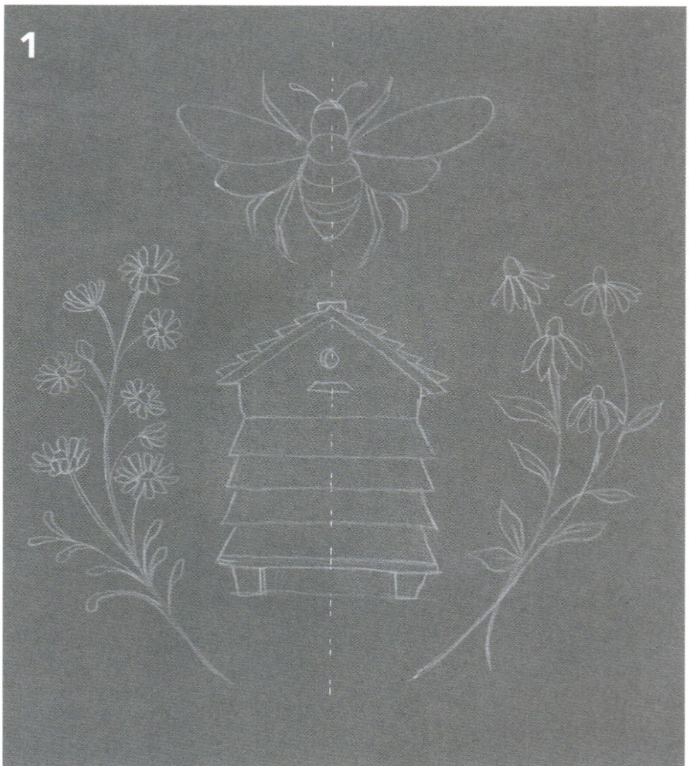

Step 1: Drawing the Elements

Using a ruler, measure and draw a vertical dashed line dividing the page into two equal halves. We will use this line as a guide to place the design on the paper, without drawing in more prominent guidelines, which may be difficult to erase. Slightly above halfway up the page, begin by drawing in the two sloping sides of the beehive roof. Complete this top part of the hive with the two short, nearly vertical lines and one long horizontal line underneath. Draw the four trapezoids below this and then the narrow rim and two small legs. Fill in the details of the roof tiles.

Draw two curved flower stems for your favorite bee attracting flowers. I have chosen black-eyed Susans for their pretty shaped flower heads and long stems and asters for their purple color, which is complementary to the yellow of the bee.

Slightly above the top of the roof of the hive, draw in the body of the bee. Our bee can be broken down into some simple shapes, starting with the small oval for the upper body, followed by a slightly larger oval below coming to a rounded point at the bottom. Add the slightly curved lines to define where you will paint in the stripes. The other details will spring naturally from the body. Lightly draw in the four symmetrical sections of the wings, six legs and the antennae.

TIP: *Notice how the elements in this piece almost form a wreath shape around the central hive. This draws your eye all around the design and balances the different shapes. Check that your own flowers are mirroring each other on each side of the beehive.*

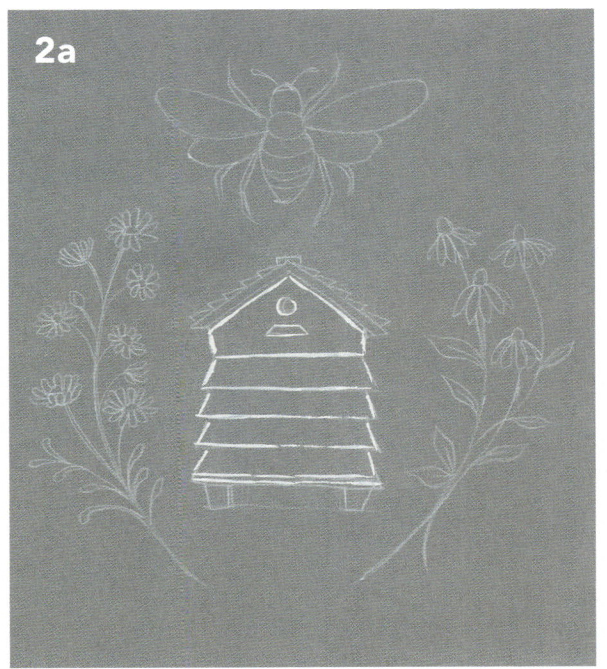

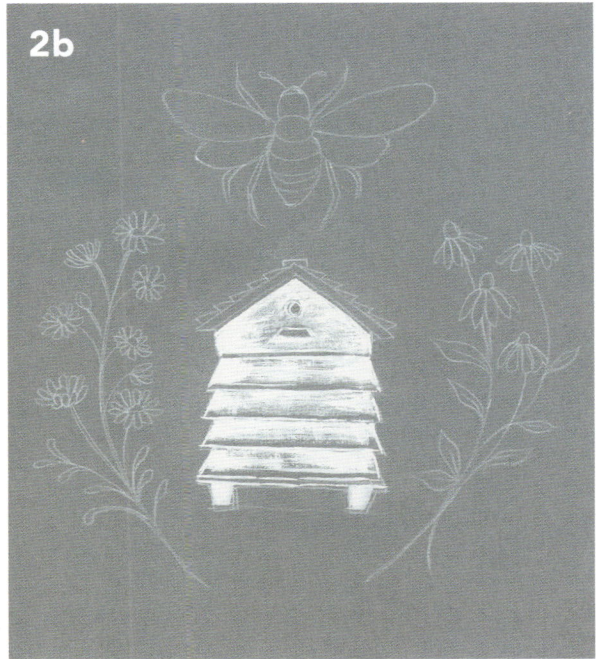

Step 2: The Hive

We will begin the painting with the pure white of the beehive. Keep a remnant of the gray paper handy as scrap to test the consistency of the paint before applying.

TIP: *Start with a fresh pot of water when working with pure white as even the tiniest speck of color can tint it slightly.*

Apply a dab of paint to a dryish brush with only a little touch of water, mixing so that it is lightly coated but not loaded. Test a swatch with the widest part of the brush and using the angle of the brush to fit the angled shape of the hive, aim to create a textured line through which you can see the gray of the paper. When you have the knack of this, begin painting on the piece.

Begin by making your brush as narrow as possible to draw the lines of the edges and slats of the hive. Using the fine pointed tip of the brush, paint round the circular hole and the wooden peg, as we need to remember to keep the insides of these unpainted.

Next, using the technique you have practiced and your medium sized angled brush, paint in the white of the slats leaving a small gap between each slat so that the dark of the paper can suggest a shadow.

Using a small flat brush, paint in the top of the hive, taking care to keep the circle and peg unpainted to suggest more shadow. Leave it to dry before beginning on the next step.

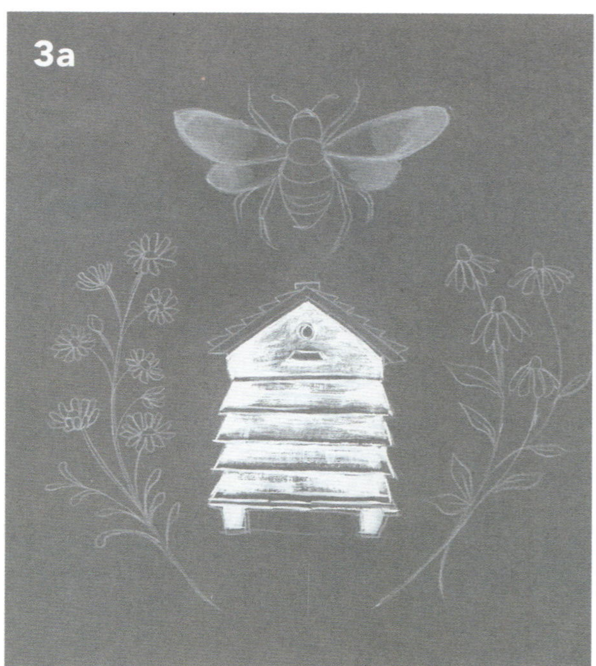

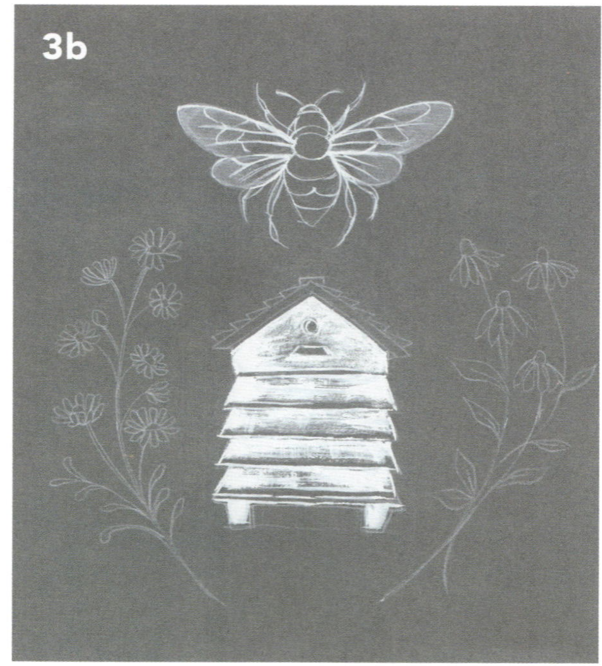

Step 3: The Bee

Next, we turn to painting the bee in a number of steps.

To create the fine gossamer wing, we will first add a very light wash of thin pure white paint before adding the details. Mix a small dot of white with a dab of water. Test several strokes and let it dry so you can check the consistency. Using your medium angled brush, lightly stroke from the tips of the wings inward, leaving the area closest to the body unpainted to suggest shadow.

As the wash will have obscured most of the drawn detail, draw it in again gently with your white watercolor pencil. Next, paint the intricate pattern on the wings with a very fine round brush and some semi-opaque white. In this way, also sketchily highlight your drawn lines of the legs, antennae and the sections of the bee's body.

We will be using a fine round brush for the remainder of the project. Using your dark gray color, paint in the alternating dark sections of the bee's body, leaving it to dry.

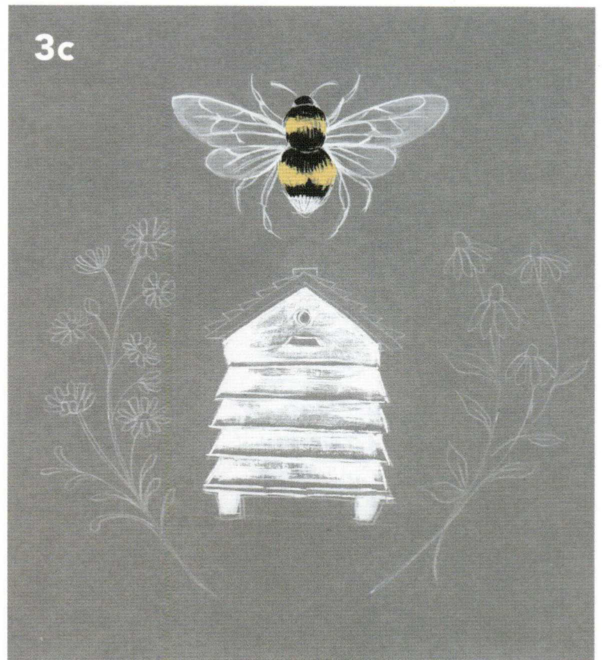

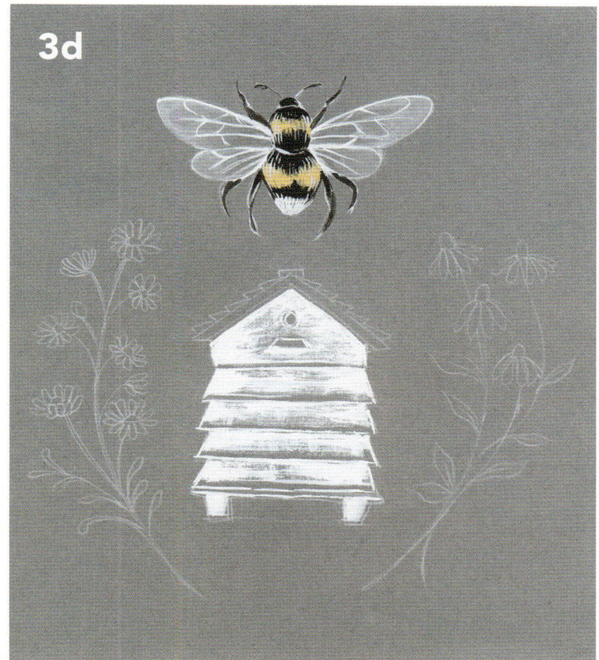

Next, using a clean brush and some of your yellow color, make tiny downward strokes to paint in the yellow sections of the body until they are nearly filled in and slightly overlapping the dark gray.

Do the same with a little pure white for the tail of the bee.

Using your pale purple, paint tiny little curved downward marks, mainly on the sides of the body, to suggest a furry texture.

Use a touch of the dark gray to paint in the legs and antennae. It's fine to leave some of the sketchy white still showing through the gray.

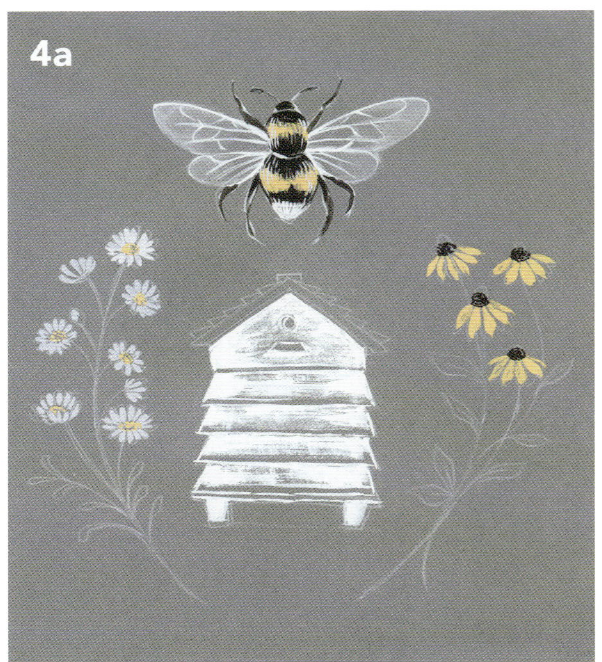

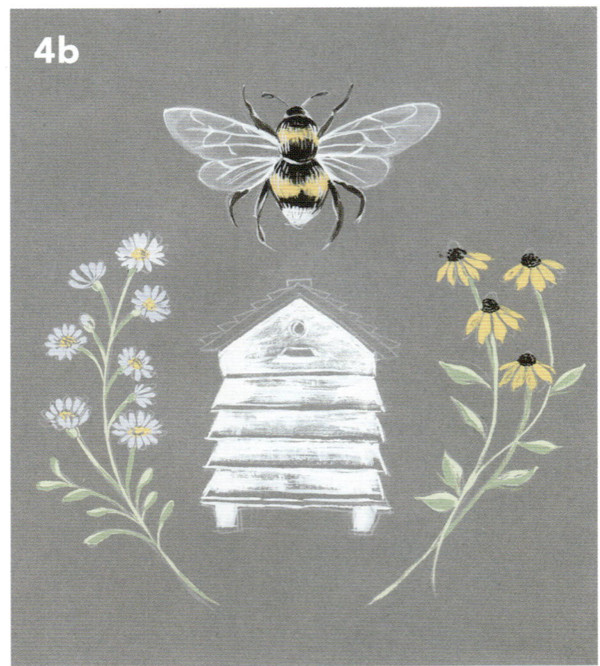

Step 4: The Flowers

Next, begin on the flower elements of the design, starting with the aster flowers on the left. With a little of the pale purple, paint single strokes for each petal and tiny dots of yellow in the centers. Paint each petal of the black-eyed Susan on the right with the yellow and the center with tiny dots of dark gray.

Turning to your pale green color, paint in the delicate curved stems of the flowers, branching out to add in the pointed and curved leaves.

With the dark green, add shadow covering half of each black-eyed Susan leaf on the right as well as on the underside of each of the aster leaves and some of the stems.

5

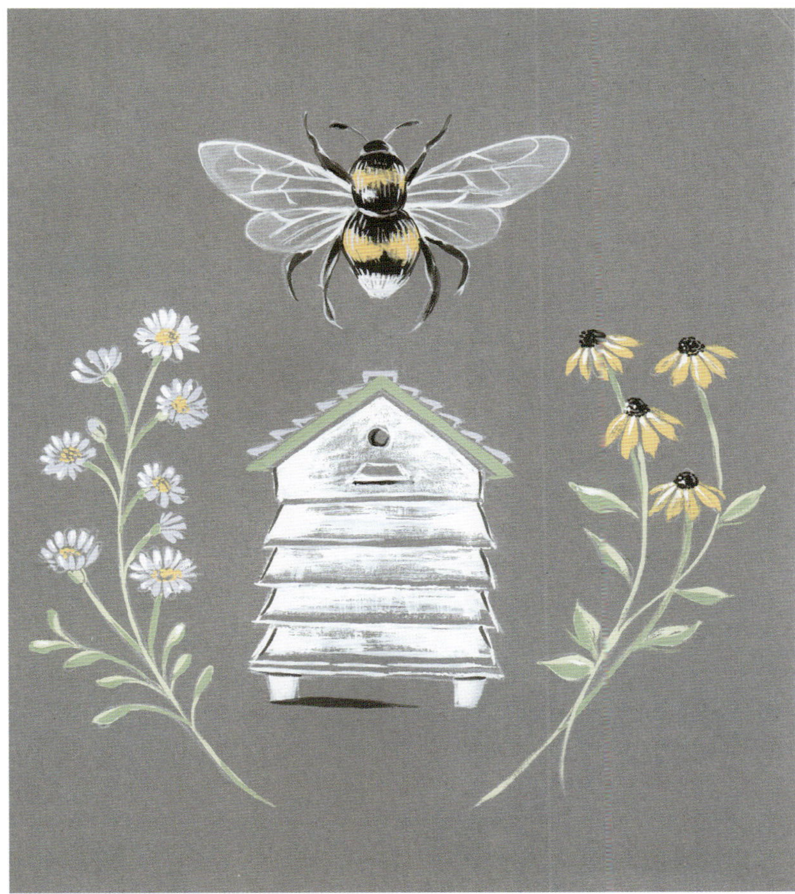

Step 5: Finishing Touches

In this final step, we add some finishing details across the whole piece. Use a little of the mixed pale purple to paint the tiles on the hive roof. Use a small amount of the dark green to paint in the sloping roof itself, being careful to leave a gap between this and the white to suggest the shadow of the roof.

Finish the hive by painting a shadow in the bee hole with faint watered down dark gray, as well as a horizontal dash on the ground underneath the hive on the left-hand side. Again in dark gray, add a few light sloping lines to add definition to the sides of the wooden slats.

Finish the piece by adding a few small pure white details to make the flower heads pop. Add lines and dots to the edges of the aster petals, the black-eyed Susan flowers and a textured dot on the body of the bee.

TAKING THE PROJECT FURTHER:

There is a marvelous array of colored paper out there, so try painting your favorite bee-attracting flower in pure white but on a different colored background. As in this project, create textures using different consistencies of paint by varying the amounts of water added.

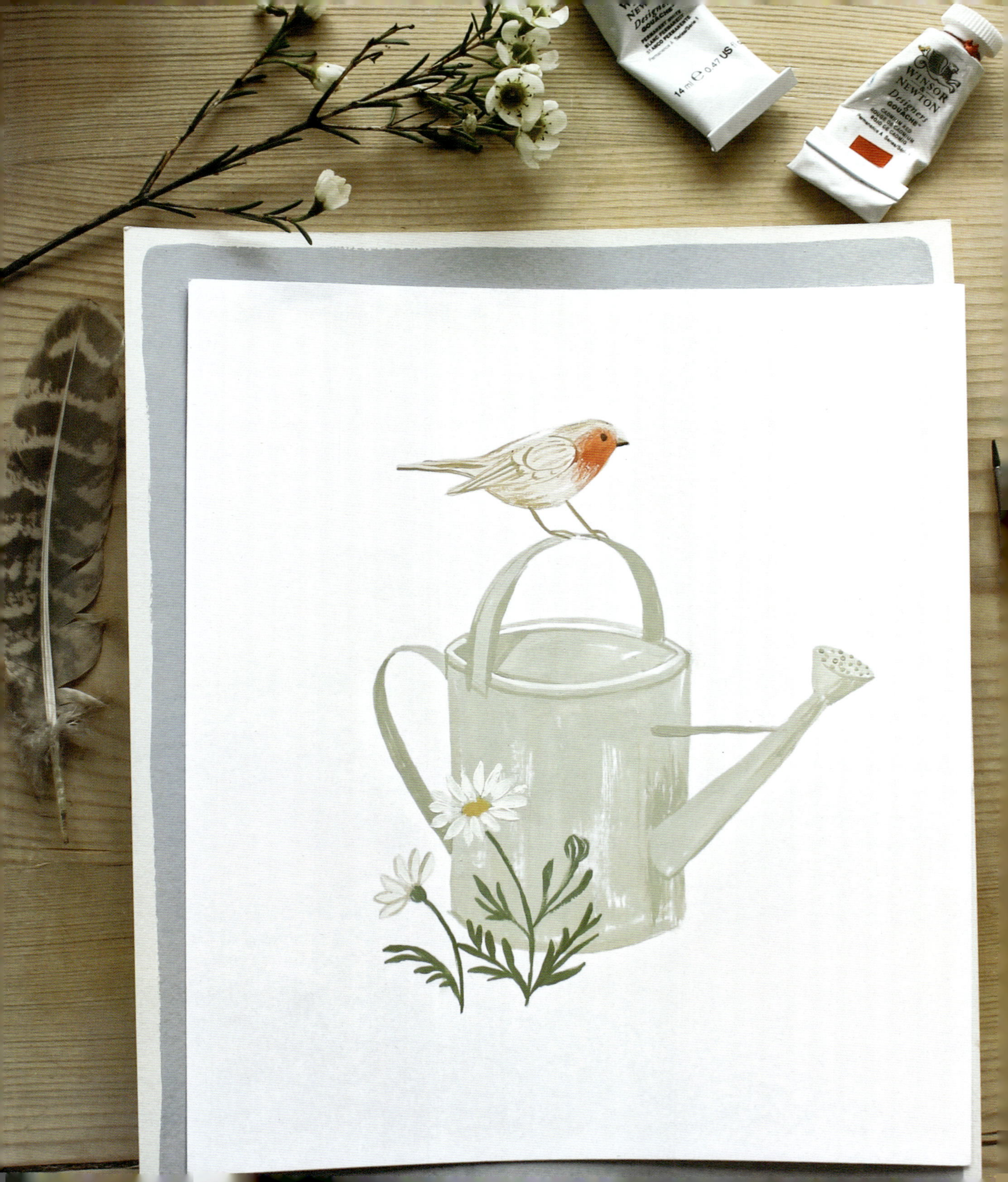
14 ml ℮ 0.47 US
WINSOR & NEWTON
Designers
GOUACHE
CADMIUM RED
ROUGE DE CADMIUM
ROJO DE CADMIO

Garden Robin

Robins are versatile little birdies who are happily featured in both summer and winter scenes. This quick little project will develop your brushwork and skills in basic composition. The watering can is the focus of the design, with the bird and flowers adding quirky interest. Daisies are wonderfully simple to paint and will break up the large flat area of the watering can. In this project, we will try using a dry-brush technique to create texture and a vintage feel.

COLOR MIXING

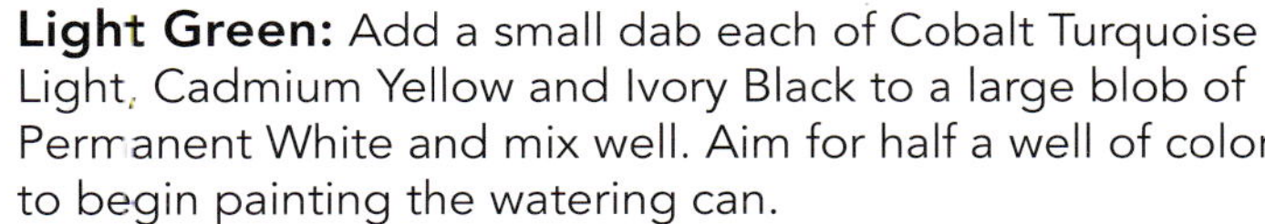

Light Green: Add a small dab each of Cobalt Turquoise Light, Cadmium Yellow and Ivory Black to a large blob of Permanent White and mix well. Aim for half a well of color to begin painting the watering can.

Darker Green: Set aside some of the light green and add a dot each of Ivory Black and Burnt Umber, mixing thoroughly. Test a swatch to make sure it's not too dark and add white to lighten if it is!

Off-White: Mix this opaque shade by adding a dot of Burnt Umber to a large dab of Permanent White.

Light Khaki: Mix a dot each of Burnt Umber, Cadmium Yellow and Cobalt Turquoise Light with a large dab of Permanent White.

Red: Add a large dot of Cadmium Red and a slightly smaller dot of Cadmium Yellow to a dab of Permanent White and the smallest speck of Ivory Black. Create only a very small amount.

Burnt Umber: No mixing needed!

Bright Green: Add a small dab each of Cadmium Yellow and Cobalt Turquoise Light, with a dot each of Burnt Umber and Ivory Black, to a small blob of Permanent White.

Mustard Yellow: Add a speck of Burnt Umber and a dot of Cadmium Yellow to a dab of Permanent White. You only need a very small amount. Test the color before painting.

Pure White: Permanent White, straight out of the tube.

SUPPLIES

Brushes: Fine round, small round, medium angled

Paint Colors: Burnt Umber, Cadmium Red, Cadmium Yellow, Cobalt Turquoise Light, Ivory Black, Permanent White

Other Supplies: Pencil and eraser, scratch paper

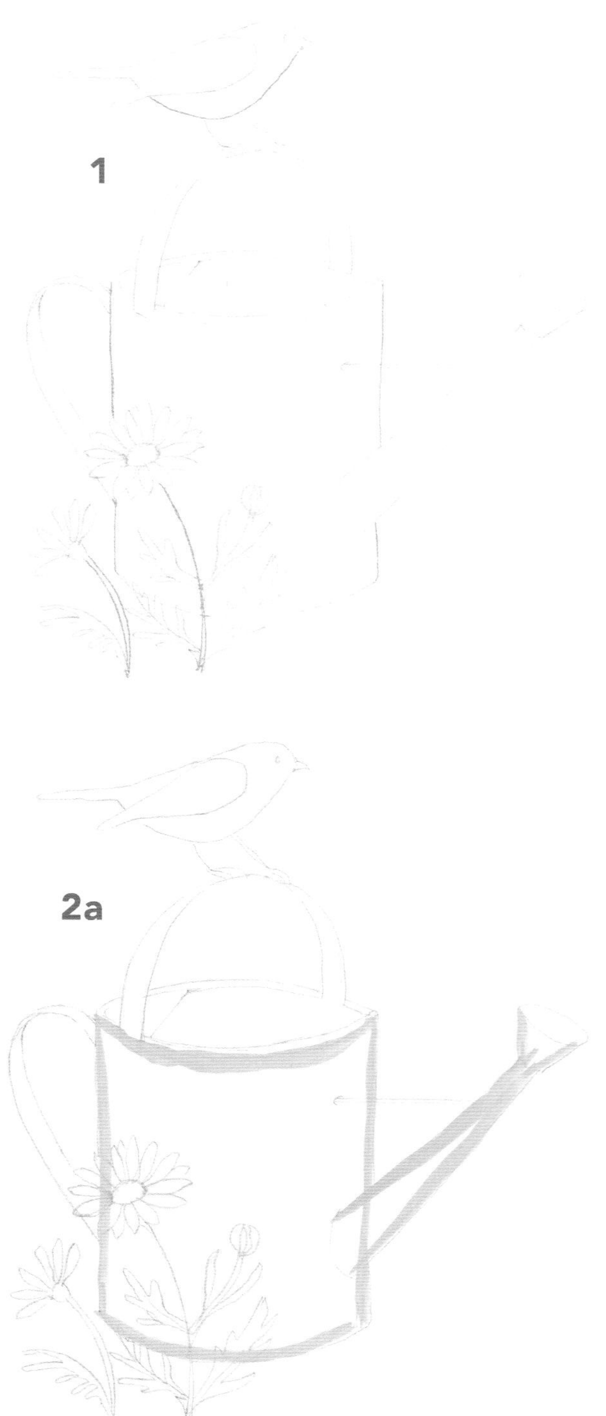

Step 1: Drawing the Scene

Draw the watering can, starting with its two vertical sides. Create perspective by joining these together using a semicircle for the base and an almond-shaped top, with a dividing line to create the opening. Add the tapering spout and a conical sprinkler end. Draw a horizontal line to connect the two together.

Add parallel lines for the 'ear'-shaped handle on the left and two arched semi-circular lines for the top handle. Notice how they narrow at the top to give the illusion of perspective.

Using my darker guidelines as reference, add the robin, starting with his legs so that he perches neatly on top of the can. The curve of his belly is a simple semicircle shape, closed with a lightly curved line for his head. Add a teeny triangular pointy beak and long thin tail. The wing is a teardrop shape on the side of his body.

Lastly, sketch in the lines for the daisy stems, setting them slightly in front of the can. The leaves curve up and outward with wavy edges. Draw in the three heads: One open flower with small oblong petals surrounding an oval center, one flower from the side and one little rounded bud. Make sure at least one of the flower heads sits in front of the body of the can to break up the expanse of green.

Step 2: The Watering Can

When dry-brushing, you tend to need a little more paint as it is applied thickly. Begin with your light green and mix a dab of the color with a wet medium sized angled brush to evenly coat the tip. The consistency should be smooth and sticky. Turning your brush to make the head as narrow as possible, draw a line down each side of the can, around the rim and up the side of the spout and head.

Then, turning the brush in your hand and with confident yet light downward strokes, fill in the body of the can. Don't worry if the paint runs out in patches, keep going until the body is covered, with some sketchy white areas showing through. Do the same with the spout, starting with a wide flat brush and twisting slightly to narrow the size of the head as the width of the spout decreases.

TIP: *Don't worry if you accidentally paint outside the lines of the can with the angled brush. It's easy to tidy up, especially with a light color. Using a little clean water, work away at the paint with a fine clean brush and blot with a paper towel to remove the color and water.*

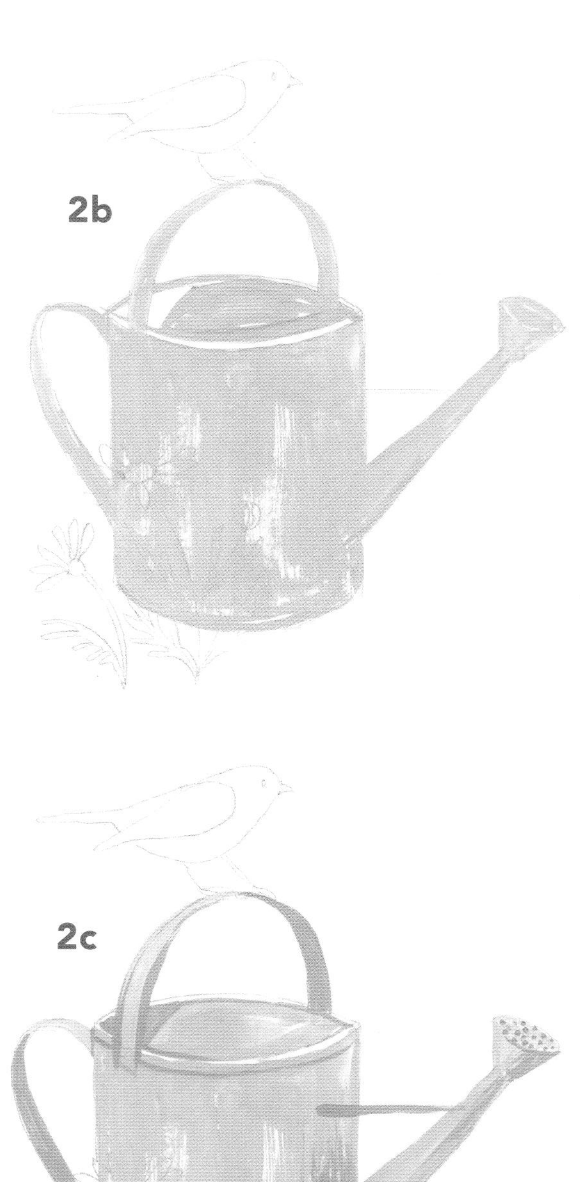

Using a fine round brush, paint in the head of the can and both handles. Try to keep the rim unpainted but don't worry too much if you go over it—we can always sort it out later.

Next, use your slightly darker green shade to emphasize the three-dimensionality of the can with shadow. Using a dry fine round brush and a dot of the paint, fill in the hole in the top of the can. Paint a shadow on the inside of both handles and very light and loose vertical lines above and below the spout to suggest a shadow.

In the same color, add detail to the rim of the can, the edges of the handles and to where the handles meet the can. Paint over the line of the spout support with a steady hand. On the underside of the spout, add loose textured shadow and add spots for the watering holes.

3

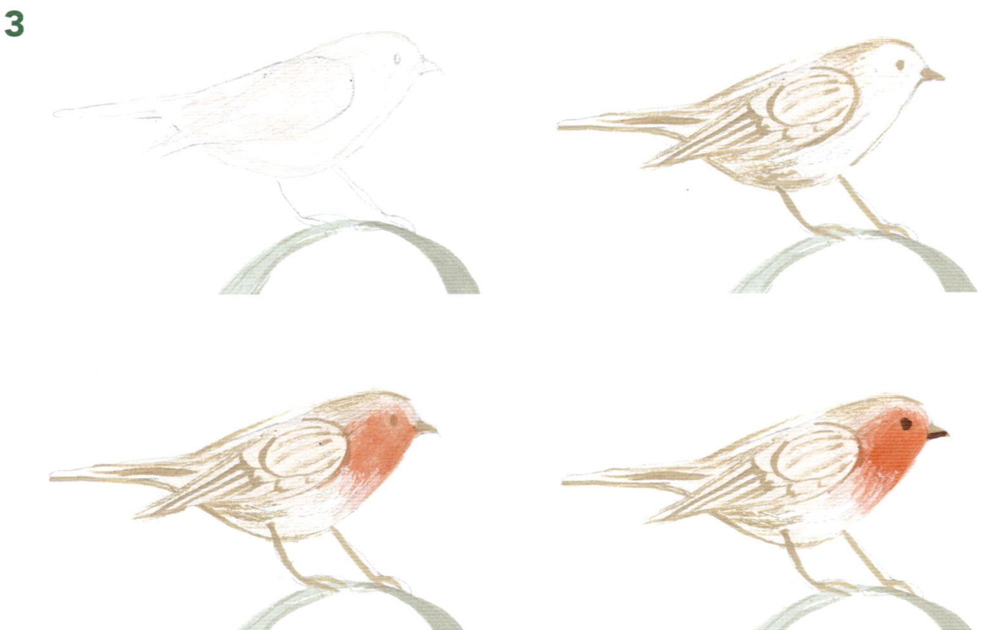

Step 3: The Robin

Turn to your opaque shade of off-white and fill in the whole robin, including the wings, tail and beak, by using a small round brush loaded with smooth dryish paint. Apply the same approach as you did with the can when using light textured strokes, not worrying too much about even coverage and leave until dry.

Next, we come to the light khaki color for the bird details. Use a fine round brush to paint in the beak, eye and legs. Sketchily outline the underside of the body and wings, lightly painting some lines to suggest the texture of feathers.

We need a very small amount of the red for the robin's breast—this will add the most impact to the piece! Water down a little of the color on the end of your brush with a touch of water, painting in the robin's breast with a few, small strokes. Use a touch of the dryish off-white to blend this into the body.

When you have done this, you can more confidently add some textured dryish red with the tip of your brush to add depth and vibrancy. Again, blend the edges with some dryish off-white.

Paint in the eye and beak with a little Burnt Umber, using the end of a fine brush.

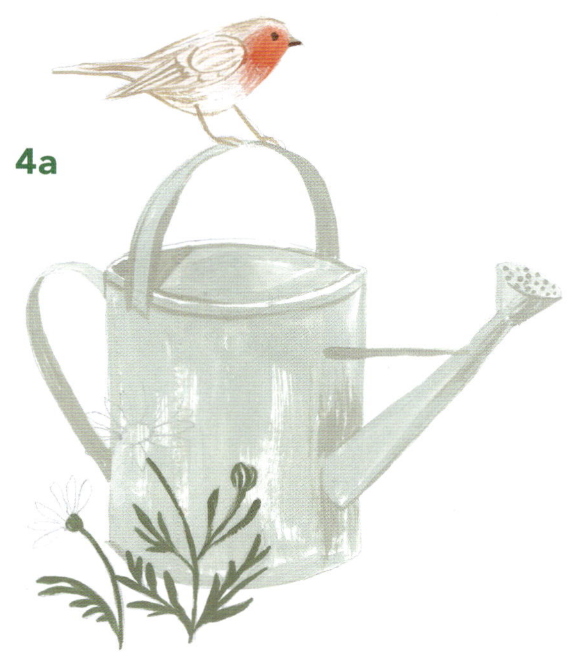

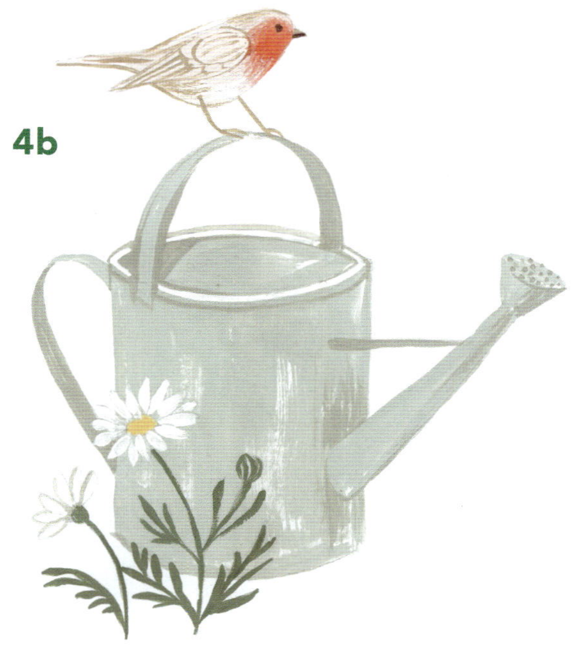

Step 4: The Flowers

The flower drawings should still be partly visible through the painted can. If they are not, very lightly sketch them back in. Next, paint in the flower stems and leaves using the bright green shade. Before you begin, test the opacity and consistency of the paint on your scratch paper. You should be able to draw a curved line without needing to reload the brush with paint. Start with the stems and then loosely paint in all the leaves with a light stroke. The darker color of the line will serve as a lovely contrast to the texture of the can.

Using a tiny amount of mustard yellow, paint in the oval flower head.

Change to a smallish round brush and with dryish pure white, paint in the petals so they have a little raised texture. Practice on your scratch paper first if you like. I find it helpful to have plenty of paint on the brush and to press down slightly more heavily in the center of the petal, creating a rounded shape with a single stroke. The white of the petals on the left can get lost on the white paper, so using your smallest brush and the lightest of touches, add a little definition to the petal edges with the light green of the watering can.

Touch up the rim of the can with pure white if you need to, using a fine brush and a steady hand. Wait until the entire piece and particularly the flower petals are dry before erasing any visible pencil lines.

TAKING THE PROJECT FURTHER:

Try painting a little garden tool scene to further develop your use of the dry-brush technique. This would make a fabulous card for the gardeners in your life! Draw in a little pile of plant pots, a hand trowel, a garden fork and a single flower and paint with a limited palette of warm browns and greens.

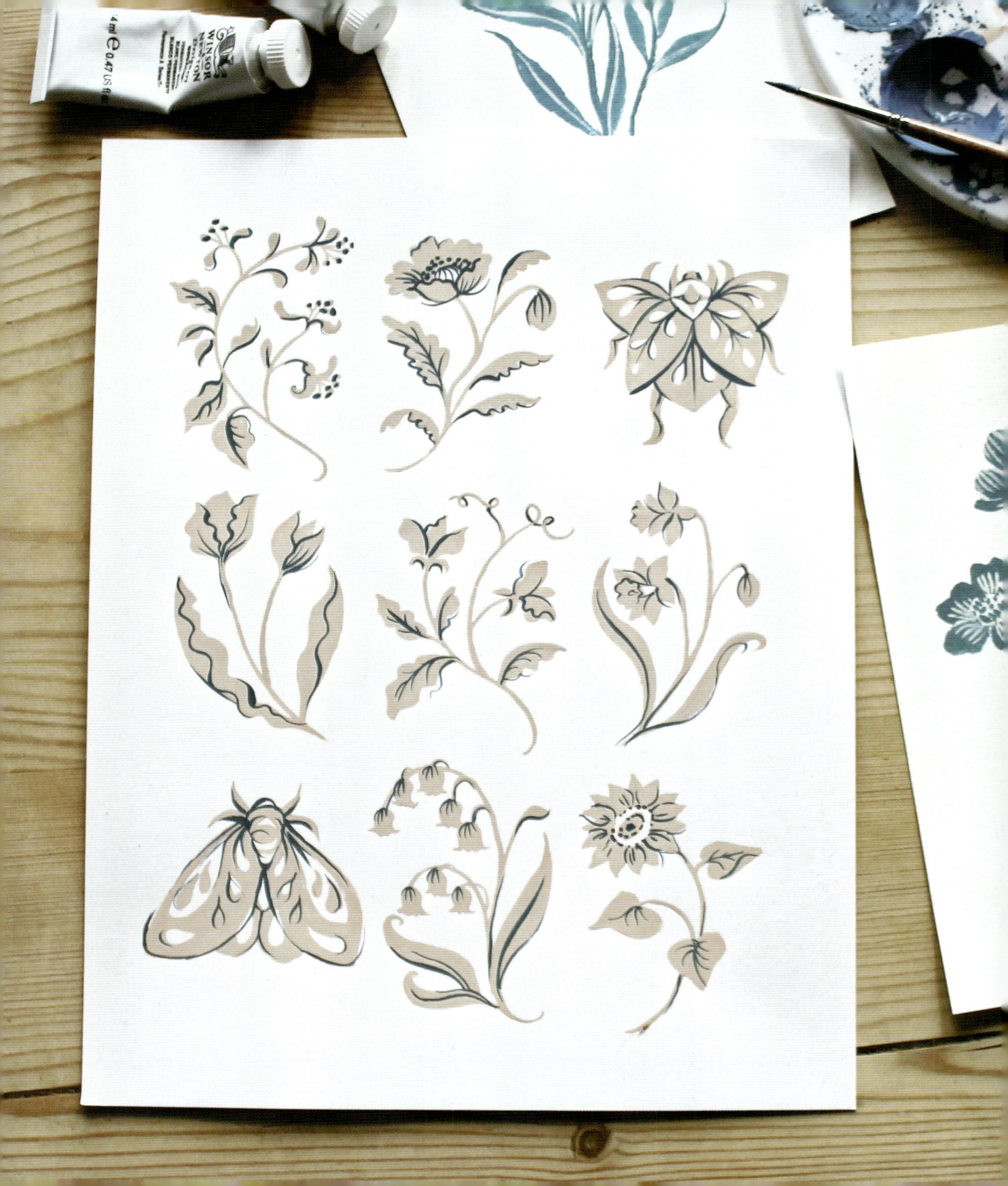
WINSOR
NEWTON

Botanical Silhouettes

Painting with two colors is so rewarding when working with gouache. It is such a simple technique and doesn't involve the faff of mixing a whole palette of colors, yet it can have a fantastic impact. I have chosen a subtle palette of taupe and stone blue, but you could choose one light and one darker shade of any two colors you like. This project is an intricate design that will naturally hone your skills using a fine brush. I have chosen several traditional garden flowers, but you may choose any flowers or creatures you fancy!

COLOR MIXING

Taupe: Add a dab of Opera Pink and a slightly larger dab of Lemon Yellow to a very large blob of Permanent White and mix. Next, add a couple of large dabs of Burnt Umber and a spot of Ivory Black and mix thoroughly. You will need nearly a full well of this so that you have enough to paint in the entire silhouette without mixing again. It may be difficult to replicate the exact same shade later, so better to make slightly more than you need and save yourself that hassle! Using a slightly different color would change the balance of the image and lose some of the crispness we are aiming for.

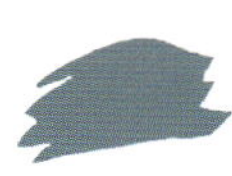

Stone Blue: Add a large dab each of Burnt Umber and Ivory Black, plus a small dab of Permanent White, to a small blob of Phthalo Blue.

SUPPLIES

Brush: Very fine round

Paint Colors: Burnt Umber, Ivory Black, Lemon Yellow, Opera Pink, Permanent White, Phthalo Blue

Other Supplies: light brown–colored watercolor pencil, graphite pencil, scratch paper

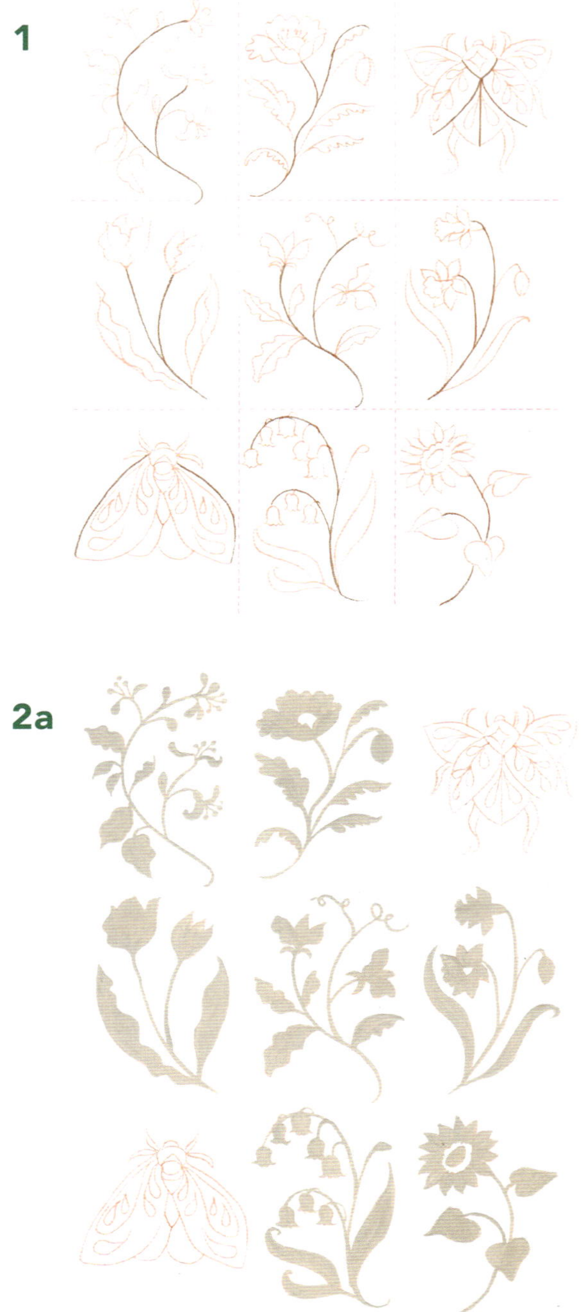

Step 1: Drawing the Flowers & Creatures

We will be using a light brown watercolor pencil for this piece instead of graphite so that it is less visible through the pale-colored gouache. As watercolor pencils are more difficult to remove with an eraser, I suggest sketching the design on some paper first so you can reference this when drawing in the lines on the final design. I have chosen a range of garden flowers so that we have the opportunity to paint some different floral shapes.

Begin by using a normal graphite pencil to very lightly draw out a grid on which to place the flowers neatly on the page. Next, with your light brown watercolor paper, draw in single lines for the stems, using my darker guidelines for reference. Pay particular attention to the differing leaf shapes and edges and try to include some that are straight-on and some from the side, as well as a variety of sizes.

All of the little details in this drawing will be important in creating a dynamic composition and taking time to draw out the elements very carefully will get you half-way there! Before you begin painting, erase the light graphite pencil gridlines and be sure to take a photo or scan—you will need this as a reference after you add the opaque taupe layer.

Step 2: Silhouettes

Mixing the paint to the correct consistency is key in this piece and we are aiming for even, opaque coverage and smooth, flat lines. The paint in your well will be thick and gloopy—dip the head of your brush in clean water and mix with a dab of the paint on the side of your palette. Paint a couple of test strokes on your scratch paper to make sure you can paint a fluid stroke in which the paint is smooth, yet still opaque.

TIP: *Every time the paint on the design starts to look a little thick, water it down by dipping your brush in water and thinning the paint a little.*

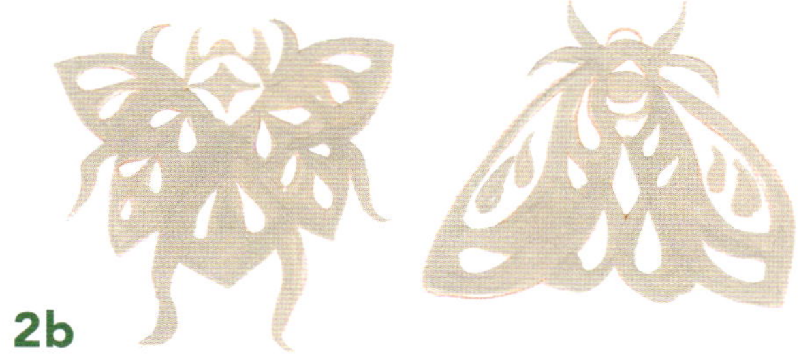
2b

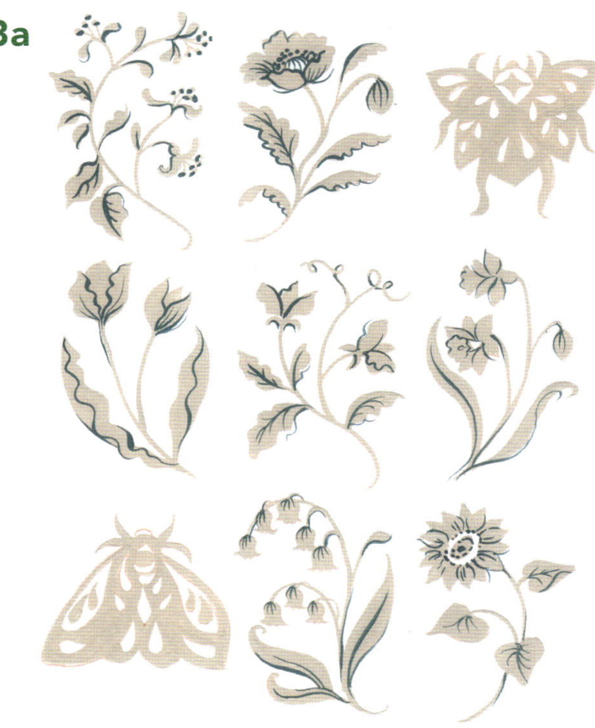
3a

Now we begin painting all the flowers in the silhouette, so set aside some time where you can do this in one go. It is a gloriously relaxing and therapeutic activity as you simply need to fill in the drawn lines!

Using a very fine round brush and your taupe color, begin by painting over the stems and little twirly bits with single fine lines. Go on to fill all the shapes completely, BUT remember to keep the centers of the flowers unpainted.

Start in the top left and move right line-by-line, or vice versa if you are left-handed. This is to minimize the chance of your hand accidentally smudging the design.

Next, we paint in the silhouettes of the two bugs, taking care to keep the pattern on their shells and wings unpainted so that the white of the paper creates a contrasting pattern.

TIP: *Taupe and stone are useful colors, so to avoid wasting excess paint, store the palette carefully and reactivate the paint at a later date with some water and a small, flat brush.*

Step 3: Contrasting Blue Linework

Turn next to your stone blue color layer, using the same techniques as you did for the taupe. When it is painted on top of the taupe, it will look a little darker than in the mixed palette or on plain paper.

We will try a freehand layer of details in the blue to complement, but not overpower, the detail in the painted floral silhouettes. The idea is to suggest stems, leaves and petals without outlining, so the fewer marks, the better. Use your initial photo as a reference so you can remember where the details go.

Start with the honeysuckle and work left to right on each row. Think of your fine brush as you might think of a pencil—we are 'drawing' little details with our brush.

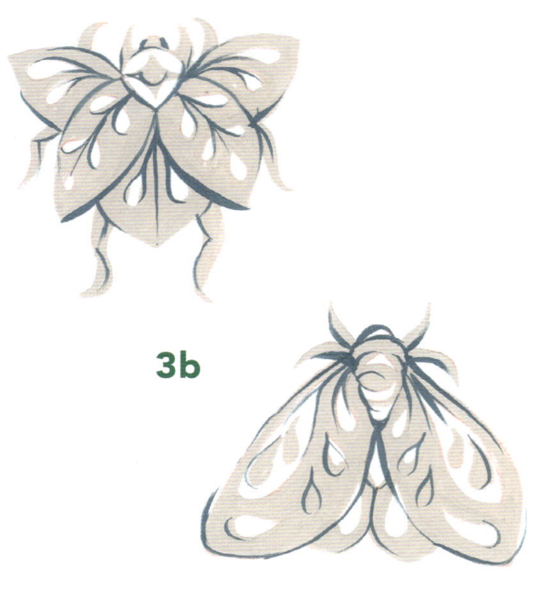

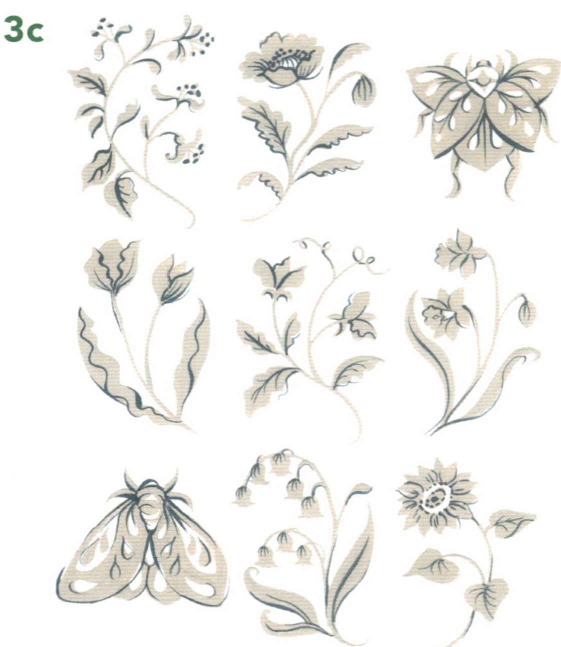

Add details on each of the leaves, be it the central and branching veins, or a little squiggle to define the underside or edge of a leaf. Some flowers, such as the daffodils, have long thin leaves that you can draw with one curved or wavy stroke.

Flower heads are a little trickier. Define the lower edges of some but not all of the petals. Create a little hatched shading on the underside of some of the larger petals to suggest that they are curved up and outward. On the bluebells, do this on the top to emphasize their curved bell shape. Add small dots to suggest the stamen, especially on the honeysuckle, poppy and sunflowers.

Finish the piece by adding details to the moth and beetle. Try to keep these as simple as possible, only partially outlining the wings and emphasizing the teardrop pattern. Don't worry about keeping lines neat or straight—the lighter, freer and more curved, the better.

TAKING THE PROJECT FURTHER:

Botanical silhouettes would work well painted onto letterheads and invitations. You could try painting a single flower with a simple dotted border as a beautiful gift. Choose one light and one darker shade of any two colors you like. These elements would also make an ideal pattern! You could choose as many or as few creatures and flowers as you like and either paint them in neat rows as we have, or more loosely in random spots or clusters.

Friendly Creatures

I have chosen two of the most common creatures for this project, a snail and a moth. They offer a great opportunity to practice adding pattern to your pieces as they naturally have such beautiful patterns on their shells and wings. In this project I will try to simplify the process, using opaque layers and a limited palette for maximum impact. I have chosen an imaginative palette of reds and blues to create a vibrant piece. Little critters are ideal for sprinkling into floral paintings, adding life and detail. Once you have the hang of these, see the reference page of drawings (page 57) so you can take the project further by painting the same creatures in other positions!

COLOR MIXING

Stone: Mix a small dab of Cadmium Yellow and a dot of Ivory Black to a small blob of Permanent White.

Off-White: Mix a dot of Cadmium Yellow and the teeniest speck of Ivory Black with a small blob of Permanent White.

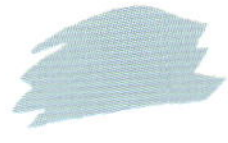

Pale Blue: Add a small dab each of Phthalo Blue and Ivory Black and a speck of Cadmium Yellow to a blob of Permanent White.

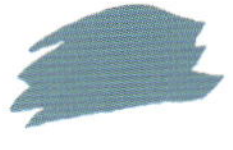

Medium Blue: Mix a small dab of Permanent White, a dab of Ivory Black and a tiny touch of Cadmium Yellow with a blob of Phthalo Blue.

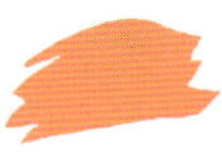

Dark Orange: Mix two dabs of Yellow Ochre to one dab each of Cadmium Red and Permanent White.

Pink: Add a small dab each of Alizarin Crimson, Cadmium Red and Cadmium Yellow to a large dab of Permanent White.

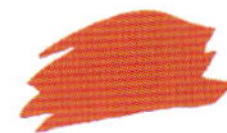

Red: Mix equal sized dabs of Cadmium Red and Alizarin Crimson with a small dab of Permanent White and a speck of Ivory Black.

Indigo: Add a small dab of Alizarin Crimson and a dab of Ivory Black to a small blob of Phthalo Blue.

SUPPLIES

Brushes: Fine round, small round

Paint Colors: Alizarin Crimson, Cadmium Red, Cadmium Yellow, Ivory Black, Phthalo Blue, Permanent White, Yellow Ochre

Other Supplies: Pencil and eraser, scratch paper

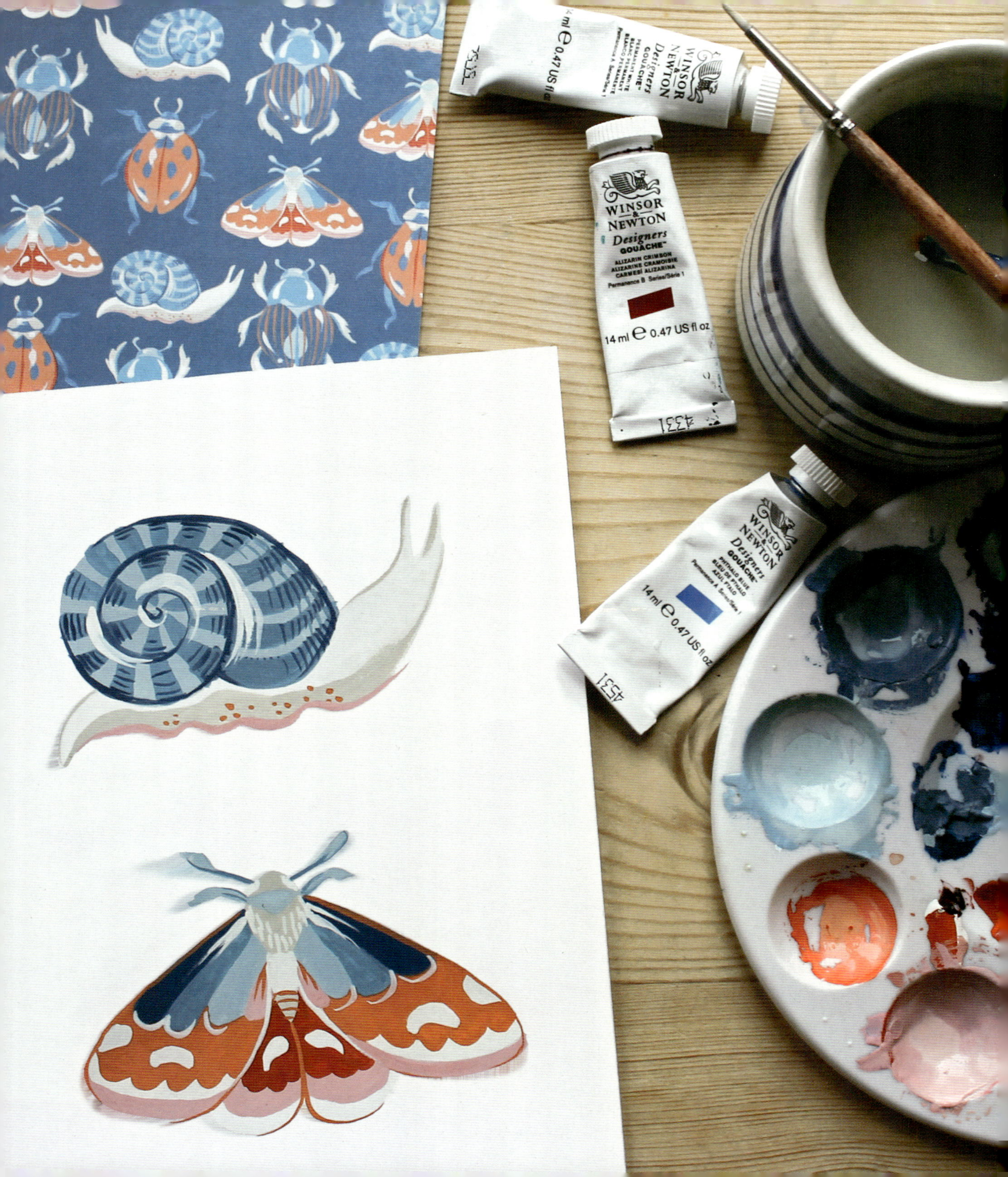
WINSOR & NEWTON
Designers
GOUACHE
ALIZARIN CRIMSON
14 ml ℮ 0.47 US fl oz

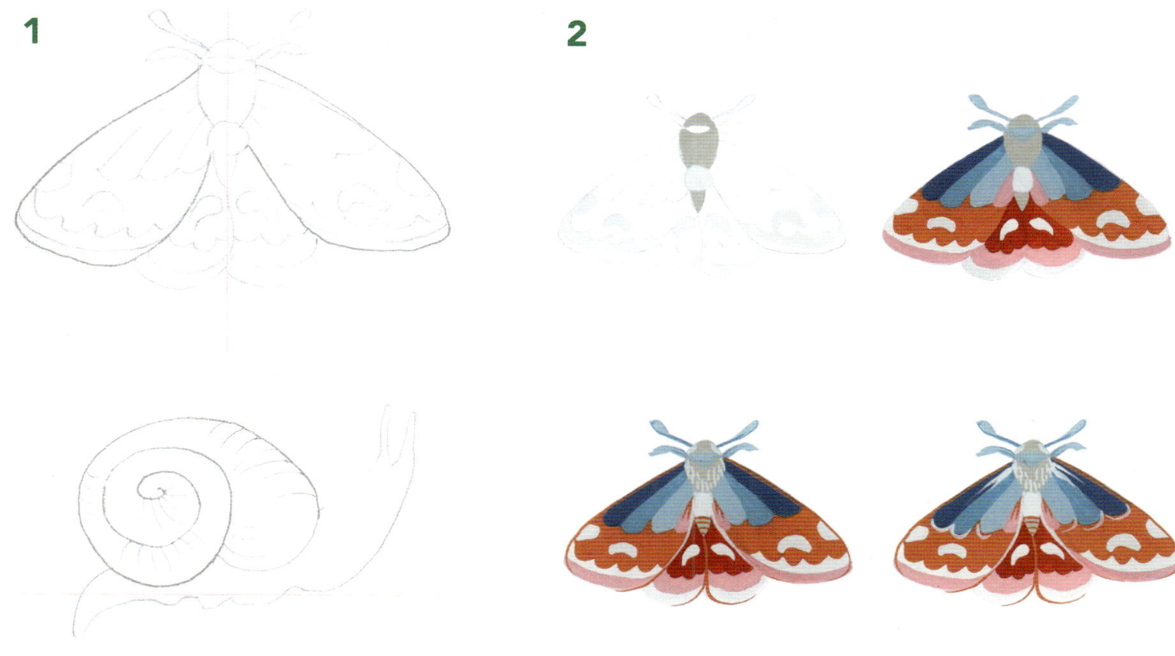

Step 1: Draw the Creatures

Start by lightly drawing out the creatures you fancy, either in a horizontal or vertical line. Drawing out the basic pattern of their bodies will make it far easier when adding color. Follow my darker guidelines to create the basic shapes and, once these are in place, think about drawing details such as legs, antennae and spots.

Step 2: Moth

We will be using a non-realistic palette to convincingly replicate colors in an imaginative way. For example, we will use medium blue and indigo instead of brown on the moth's wings, and pale blue for the legs and antenae, but it will still be easily recognizable as a moth!

Use a fine round brush for the entire moth. Paint the body in stone and off-white. Add off-white detail to the pattern on the wings.

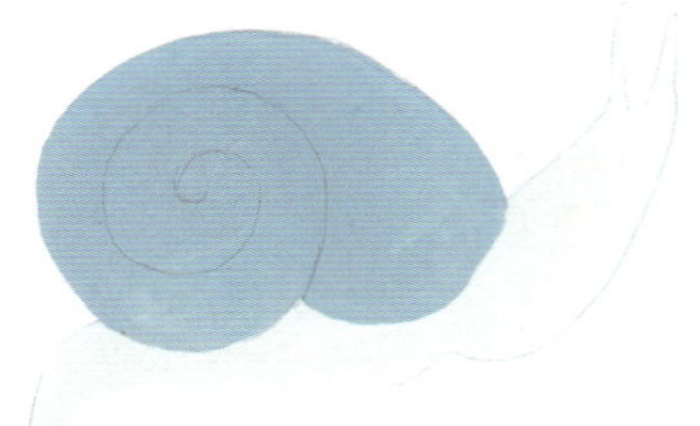

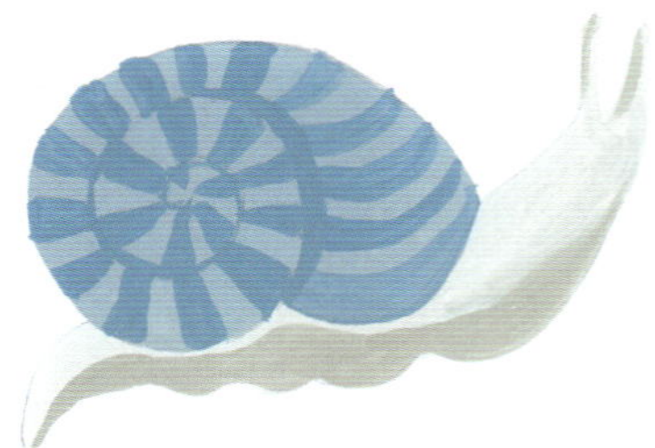

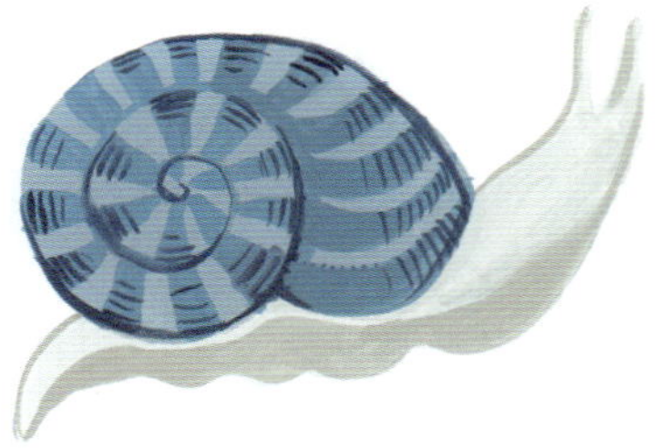

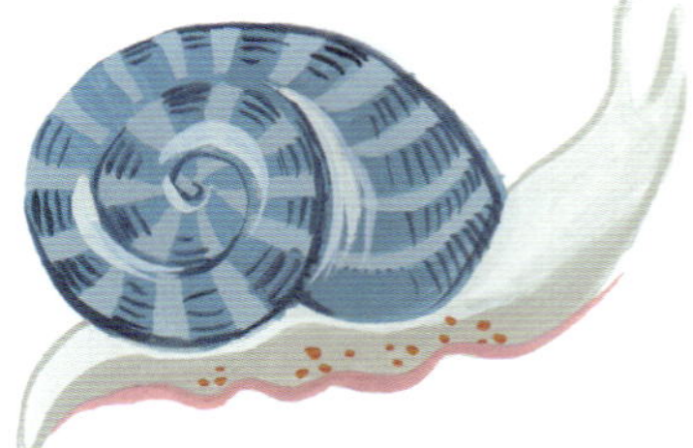

This step will involve almost all the colors in your palette so be sure you have fresh water in your pot and some tissue to blot after cleaning your brushes. Taking one color at a time, fill in the pattern on the moth, starting with the blues, the lightest shades first. Next, dark orange, then pink and then red.

Using a light stroke and some dark orange paint, draw some line detail on the wings and stripes on the body. Try not to outline, but rather use the line to emphasize the curved shape of the wings. Use a tiny bit of off-white to draw some feathered detail on the body. Paint a tiny amount of medium blue line detail on the antennae and legs.

Paint small strokes of off-white highlights on top of the indigo and on the dark orange.

Step 3: Snail

Using a small round brush and, after making sure that the consistency is opaque on some scratch paper, fill the shell of the snail in pale blue and the body in off-white. You will lose the curl of the shell, so once the design is dry, lightly draw this back in with your graphite pencil.

Begin layering with a fine round brush and, using the medium blue, lightly paint a line over the pencil curl. Paint narrow, curved stripes, thinking about the rounded nature of a snail shell.

Blotting the brush and then loading it with dryish stone-colored paint, add a long wiggly shadow to suggest the snail's underside.

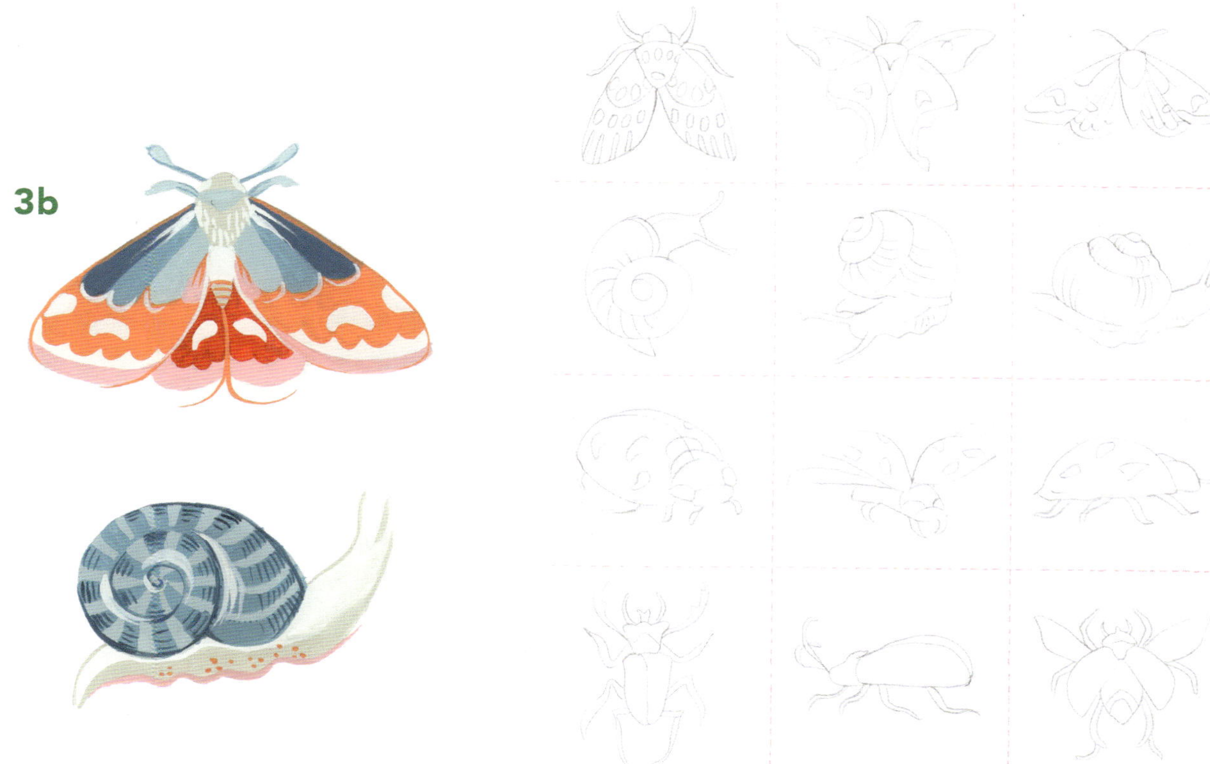

Using the indigo, begin by adding a curved stroke from the left down to where the bottom of the shell meets the body, adding a mirrored line above with a small fine curl. Add one further stroke from the top of the shell down toward the head. Add fine hatched lines to suggest the shadow of the shell.

Using the stone color, give a little definition to the tail and eyes.

With dark orange, add tiny dotty details to the body. Use a pink wiggly stroke to ground the snail.

Using off-white and a dry brush, add a few light textured strokes to suggest volume on the shell.

TAKING THE PROJECT FURTHER:

Have a go at a few different creatures such as a ladybug or beetle, using a more realistic color palette including black, brown, red, cream and white, to create a more traditional design. The elements will work wonderfully in whatever configuration you choose! How about three in a row, or a pair or maybe just one on its own with an oval border.

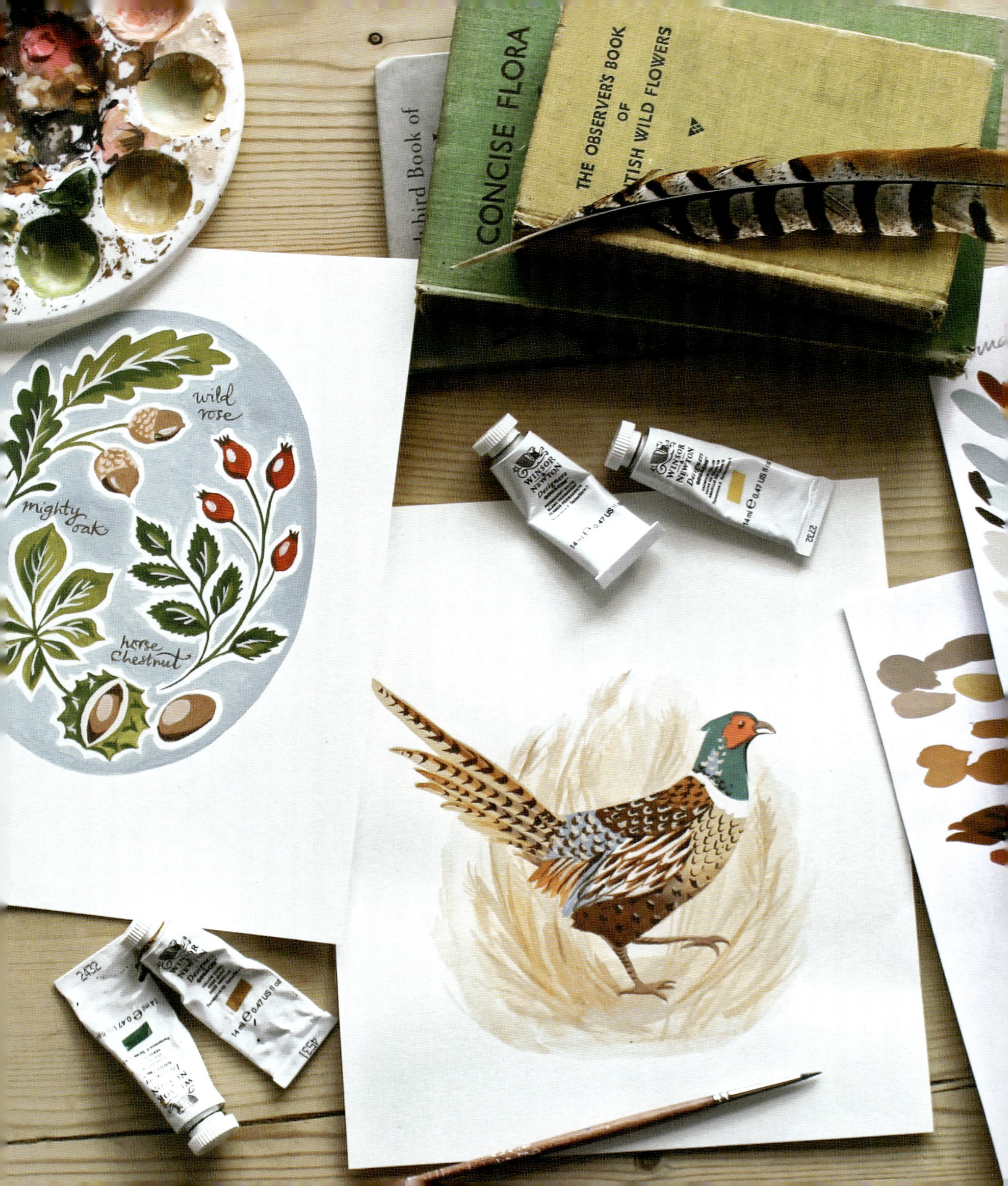
CONCISE FLORA
THE OBSERVER'S BOOK
OF
TISH WILD FLOWERS
wild rose
mighty oak
horse chestnut

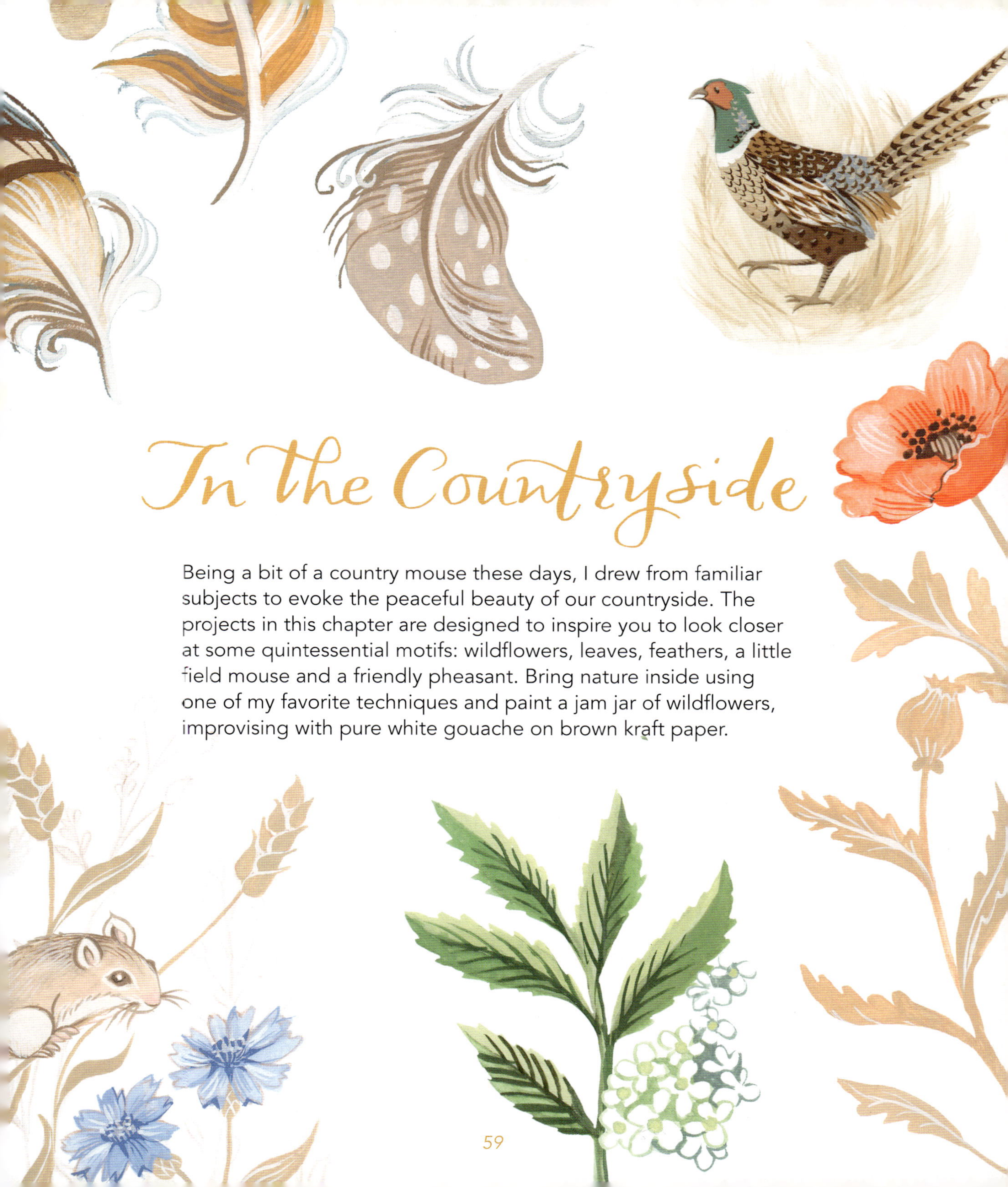

In the Countryside

Being a bit of a country mouse these days, I drew from familiar subjects to evoke the peaceful beauty of our countryside. The projects in this chapter are designed to inspire you to look closer at some quintessential motifs: wildflowers, leaves, feathers, a little field mouse and a friendly pheasant. Bring nature inside using one of my favorite techniques and paint a jam jar of wildflowers, improvising with pure white gouache on brown kraft paper.

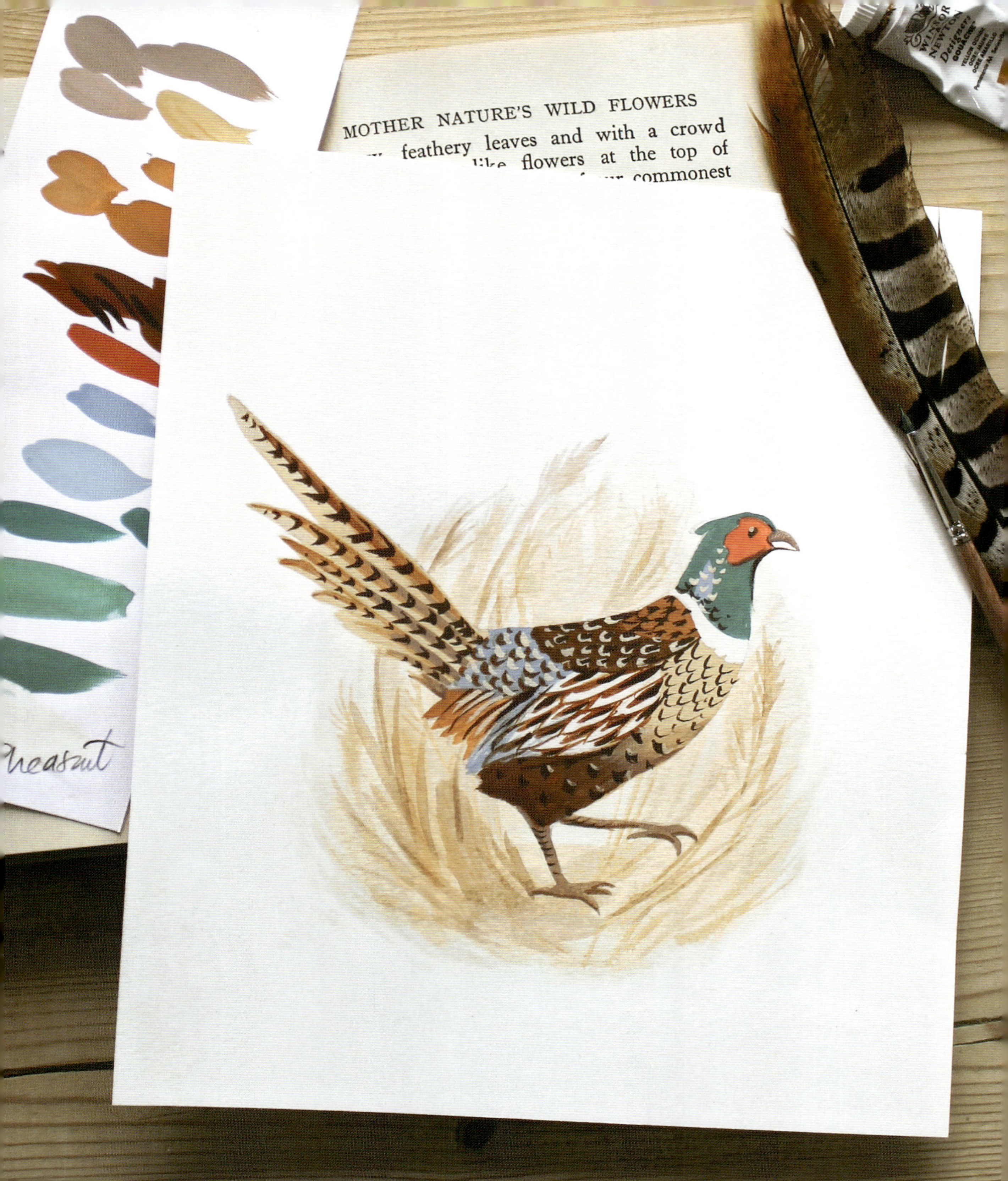

MOTHER NATURE'S WILD FLOWERS
feathery leaves and with a crowd
flowers at the top of
commonest

Pheasant Portrait

Cock pheasants have a wonderfully jaunty attitude and are great fun to paint. Last year we had a friendly resident in our garden who strutted up and down the lawn every morning. We named him Percy and this is a homage to him! In this project, we will use two contrasting techniques to great effect. The first is a loose wet-on-wet wash to create a soft imaginative background and the second is a controlled wet-on-dry layering of opaque color to create pattern and volume. Together, they create a lively scene that is full of texture and movement.

COLOR MIXING

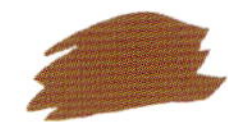
Burnt Sienna: No mixing needed.

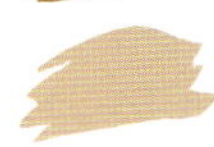
Medium Brown: Mix a dot each of Burnt Sienna and Burnt Umber together. We only need a very small touch of each of these, so only mix a little of each color. Test each color with a little swatch on some scratch paper.

Off-White: Add the tiniest speck of Burnt Umber to a large dab of Permanent White, mixing thoroughly.

Bright Green: Mix a little Cobalt Turquoise Light with some Yellow Ochre, a touch of Ultramarine and the smallest speck of Permanent White.

Warm Red: Add a small dab each of Permanent White and Burnt Sienna to a dab of Cadmium Red.

Dark Orange: Mix two dabs of Yellow Ochre to one each of Cadmium Red and Permanent White.

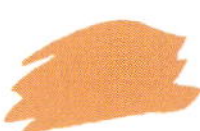
Pale Yellow: Add a dab of Yellow Ochre to a small blob of Permanent White.

Burnt Brown: Add a dot each of Burnt Umber and Permanent White to a dab of Burnt Sienna.

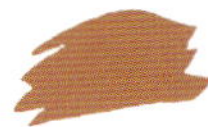
Pale Blue: Add a dab of Ultramarine and a small dab of Burnt Sienna to a large dab of Permanent White.

Taupe Brown: Add an equal dab each of Burnt Umber and Ultramarine to a large dab of Permanent White.

Dark Brown: Add a dab each of Burnt Umber and Ivory Black to a dot of Permanent White.

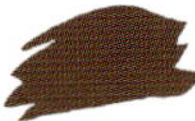

SUPPLIES

Brushes: Fine round, medium filbert, small flat

Paint Colors: Burnt Sienna, Burnt Umber, Cadmium Red, Cobalt Turquoise Light, Ivory Black, Permanent White, Ultramarine, Yellow Ochre

Other Supplies: Pencil and eraser, Yellow Ochre watercolor pencil, watercolor scratch paper

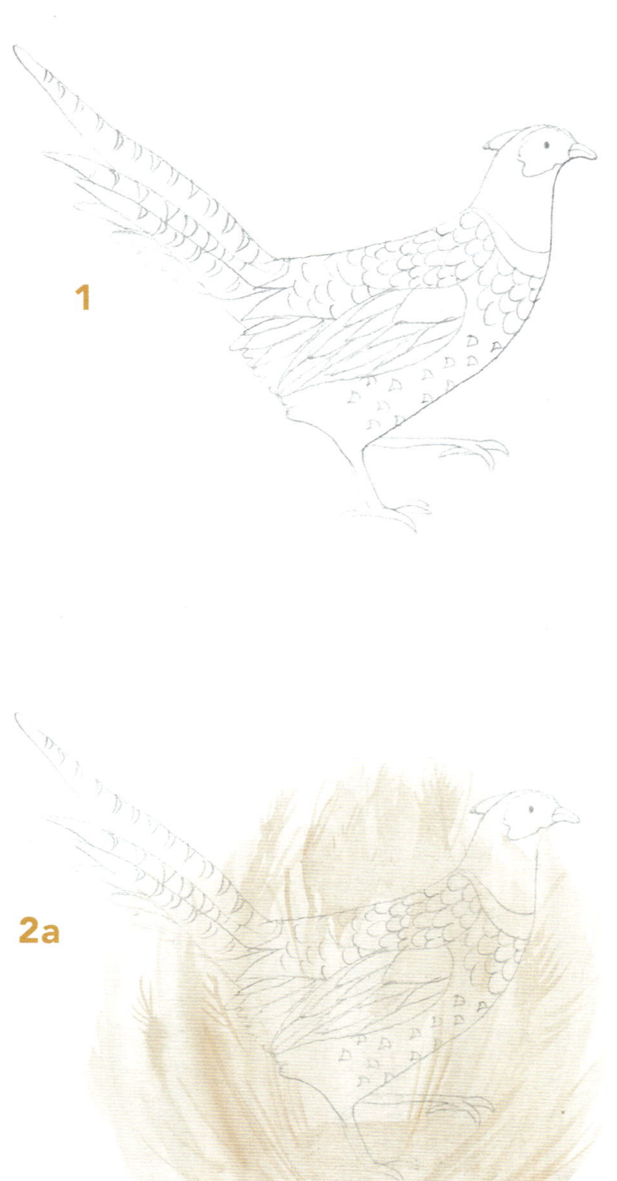

Step 1: Drawing the Pheasant

The washy ground will be created using a wide brush and plenty of water, so I suggest that you use watercolor paper to avoid wrinkling.

Begin by drawing your pheasant. Use a light graphite line, placing him squarely in the middle of the page. Use my slightly darker guidelines for reference to draw in his rectangular body with a curved breast and head and downward-pointing beak.

Draw in the tall tail feathers pointing up at an angle, then one little leg going down to meet the ground, with one claw at the back and the other three facing forward. Draw the other leg straight out in front—with only three visible claws—to give him a jaunty little strut.

Next, focus on adding detail to describe his unique feathers. Draw in a wavy wattle and eye. Give him two waved lines for the white collar and then two curved lines to define his mantle, rump and wing feathers. Fill him in with pattern—little scale-like semicircles below the collar and on his back, longer thin shapes on his wing, stripes on his tail feathers and tiny shapes like triangles with curved sides for the lower breast feathers.

Step 2: Washy Background

Our drawing starts this step dry but we will be painting over it using a wet-on-wet technique. This involves first painting a washy background over the pheasant drawing and then while this is still wet, adding more painted detail to create texture.

> TIP: *Throughout the piece, test your colors and paint consistency on some watercolor paper. We are aiming for the background to remain light and washy, despite adding three layers.*

Make a warm watercolor-like wash by mixing a tiny speck of Burnt Sienna with plenty of water to give a very transparent mixture. Using the edge of a medium sized filbert brush, draw a short horizontal line about ¾ inch (1.9 cm) below the lower foot.

Next, with the brush flat and loaded with plenty of watery paint, draw a small rounded spiky 'fire' shape over the body, except for his beak and tail feathers, which should remain unpainted. With a light curved stroke, blend the original line so it is no longer clearly visible.

Working quickly, while the brush and paper are still wet, use a smallish round brush to add a slight touch more of the Burnt Sienna to the watery mixture. Working from left to right, cover the whole painted 'fire' shape with thin and confident curved, upward strokes of different heights to suggest stalks of wheat. The painting should still be very light.

Allow some lines to extend out beyond the washy area to give a natural leafy feel and add in some little bushy seed heads. The darker color will bleed and bloom, but this will add to the natural feel of the grasses. Leave it to dry completely before moving on to the next layer.

Mix a little of the medium brown with some water to create a faintly opaque color. With a fine round brush and thinking about the shape of the bird, add some shading below the bird to ground it. Also add some light curved stalks and seed heads. Don't be afraid of painting over the bird's body again. Leave it to dry completely before moving on to the pheasant.

TIP: *As there are several similar colors, it is important to keep them as clean as you can and avoid them blending into a generic brown. Try using two pots of water, one to clean the brushes and the other for a second rinse. This pot can also be used when mixing a transparent watery wash.*

2b

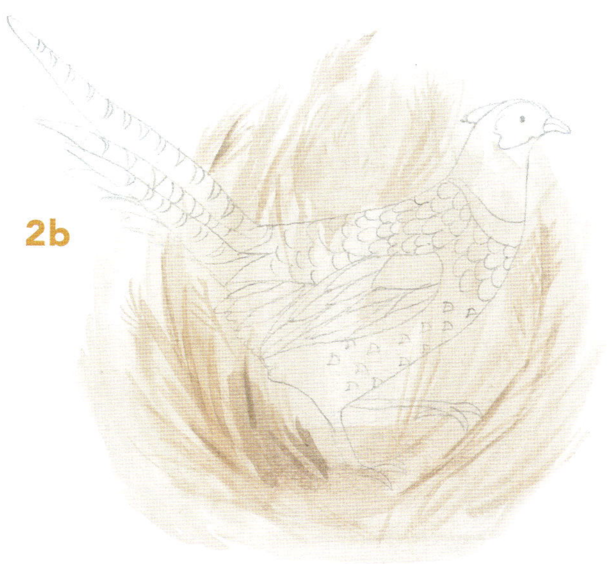

Step 3: Painting the Pheasant

Using a small flat brush, begin with the lightest color, the off-white of the collar and wing. When filling in narrower areas, twist the brush in your hand to use the tip edge as a liner.

Paint in the bright green and warm red of the head and neck. Add the dark orange below the collar and to the feathers below the tail.

3a

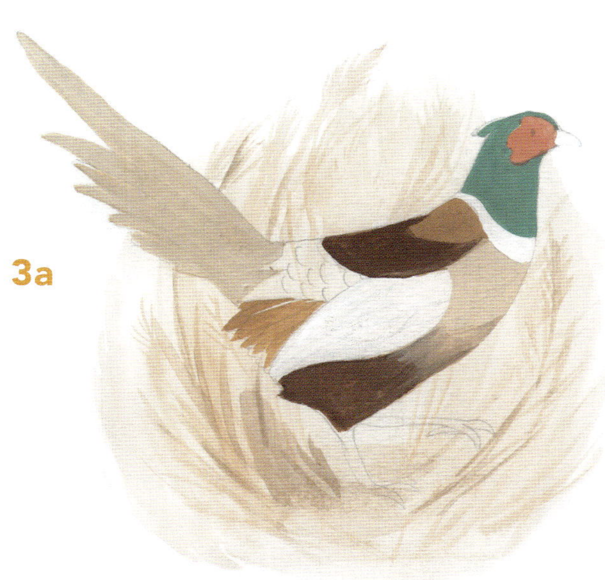

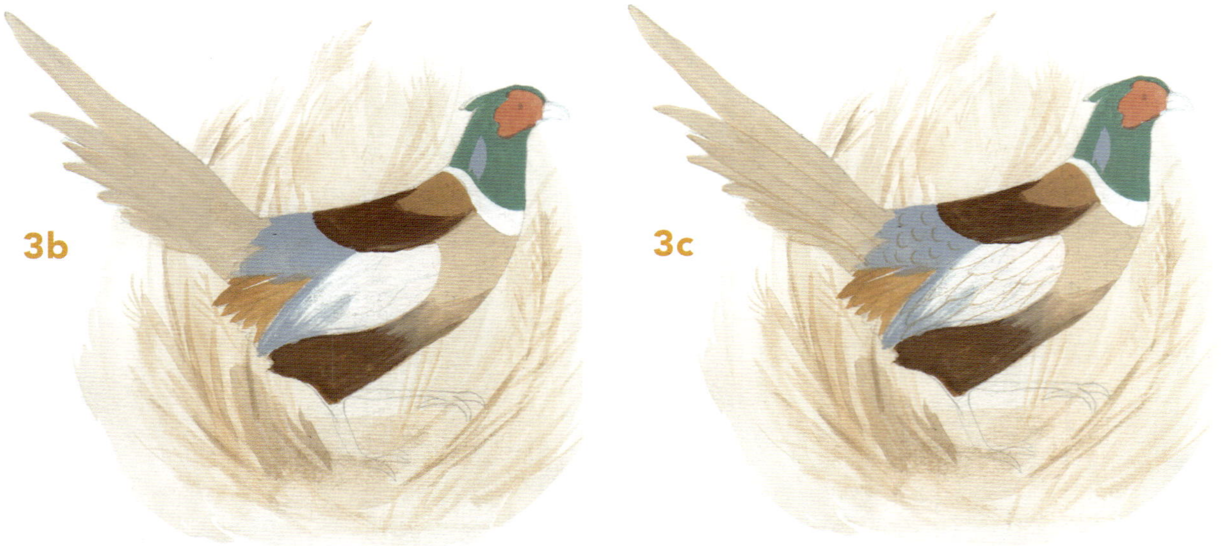

Paint in the tail feathers and upper breast with pale yellow. Add burnt brown to the lower breast and across the back. Where these last two colors meet on the breast, use a little pale yellow and a damp brush to blend the two together to create an ombré effect.

For the rest of the details, we will use a fine round brush. Add a textured pale blue layer for some of the feathers over the bright green on the lower back and on the tip of the wing.

Using a Yellow Ochre–colored pencil, redraw the feathers on the top of the back as you might draw the pattern of fish scales, as well as the long feathers on the wing and the tail.

Using the pale yellow color, taking care to be neat, redraw the centers of the back feathers.

Using the burnt brown shade, draw some detail lines on the tail feathers, on the pattern of the wing feathers and a few little curved lines on the lower back.

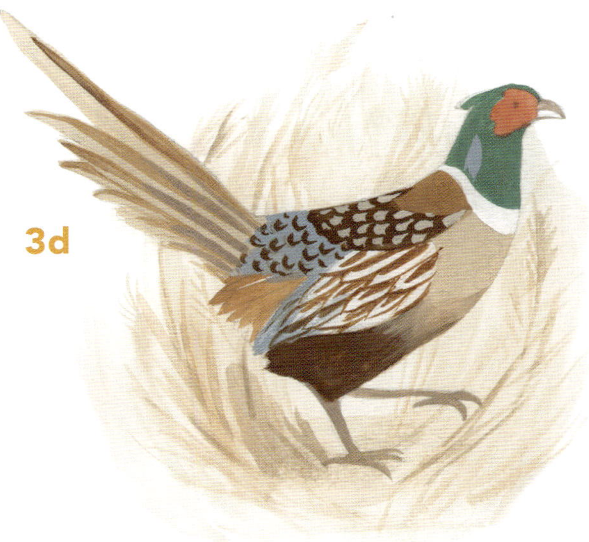

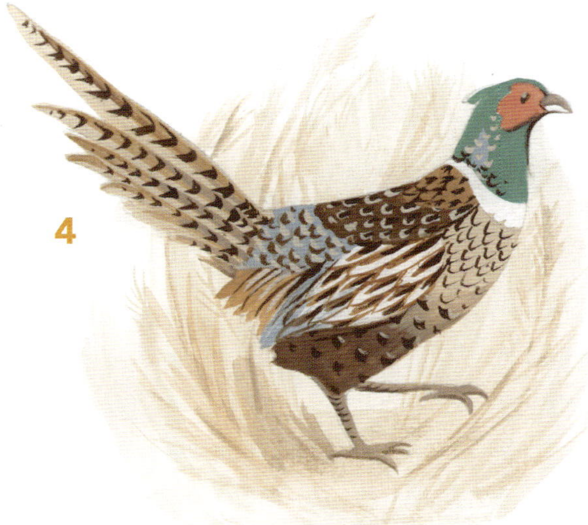

Use the taupe brown shade for the legs, feet and topside of the tail feathers. Define the beak and paint the upper beak brown.

Step 4: Pheasant Details

This last step ties the whole piece together with some detailed dark brown marks. I would suggest using a fine round spot brush and paint that has an opaque yet fluid consistency.

Start at the pheasant's head and work your way down, filling in all the details. Add in the eye and then add a few tiny details under the beak and on the neck. Paint in small line details on the breast, moving into the tiny triangles.

With varying strokes, add tiny details all the way down the back and add tiny lines to the legs. Lastly, we add the dark brown of the tail feathers, tilting the brush and using its side length, one single stroke for each feather.

Complete the piece by using a little of the pale yellow to add tiny strokes to the neck over the blue, as well as over the blue and brown on the pheasant's lower back and lower tail feathers.

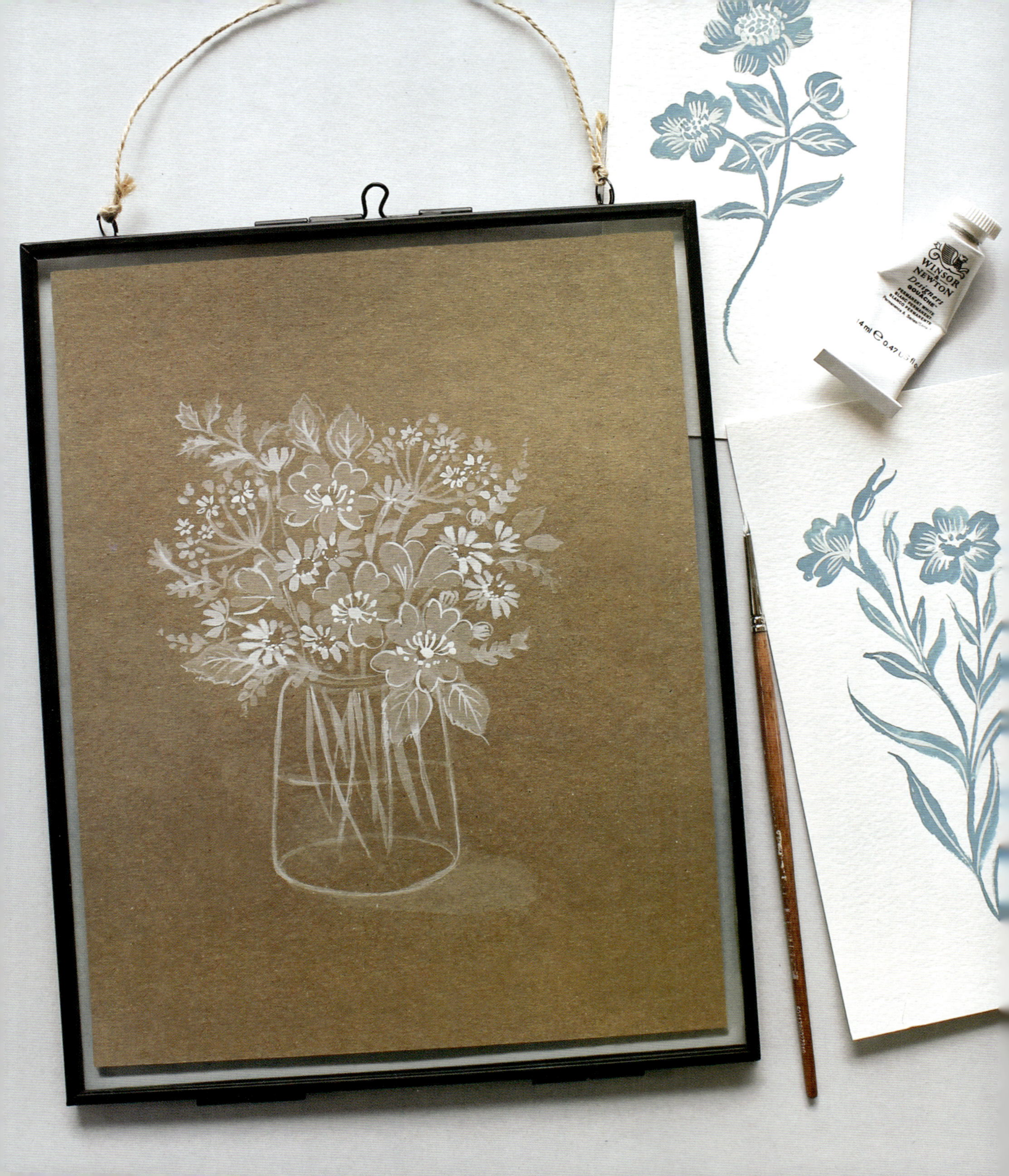
WINSOR & NEWTON
Designers
GOUACHE
PERMANENT WHITE
BLANC PERMANENT
BLANCO PERMANENTE

Jar of Wildflowers

This project is one of the simplest in the book, but requires real care and thought as it involves some detailed linework. White gouache on brown kraft paper is a very satisfying technique because it gives a sophisticated result without the effort of mixing colors. It is super easy to get your hands on kraft paper in art supplies shops or even supermarkets and hand-painted designs make beautiful cards for special occasions.

The main technique we will be practicing here is painting the whole floral design freehand with no preliminary sketching. This gives us the chance to loosen up, not worrying about creating something neat and perfect. We can turn mistakes into flowers and wonky stems into wild grasses!

COLOR MIXING

White: Pure white, glorious white!

SUPPLIES

Brushes: Very fine round, smallish round

Paint Colors: Permanent White

Other Supplies: Kraft paper, kraft scratch paper, blotting tissue

Step 1: Testing, Testing!

First things first, no mixing! Squeeze out a smallish blob of Permanent White in the middle of your palette with plenty of room around to water down and play with a variety of consistencies. It is essential that your water, brush and the edges of your pot are sparkling clean.

For the drawing of the jar and tiny flowers, we will be using a very fine round brush to give as much control as possible. Mix a dab of the white paint with a wet brush a couple of times to thin it down and check its consistency on some scratch paper. Ideally, it should be loose enough to draw with but still have a high pigment. In other words, it should still be quite white.

TIP: *As you go along, you'll need to mix more of this and the intensity of the white will vary. This is not a problem at all—embrace the lovely variety of the strokes and details you can create!*

Before we begin the piece and to help get used to this new way of working, we will practice a few strokes on your scratch paper to see how it looks when you draw a line with your brush. In one single stroke, try varying the weight of the line by pressing down gently at first and then more firmly as you go along.

When working with really watered down white, make sure that there is not a watery blob on the end of your brush after mixing or it will immediately pour onto the page. Always have some tissue on hand ready to blot!

Next, with the tip of your brush, try creating a tiny flower head by painting five little circles, leaving a hole to suggest the center of the flower. Repeat this with a variety of different watered-down whites, leaving them to dry so you can see how they look on the page.

By the time you've finished this, some of the first flowers should have dried. Return your attention to your palette and with a slightly drier loaded brush, paint a circle of dots around the central brown of the hole on top of the petals to add definition to the flower heads.

Doing these little warm-up exercises will really help you understand what happens when you mix the white with water and you will feel more in control of the paint before you begin the piece.

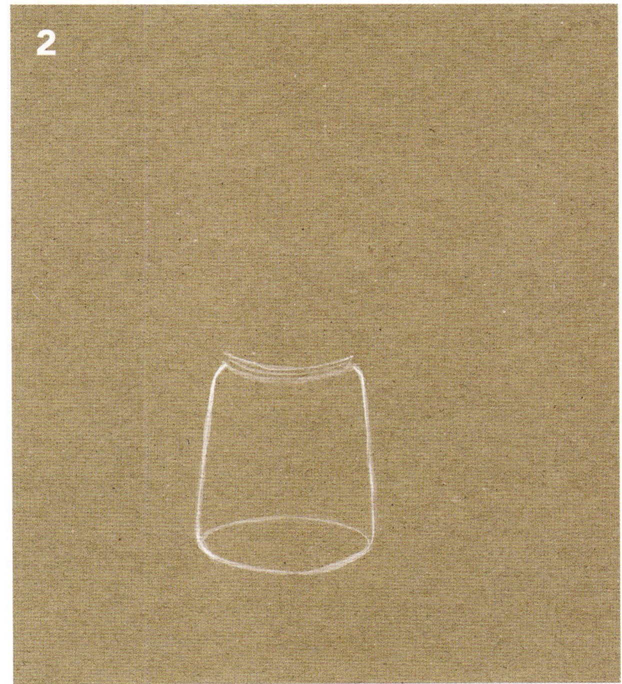

Step 2: The Jar

The jar will ground the design and inform the rest of your decisions, so be sure to place it well on the page. Imagining that the page has been divided into five parts horizontally, I have placed the line of the bottom of the jar approximately one-fifth of the page from the bottom.

Begin by drawing in the semi-circular line of the base of the jar with a fine stroke. Next, paint in the sides of the jar, which should be ever so slightly leaning inward to create the illusion that we are looking down at the jar from above. Draw in several curved lines mirroring the base to suggest the rim of the jar where you screw the lid on. Also paint a faint line to complete the curved ellipse of the base.

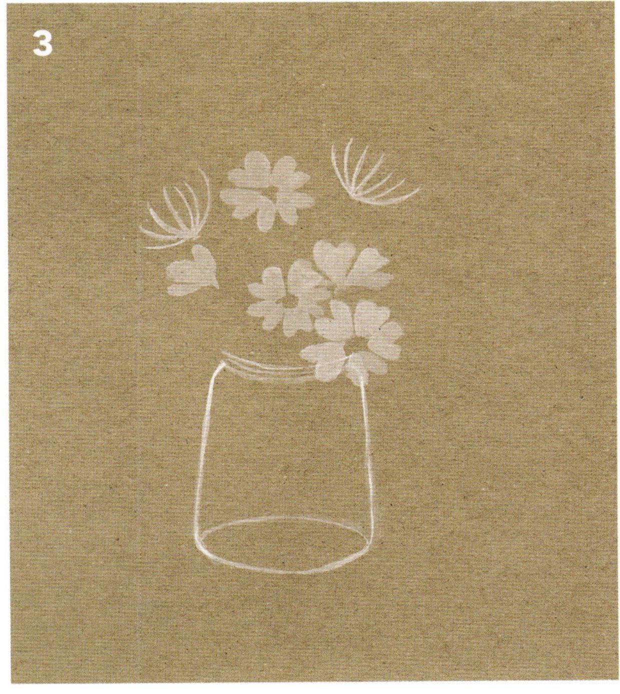

Step 3: Dog Roses & Queen Anne's Lace

TIP: *If you would like to look for some different shapes to draw from, look online for botanical black and white drawings. The vintage etchings you will find offer a wealth of inspiration!*

Next, we will paint in dog roses as the central flowers using a smallish round brush and a very watered-down white. The petals are essentially heart shapes and each head has five of them. Paint several flowers as if they are floating in air, including one overlapping the rim of the jar.

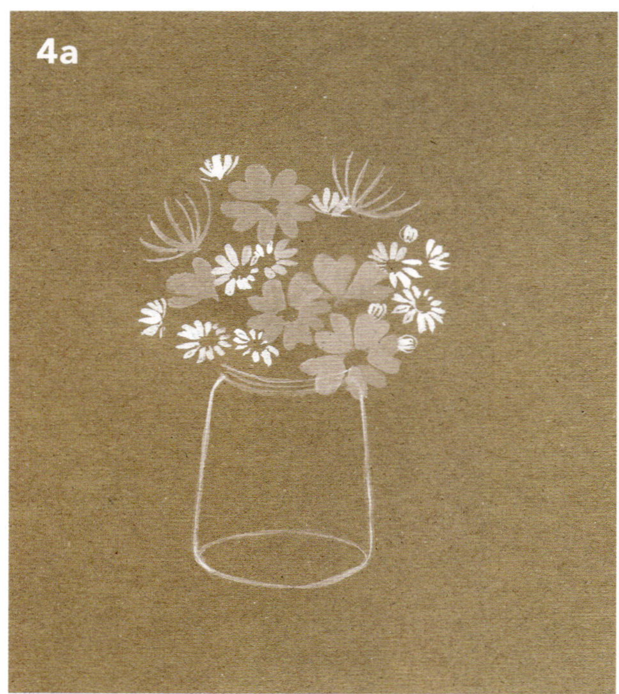

TIP: *As you paint, think about how a real flower might look—some will be straight on, others from the side or half open—try to include a variety.*

The next wildflowers we will be painting are Queen Anne's Lace. Using a very fine round brush, start with their head-stems, which are a little like upside-down umbrellas.

Step 4: Tiny White Flowers

Now we turn to the daisies. These give the opportunity to practice lots of tiny, delicate details. Using a slightly more opaque white, paint small, thin petals around an unpainted center circle. Dot these in and around the dog roses, not worrying if the petals overlap.

Go back to the Queen Anne's Lace and paint the head and buds at the end of the stems with teeny little flowers and dots.

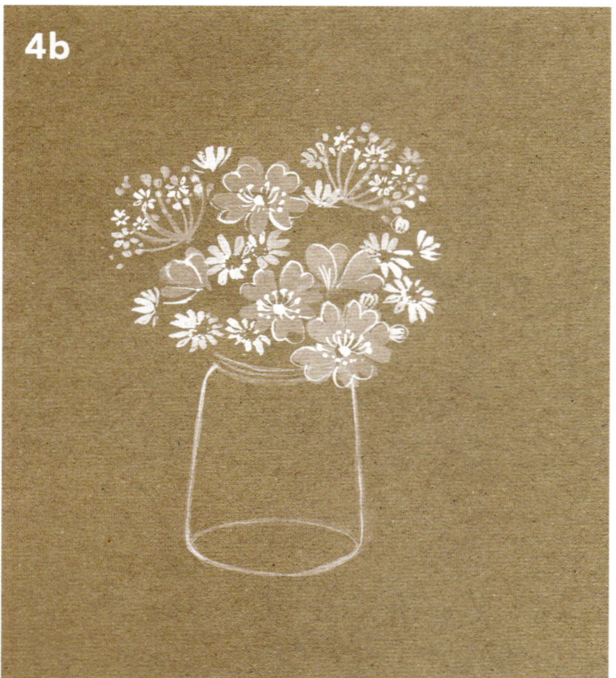

TIP: *If you make any real bloopers, don't worry! Just clean your brush thoroughly in a new pot of water and remove the paint gently with your brush, using some water and plenty of blotting. Be patient and wait until it is dry before painting over, otherwise the new lines will bleed.*

Mix some slightly thicker and more opaque white with just a dab of water to add definition to the flower heads and make them pop. On the dog roses, very daintily draw a little dot in the middle of the brown paper center and then small lines radiating out with tiny dots on the end.

Using thin, opaque, light strokes, draw in some definition lines on the edges of all of the petals. Paint the dotted details on the centers of the daisies and white dots to add depth to the Queen Anne's Lace flowers.

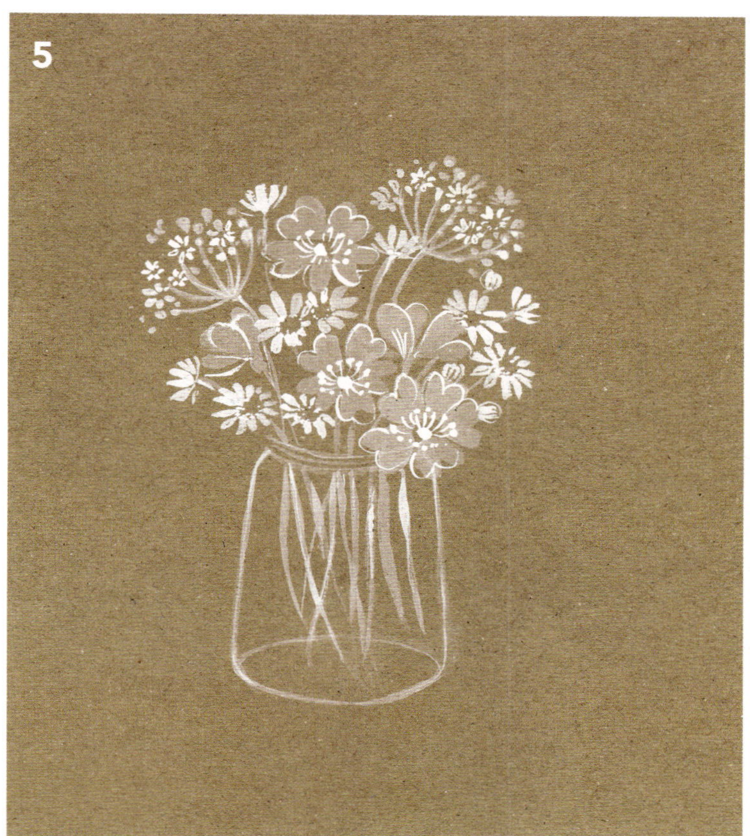

Step 5: Stems

Stems are next and we will use the technique of varying the weight of the line during a single brushstroke, which we practiced in step 1. Taking one flower at a time, follow its stem from the flower into the neck of the jam jar with your brush. There will be plenty of flowers and lines in the way, so only paint where there is empty kraft paper!

When you paint the stems in the jar, think about varying the thickness of your line. Imagine that they have been popped into the vase quickly so that the stems are not perfectly straight or of even heights. Paint these in from the rim to just above the bottom of the jar.

TIP: *If you paint a flower you're not happy with, it is easy to incorporate mistakes. Wet and blot, removing as much excess paint as you can, then wait until it is dry. Embrace the remaining faint marks by painting over the top with other textured flower shapes, little dots, tiny seed heads or wild grasses.*

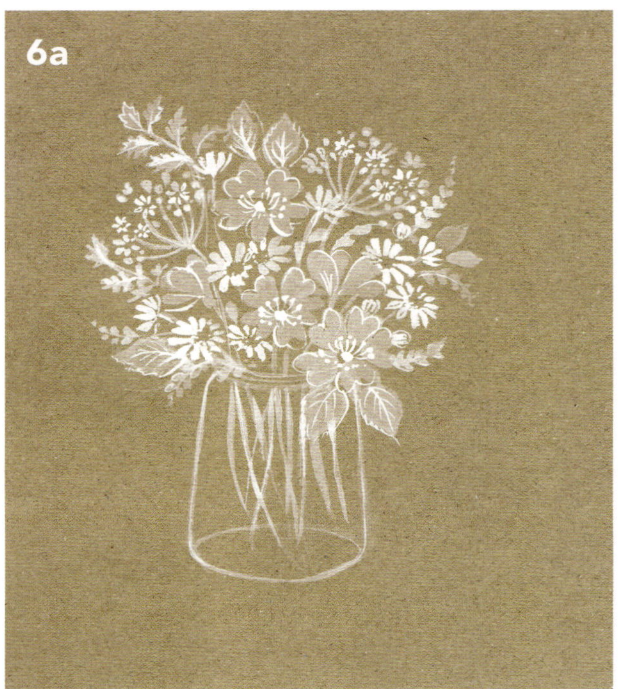

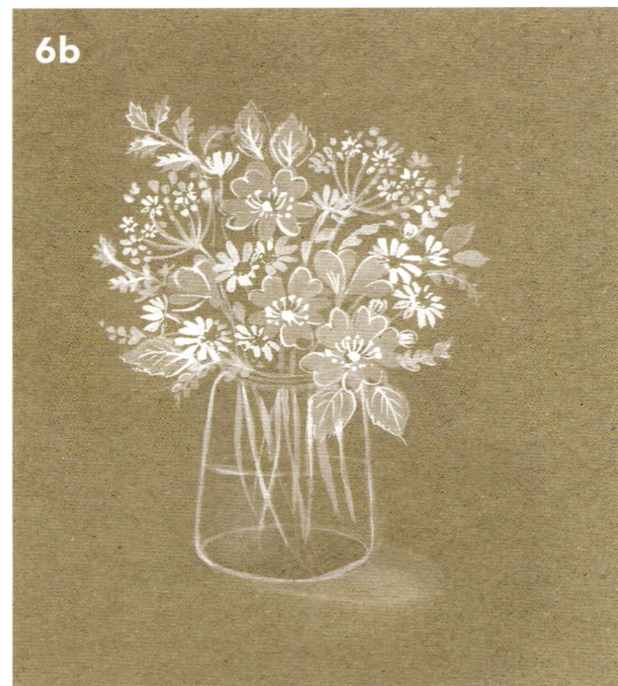

Step 6: Leaves & Details

Paint in the leaves for the flowers. This will add some contrasting shapes and make the flowers look wilder and fuller. Using a moderately watered-down white, paint in leaves to poke out from wherever you fancy, not worrying at all about things overlapping or looking unbalanced. When dry, add in some fine and slightly more opaque white veins on top.

Lastly, add a couple of finishing touches to complete the painting. Using your smallish round brush and some very watered-down white, paint a faint ellipse to suggest the line of the water in the jar. Add a little more white highlight to make this waterline thicker on the left side of the jar. Again, using a very faint watery white, loosely paint some white shading to suggest the water below the line.

Finally, I like to ground my designs with shadow so I have used a light wash to create a suggestion of shadow on a table surface with a white ellipse. You can do the same or leave it without if you prefer.

Floating Feathers

In this project, we will be looking closely at several feathers of different shapes and sizes. Feathers lend themselves to being painted in gouache, as you can build up texture and detail so easily just by varying the thickness of your brush strokes and the consistency of the paint. They are also a great element to sneak into designs since they have such fantastic movement and pattern. We will use a wet-on-wet ombré technique to add shading across some of the feathers and fine detailing for the feather barbs.

COLOR MIXING

Pale Stone: Add a dot each of Burnt Umber and Yellow Ochre to a blob of Permanent White.

Teal Blue: Add three large dabs each of Permanent White and Burnt Umber to a large blob of Phthalo Blue. Mix a very full well for the entire background of the piece.

Light Ochre: Add a dab of Yellow Ochre and a dot of Burnt Umber to a small blob of Permanent White.

Light Brown: Add a dot of Yellow Ochre and a small dab of Burnt Umber to a small blob of Permanent White.

Medium Brown: Add four large dabs of Permanent White and two dabs of Yellow Ochre to a large blob of Burnt Umber.

Yellow Ochre: Pure out of the tube.

Medium Blue: Mix a little Phthalo Blue and some Burnt Umber with a small blob of Permanent White.

Dark Brown: Add a dot each of Permanent White and Yellow Ochre to a dab of Burnt Umber.

SUPPLIES

Brushes: Small round, fine round, small flat, medium angled

Paint Colors: Burnt Umber, Permanent White, Phthalo Blue, Yellow Ochre

Other Supplies: Pencil and eraser, scratch paper

TIP: *Be sparing when adding dark colors to white and creating pale tints, or you end up having to add heaps of white to lighten! Try painting over some pencil lines on your scratch paper to check the consistency before starting on the design.*

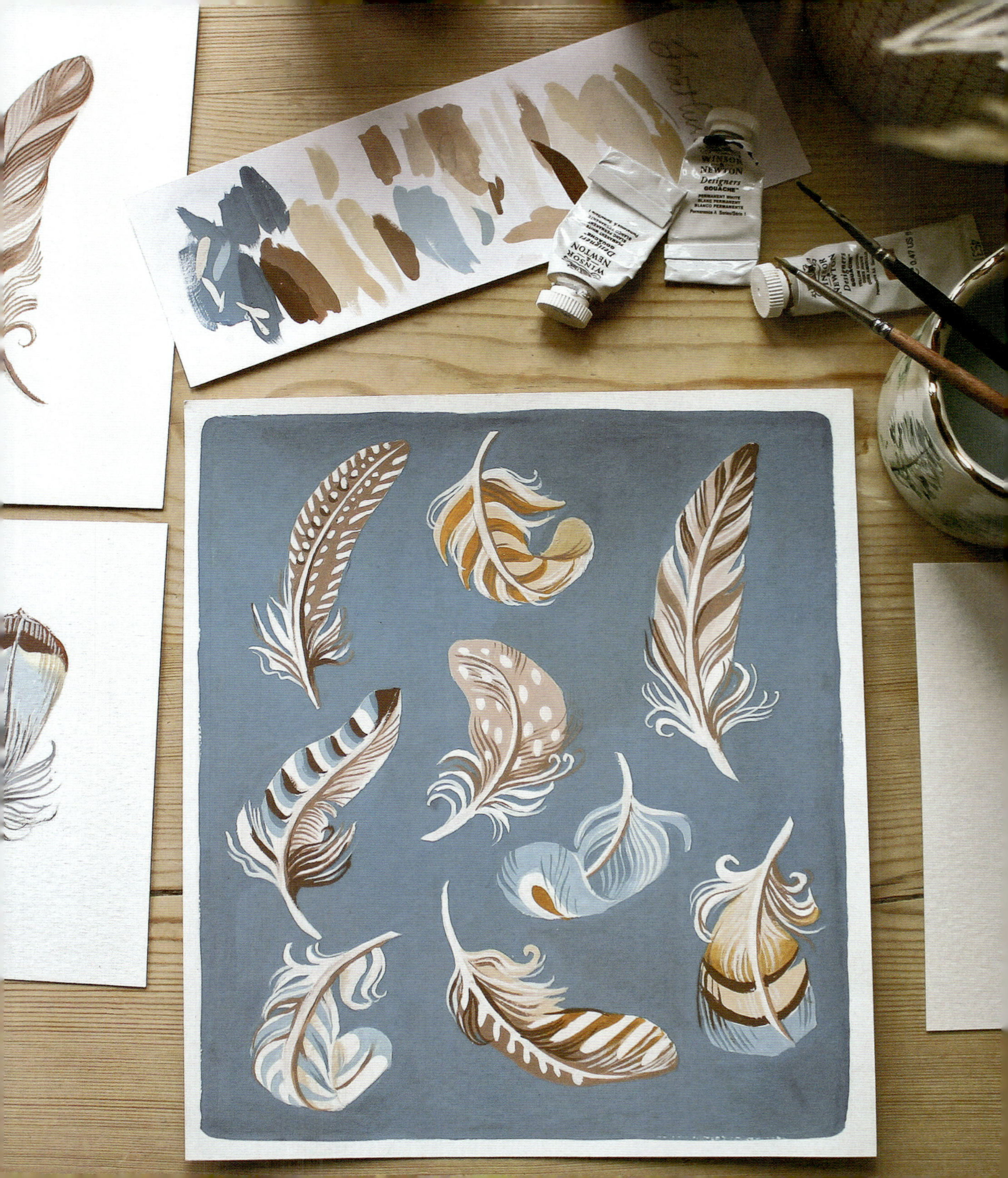
WINSOR & NEWTON
Designers
GOUACHE
PERMANENT WHITE
BLANC PERMANENT
BLANCO PERMANENTE

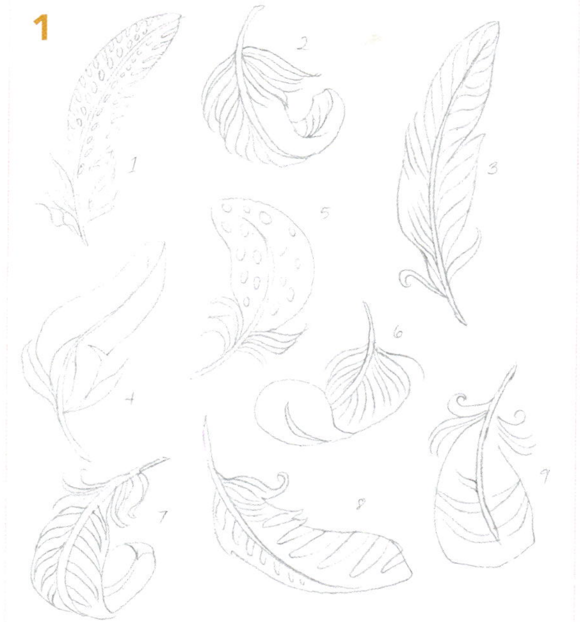

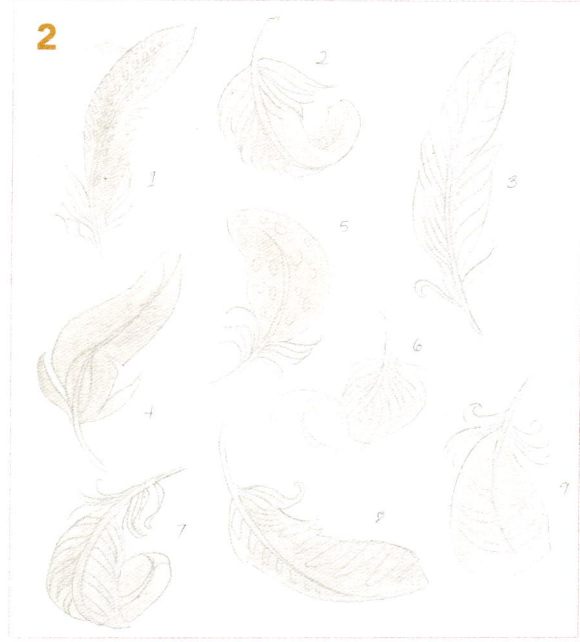

Step 1: Draw the Pattern Elements

The placement of the feathers on the page is similar to how I might draw elements for a repeating pattern. They are seen from a mixture of angles— straight on so that the whole feather is visible and from the side as if the feather is curling up. Notice that even in those that are straight on, we create movement by gently curving the line of the central quill shaft.

Draw your feathers out lightly with a pencil, using mine as a reference if you like. Working feather by feather, draw in as many details as you can, trying to make them as unique and varied as possible! You can use images of real feathers or make them up. I have numbered mine for ease of reference when describing painting details.

Step 2: Pale Underpainting

The base color for all the feathers is a pale stone color. Use a dab of color on a lightly wetted small round brush and loosely paint in all seven feathers so that they are covered semi-opaquely, with the drawn lines just about still visible through the paint. When you reach a feather with downy barbs at the base, work from the center outward in light, wavy strokes.

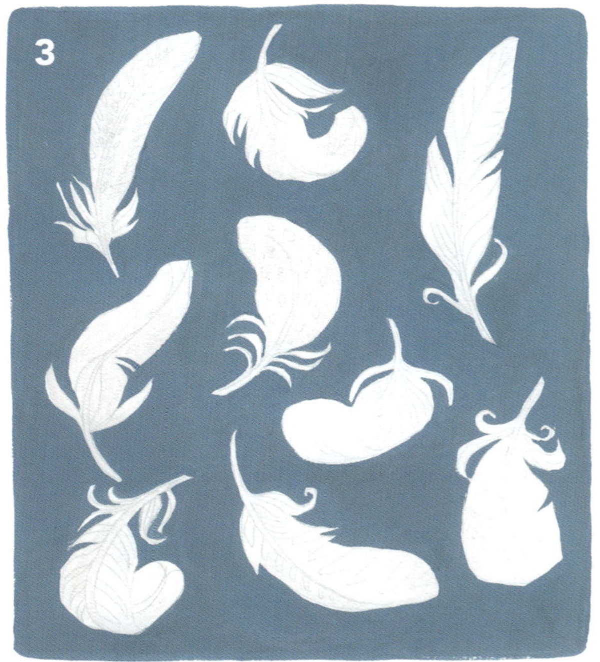

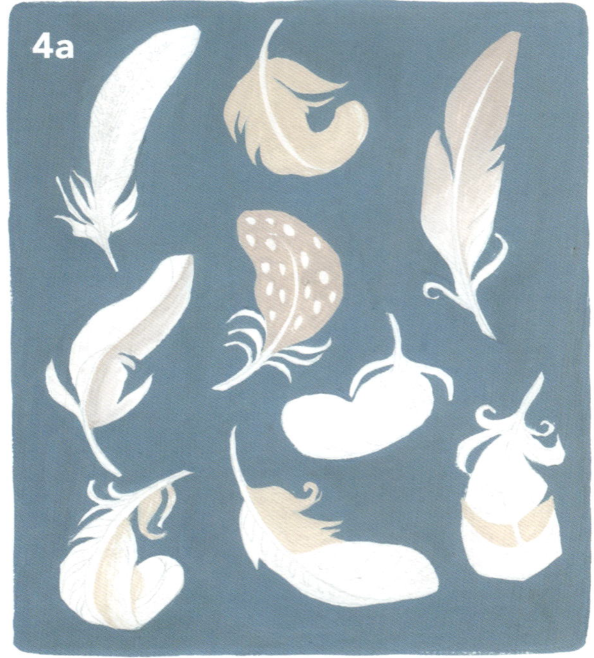

Step 3: Background

Our teal blue should be even and consistent throughout the well to avoid streaks and patches of uneven color. Test a couple of large swatches on some scratch paper and leave them to dry so you can make sure you are happy with the color and adjust if necessary. We will use these swatches in the next stages.

Using a small flat brush, draw a smooth, round-cornered, relatively neat rectangle to box in the feathers. Next, painting right up to the edge of the feathers, paint a smooth but not meticulously neat outline. When you meet a tricky area such as the down feathers, don't worry too much about making everything perfect and exact—we will have plenty of scope to paint over any imperfections later.

Once all the feathers are outlined, load a medium angled brush with some paint to fill in the gaps and create a smooth background with no visible strokes. Leave it to dry completely and notice the color lighten slightly as it dries.

Step 4: Light Browns & Ochres

In the next step, we will paint in some of the lighter shades of color. The feathers are quite complex so I will be walking you through how to paint the same ones I have illustrated. I have taken a 'color-by-color' approach, mapping out layers of both flat and blended color on which to add some detailed linework. I will be describing the feathers by the numbers in step 1.

With a small round brush, use the light ochre to paint in feather 2, a line on feather 7, the top right of feather 8 and the central band of feather 9, excluding the spines.

On feather 3, but again excluding the spine, use the light brown color to paint the top half. Then, using some of the pale stone, blend up from the bottom vertically to create a seamless ombré.

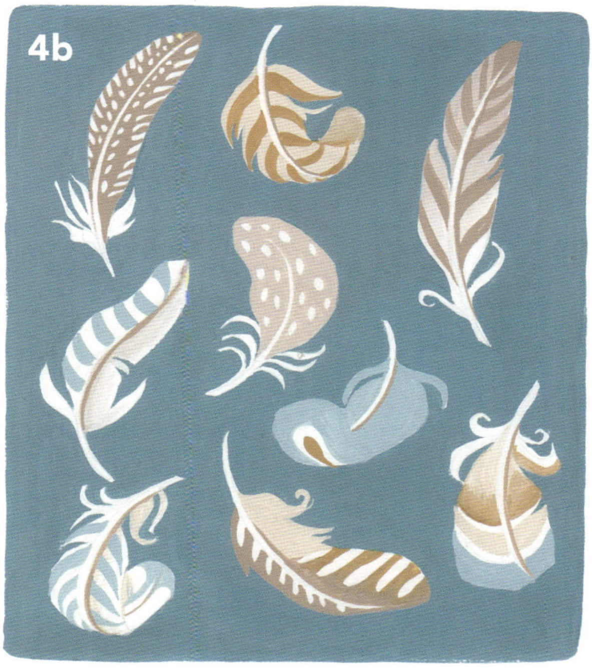

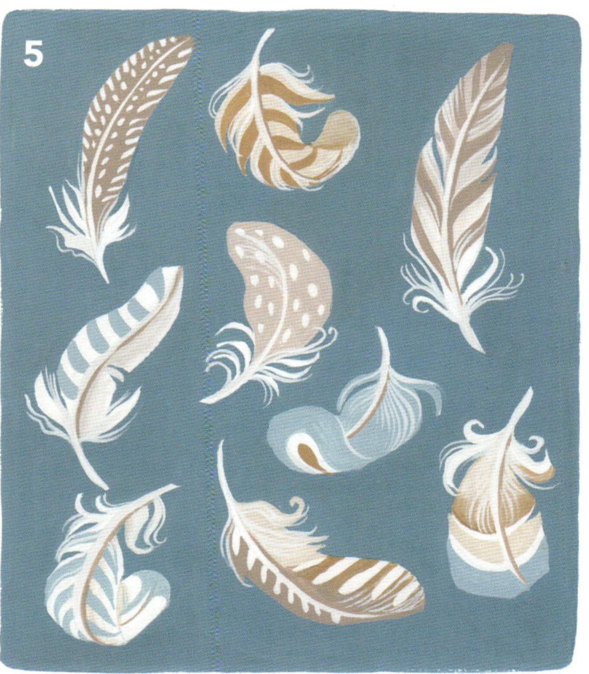

On the right side of feather 4, we will create another ombré blend of light brown to pale stone, but this time blending horizontally. Fill the whole of feather 5, taking care to paint around the little dots.

Next, we paint some of the medium and darker shades of blue, ochre and brown. Use medium brown to carefully draw around the patterns on feathers 1 and 3 and paint in the arrow-shaped stripes all the way down the feather until you reach the fluff at the bottom. Paint in the pattern on the left side of feather 8 and on the right side, create an ombré from the center to the edge with some medium brown and Yellow Ochre. With a smooth fine line, use a little pale stone to define the right side of all the feathers' central quills.

On feather 4, use medium blue to paint in the stripes on the left-hand side. On feather 6, paint in the whole feather, leaving the rounded tip pattern unpainted. Paint in narrow stripes on feather 7 and the very tip of feather 9.

With Yellow Ochre, paint in the stripes over the pale ochre in feather 2 and paint the center tip of feather 6. On feather 9, blend the light ochre and Yellow Ochre to create an ombré. Leave all the layers to dry completely.

Step 5: Light Downy Feather Detail

Using a fine round brush, load the tip with fluid but opaque pale stone-colored paint. Paint in light-colored spines to really neaten up all the central quills.

In the final step, we will be thinking about adding light-on-dark details that will really pop against the dark ground and finish the piece by tying the background and foreground together.

6

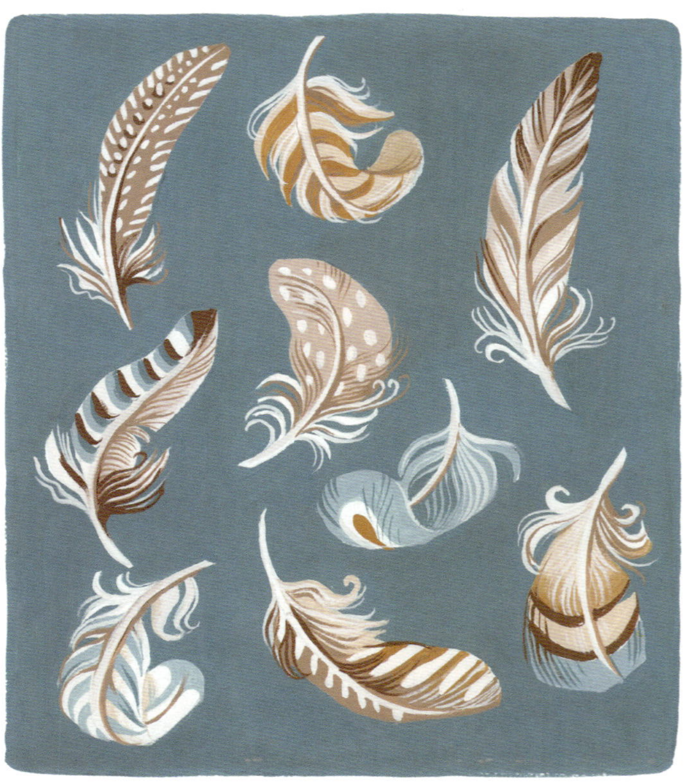

We need to make sure that the paint is relatively dry or it will move and smudge the blue ground. Test a little white on top of the swatches that you did in the last stage. Starting at the base of the feathers, where the fluff meets the quill, paint in a mixture of fine wavy and curved lines, taking care to overlap all the pencil lines. When you meet the blue ground, paint a couple of light lines into the color. Repeat on all of the feathers.

Step 6: Darker Final Details

To complete the piece, we will paint in some fine details with medium and dark brown as well as the background teal.

Working feather by feather, really enjoy adding all the tiny little line details. This part brings out the very small perfectionist side of me and you can make these as intricate as you like.

Using my design as a reference, add teal blue on top of the medium blue color to separate each of the barbs. Next, using the medium brown, paint in tiny lines on some of the lighter fluffy feathers to add definition to the spine and lower half of feather 5.

Next, paint in a few dark brown accents to pull together the whole pattern. I have defined the central quills, but also added lines on the tips of feathers 3 and 4 and the stripes on feather 9.

I often like to finish my pieces by taking a step back and looking to see where I might need to add a little touch or line. Take a look at your own painting and add in any details needed to complete the design in a way that's pleasing to you.

Harvest Mouse

This project develops some more advanced composition skills by building the scene in two parts or layers. First, we will create a background of a simple wild grass silhouette, setting the scene for a painting of a country mouse climbing a stem of wheat. The colors we will be using are rich warm earthy tones, with the poppies and cornflowers adding a vivid contrast to the otherwise muted palette. This is an opportunity to practice a variety of brush marks, from loose gestural strokes to the detailed strokes of the mouse's furry coat.

COLOR MIXING

Pale Yellow: Add a tiny dab of Yellow Ochre and a very slightly larger dab of Burnt Umber to a small blob of Permanent White.

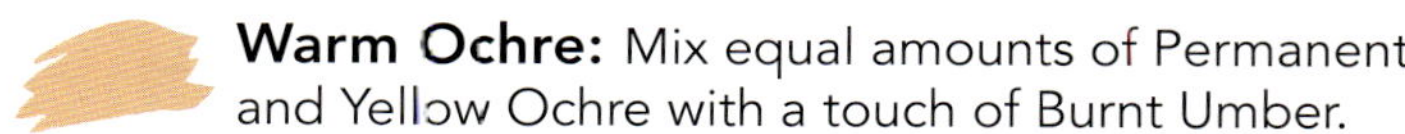

Warm Ochre: Mix equal amounts of Permanent White and Yellow Ochre with a touch of Burnt Umber.

Light Brown: Add a dab of Burnt Umber and a small amount of Yellow Ochre to a little blob of Permanent White. It should have a slightly grayish tone.

Warm Brown: Take a dab of the mixed pale yellow and add a dab of Burnt Sienna.

Off-White: Take a dab of the mixed pale yellow and add a dab of Permanent White.

Medium Brown: Take a dab of the mixed light brown and add a dab of Burnt Umber.

Red: Add a couple of large dabs of Permanent White and one of Burnt Sienna to a small blob of Cadmium Red.

Blue: Mix a small dab each of Ultramarine and Burnt Umber with a small blob of Permanent White.

Pale Pink: Take a tiny speck of the mixed red and mix thoroughly with a dab of Permanent White.

Dark Brown: Mix a speck each of Permanent White and Ultramarine with a small amount of Burnt Umber.

Dark Blue: Mix a dab each of Permanent White, Ultramarine and Burnt Umber together.

SUPPLIES

Brushes: Very fine round spot, fine round, small round

Paint Colors: Burnt Sienna, Burnt Umber, Cadmium Red, Permanent White, Yellow Ochre, Ultramarine

Other Supplies: Ruler, graphite pencil, light brown watercolor pencil and eraser, scratch paper

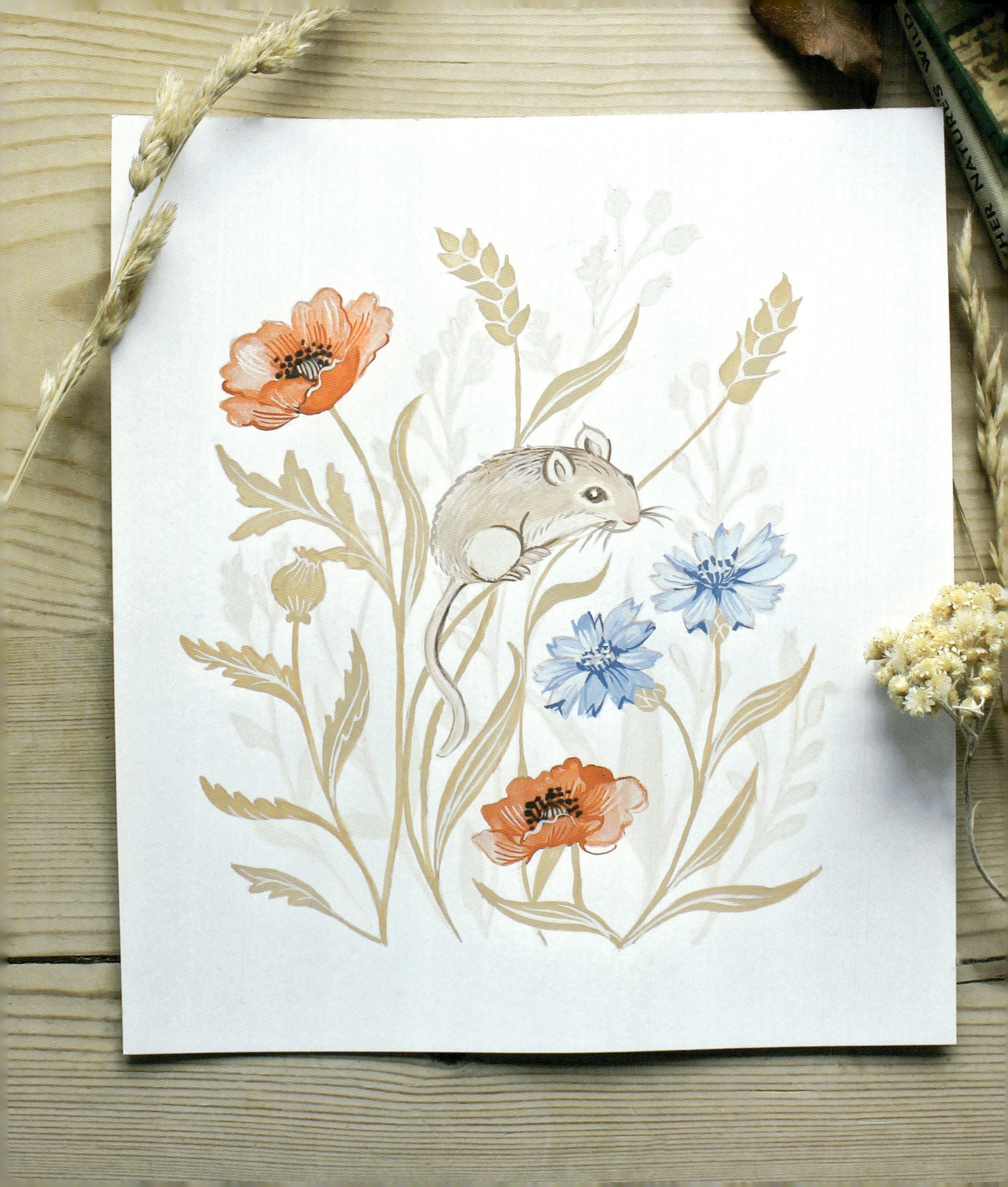

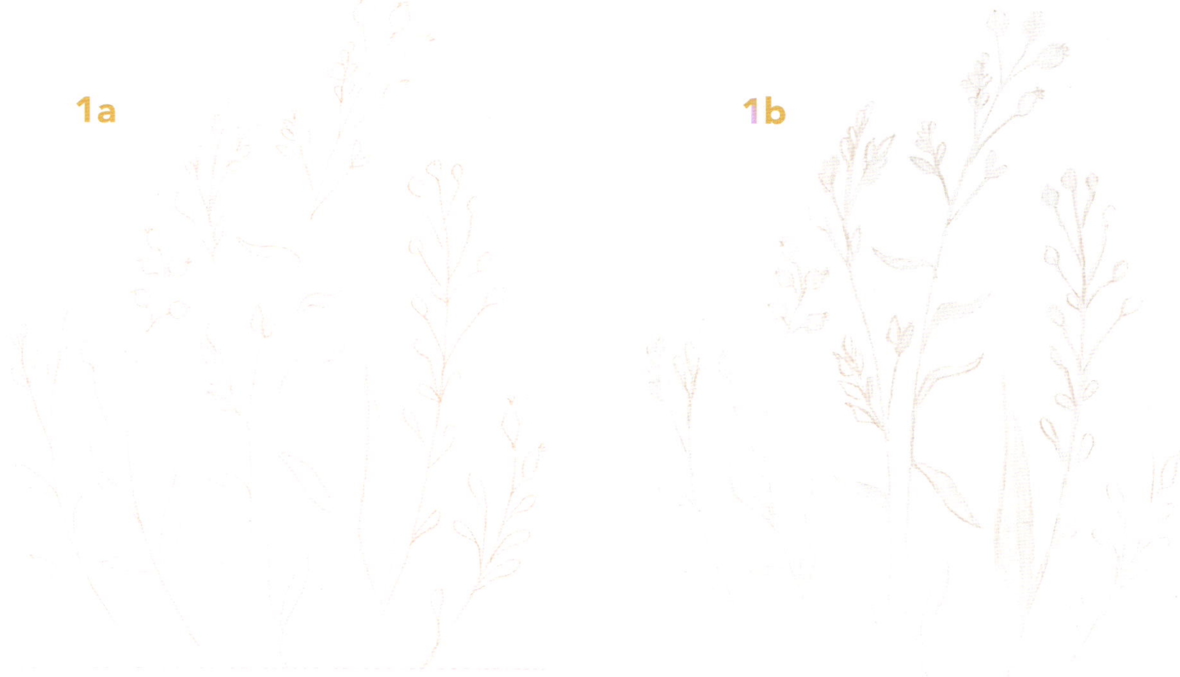

Step 1: Draw & Paint the First Layer

Begin by drawing a very faint pencil guideline a little way up from the bottom of the page, which will serve for both layers. As we are using a pale palette with plenty of water, draw out the scene with a light brown watercolor pencil so the line blends in as we go along.

Next, very faintly indeed, draw in six stems with their tiny little seed heads on the end of each one. Add a variety of long slightly pointed leaves lower down on the stems.

Mix a little of the pale yellow color with a large dab of water so the consistency is barely opaque, loose and very fluid. It should be a very pale silhouette so that the design does not look confusing when combined with the top layer. Test on your scratch paper and add more white if necessary—bear in mind that the paint will dry darker than you think.

TIP: *To make sure that you don't smudge the paint, begin on whichever side is the opposite to your dominant hand, that is—left to right for right-handed folk and the opposite if you're a lefty.*

With a fine round brush start with loose single lines for the stems and, as you go, work to blend the light brown pencil into the gouache. When you reach the seed heads, flick your brush out a little using small upward strokes. Fill in the little seeds with tiny round strokes. When the whole design is painted, you will see that your brown watercolor pencil line is still a little visible, so using a light touch, add another thin layer here and there to cover the lines. Wait until completely dry before beginning on the mousey layer.

2

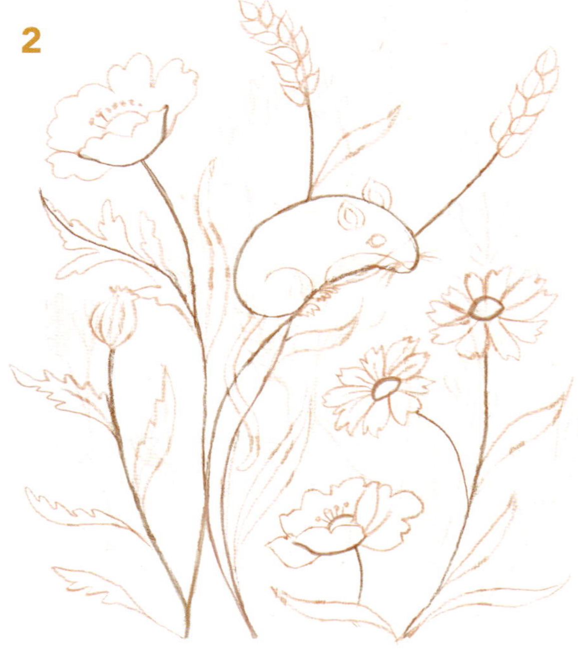

3

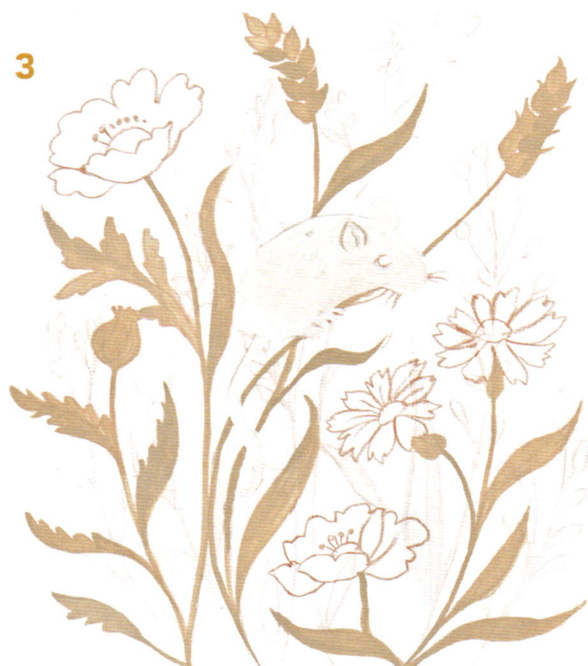

Step 2: Draw in the Top Layer

Next, we draw in the top layer with your light brown pencil. I have added some darker guidelines to help you along. This will seem quite daunting as there is already a layer of painting, but don't worry—as soon as you add some darker painted lines, the piece will begin to pull together.

Just be mindful as you draw this second layer that we want it to sit neatly and harmoniously on top of the first. Make your first line start at the base of the third grass stem from the left and curve across to meet the top of the fifth stem. Draw on a corn head with small teardrop-shaped grains.

The mouse will sit on the middle of this stem and is essentially a jellybean shape with a slightly pointy nose peeping over the stem on the right. Add little eyes, whiskers, ears, feet and a long curling tail. Add another stalk and curved wheatsheaf appearing from behind the middle of the mouse's back.

Draw in the tall poppy on the left, sitting the flower head in the plain paper gap above the background. Start with the bottom petal first, then the curved and dotty center, followed by a fan of wavy-edged petals. Add a shorter stem topped with a round seed head to the left. To the right of the mouse, first draw the branching stem followed by an oval floating slightly above, surrounded by rings of jagged edges of petals for the two cornflowers' heads. Finally, a small poppy tucks into the remaining space. All stems are given long curved leaves as per my drawing.

Step 3: Paint the Wheat Stems & Mouse

Mix a dab of the warm ochre with a touch of water—we will add this lightly but with an opaque consistency to really bring these elements into the foreground. Paint in all the stems and leaves, leaving the flower heads unpainted.

Next, with some opaque pale yellow, paint in the mouse's body and tail.

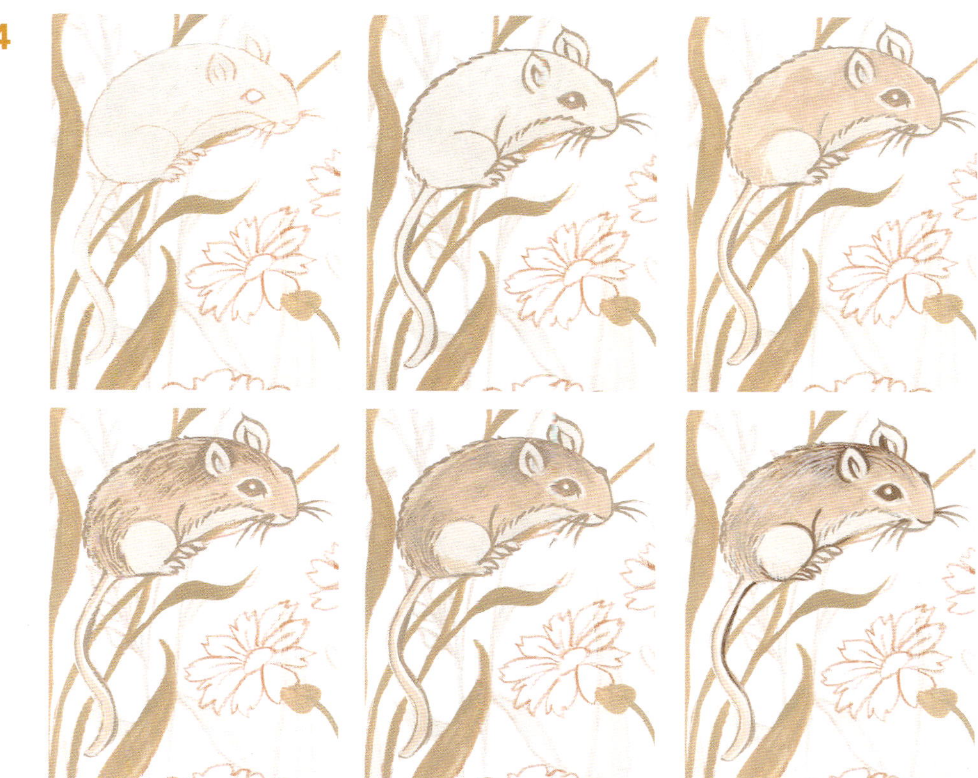

Step 4: Painting the Harvest Mouse

First, redraw some details on the mouse such as the ears, whiskers, nose, a little semi-circular curve of the leg and a line to show where the light part of the belly will be.

Use the light brown color and a touch of water to create furry details on the outline of the mouse. Using a fine brush and fine broken lines made up of tiny dashes, paint over the mouse's pencil lines to define her outline and details, creating the feeling of fur.

Using a slightly watery consistency of warm brown paint and a small round brush, add a wash to the mouse's body by following its curve, leaving the haunches, underbelly, ear and outline of the eye unpainted.

Return to the light brown of the mouse outline and use tiny little broken strokes to suggest the fur on her coat, painting a little shadow to make it appear darker on the back and between the ears. To make the coat look smooth and not spiky, paint the fur all going in the same direction, following the curve of her body.

When dry, go back to the warm brown and with a touch of water, add a light wash to smooth and blend in the texture a little.

Add a dab of white to some pale yellow to create an off-white color and add tiny highlights on her furry coat. Use a touch of medium brown for the eyes and definition around the ears, back and tail.

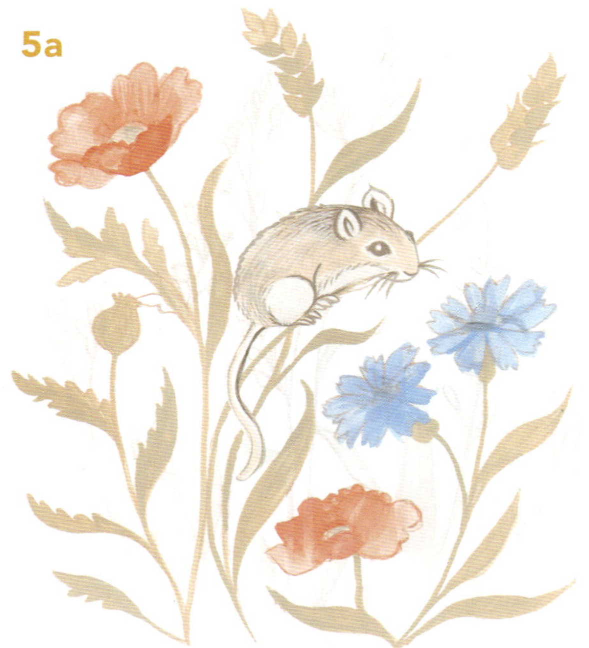

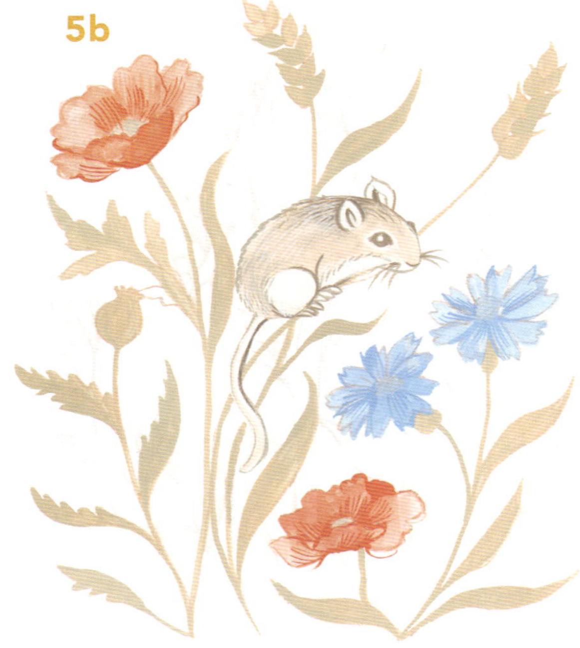

Step 5: Poppies & Cornflowers

Turn your attention next to the poppies and cornflowers, for which you will need to mix a warm red and blue. Water some of the red color down a touch and paint in the heads of the two poppies with a slightly translucent layer, not worrying at all if it looks lighter in some areas. Some of the underpainting might show up on the lower poppy—if so, just blend it in a little. Again, water down a little blue and loosely paint in the petals of the cornflowers.

Using a little of the mixed red, with a fluid but completely opaque consistency, add line details on top of the washy layer. Do the same with some thicker blue on the cornflowers.

Use a little pale pink to add details on the mouse's nose, ears and feet.

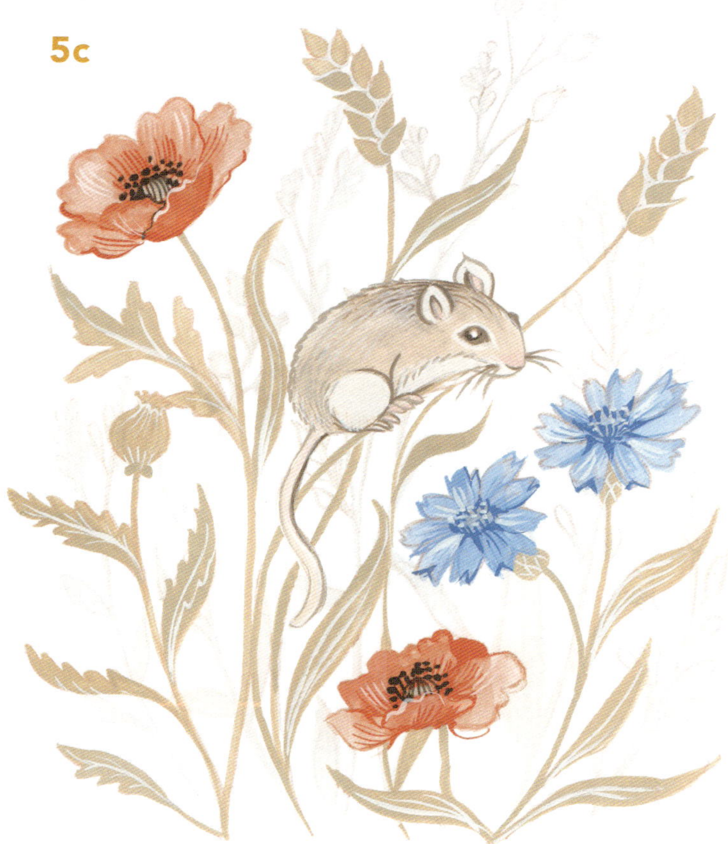

Next, use a dark brown for dotted and line details on the centers of the poppies.

Use dark blue for the center of the cornflowers, painting in the little dots for the anthers.

To finish the scene, we need to add detail to the ochre stems. Reactivate the pale yellow of the background layer with a couple dabs of water. Using a fine brush coated with fluid yet completely opaque paint, draw in lines for the veins on the leaves and the poppy heads. Use a little of the color to add light highlights on the petals and define the wheat ears by outlining the grain cases.

TAKING THE PROJECT FURTHER:

This is a brilliant technique to transfer into other scenes. You could have a wildflower silhouette with a bunny in the foreground, or a leafy silhouette behind a songbird or squirrel.

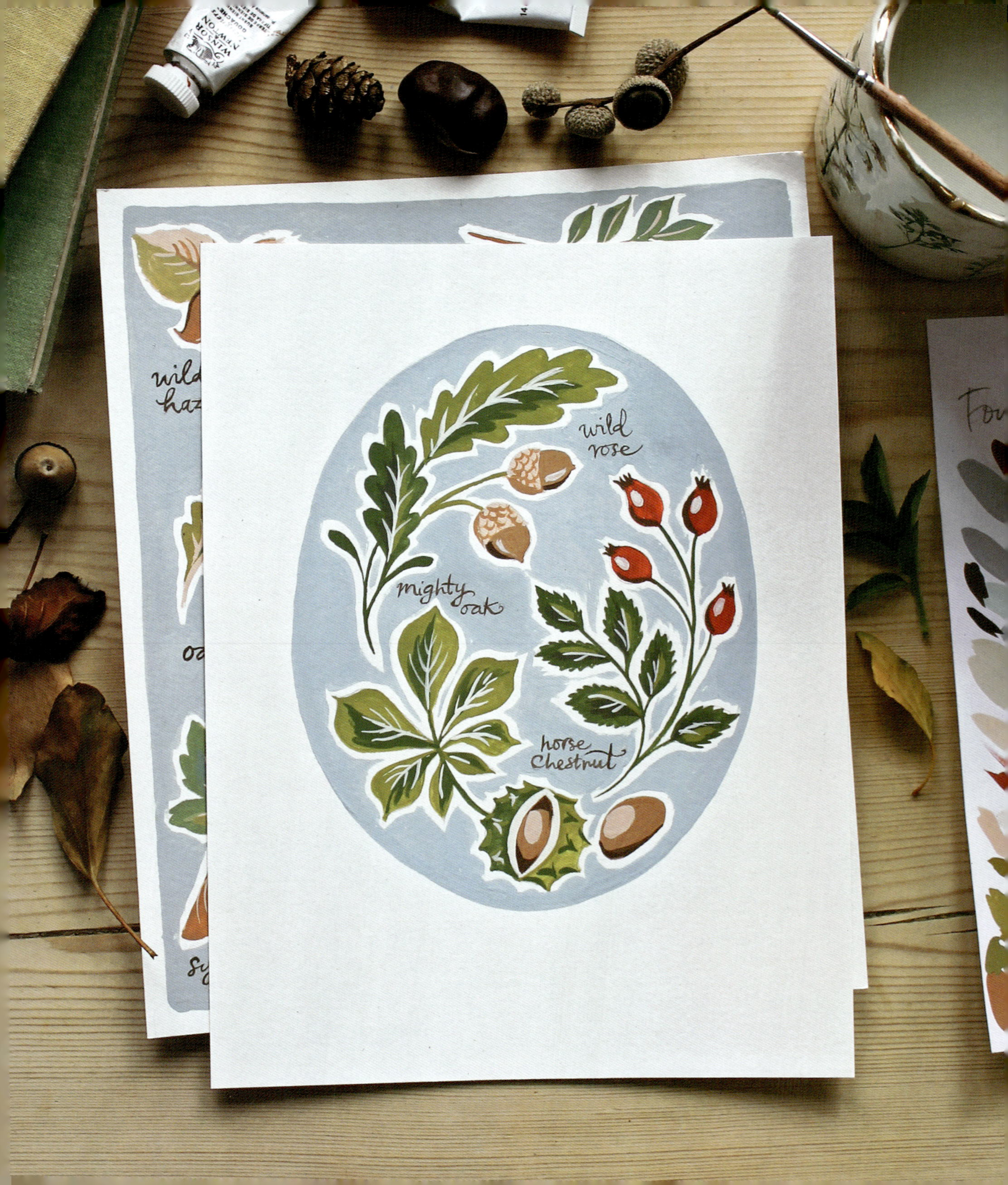
wild rose
mighty oak
horse chestnut

Found & Foraged

Living in the countryside with little ones means I spend a lot of time wandering the lanes and fields collecting leaves and wild fruits, some of which have inspired the subject of our painting here. The composition is wonderfully versatile and easy to adapt—you could replace leaf sprigs and berries with flowers or other foraged delights and still keep the same effect. We will take a multi-layered approach, building flat layers of colors to create volume without blending.

COLOR MIXING

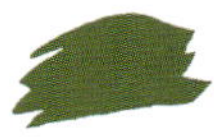

Medium Green: Add dabs each of Yellow Ochre, Permanent White and Olive Green together with a large dab of Phthalo Blue.

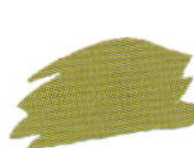

Moss Green: Add a large dab each of Phthalo Blue, Cadmium Yellow and Yellow Ochre together with a dab of Permanent White. This color should be really vibrant and bright.

Peach: Add equal specks each of Alizarin Crimson and Cadmium Yellow to a large dab of Permanent White. You only need a small amount of this!

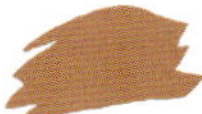

Burnt Sienna: Add a small dab each of Burnt Sienna and Burnt Umber together with a large dab of Permanent White.

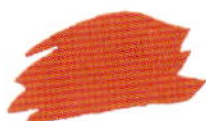

Red: Add a dab each of Permanent White, Burnt Sienna and Alizarin Crimson together. You only need a tiny amount of this color.

Off-White: Take a dot each of the mixed peach and moss green and combine thoroughly with a large dab of Permanent White.

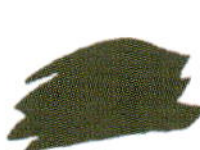

Dark Green: Add a dab of Phthalo Blue to a small dab of Yellow Ochre and mix with a dot of Permanent White. Darken with a dot each of Burnt Umber and Ivory Black.

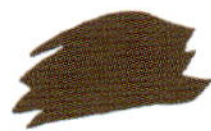

Brown: Add a dot of Ivory Black together with a dab each of Permanent White and Burnt Umber.

Blue Gray: Add a dab of Burnt Sienna and a couple of dabs each of Ivory Black and Phthalo Blue and mix thoroughly. Add in a large blob of Permanent White and more to lighten further if needed. We will need plenty of this color to ensure we have enough to paint the whole background in without mixing again. Remember to test a swatch before starting on your piece.

SUPPLIES

Brushes: Small flat, very fine round, fine round, small round

Paint Colors: Alizarin Crimson, Burnt Sienna, Burnt Umber, Cadmium Yellow, Ivory Black, Olive Green, Permanent White, Phthalo Blue, Yellow Ochre

Other Supplies: Pencil and eraser, scratch paper

1a

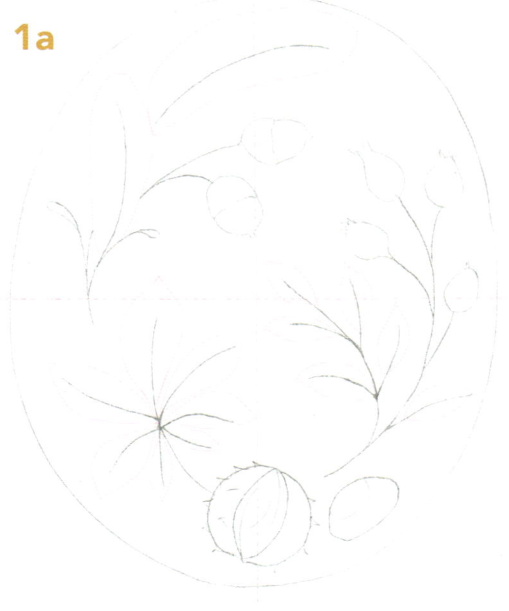

1b

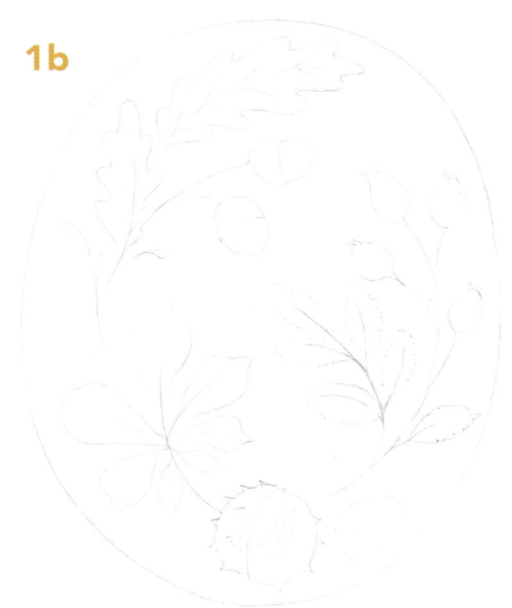

Step 1: Pencil Drawings & Labels

I will describe how I created my layout, though yours may be slightly different depending on the scale or the direction in which each element is facing. I have used a large portrait oval for this piece and you can do the same or adapt it to whatever size you like. Try not to get too worried about copying exactly and feel free to use your creative intuition.

The aim of the composition is to create flowing and harmoniously spaced elements. To do this, you need to really think on your toes and add in the elements to suit the space available—a little like a jigsaw puzzle!

TIP: *If in doubt, or if you have a rogue space where nothing fits, draw in a little leaf or two!*

Using my darker guidelines as reference, begin placing the sprigs, with curved lines for the main stems and then the offshoots. The leaves each have quite complex structures so we will work one by one, starting with the oak and acorns.

Looking at my pink guidelines in image 1a, very faintly draw in two shapes that look a little like fat sausages to place both leaves. The acorns are essentially a small oval with a little semicircle at the end. Separate the cup and acorn with a lightly curved line.

The rosehip is slightly less complicated. We have one small stem on the left that is made up of five leaves and a single one on the right. Again, very lightly draw them in as pointed almonds and these will be your guide when adding a more realistic edge.

The horse chestnut leaf has seven blades—or mini-leaves—making up the whole leaf shape. Draw them in as pointed basic almond shapes, placing them neatly. Next, draw a slightly off-center oval at the bottom of the horse chestnut stem, with an 'eye' in the middle to show the conker poking out. Add another oval for the conker.

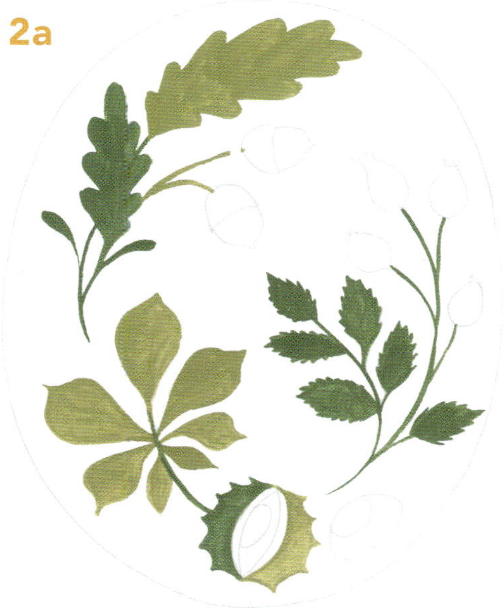

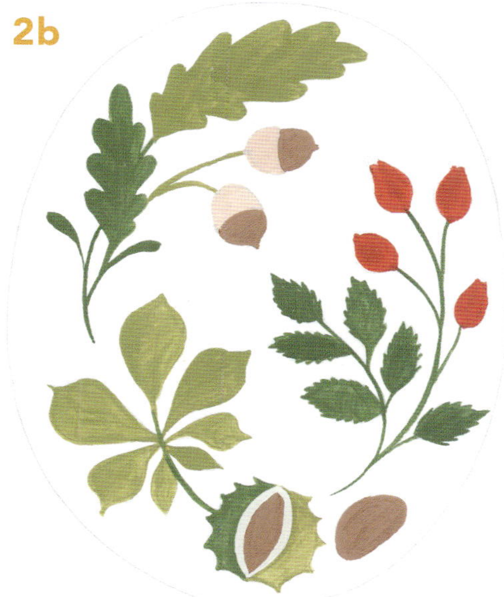

Next, we draw in the more realistic edges to the leaves as per my drawing. For the oak, firmly draw in wavy edges of the leaf. In real life, these would not be perfectly straight on, so embrace the wonkiness! The lines for the veins fan out from the central one. For the rosehip, add a fine serrated edge to each leaf, trying to also curve where you can.

The horse chestnut leaves are actually fatter at the top than your original drawing, so draw over the top slightly. Add little pointy 'v's to the shell to suggest spikes on each side.

Erase the original faint guidelines.

Take a photo of the design for reference later!

TIP: *If you are going to try painting your own collection of sprigs, I would suggest sketching out the layout of the elements first on scratch paper so you don't get muddled. When you are happy, copy the drawing lightly and neatly onto some watercolor paper.*

Step 2

In the next step of the piece, we will use a small round brush to paint a layer of flat green colors across several of the elements as a base coat to which we can add details.

Use the medium green to paint in the stems of the oak sprigs, excluding the acorn stems and the lower leaf. Next, paint in the entire stem and all the leaves of the rosehips. Paint the stem of the horse chestnut and the left side of the shell as well.

Paint in the top oak leaf and acorn stems with the vibrant moss green color, as well as the entire horse chestnut leaf and the right side of the shell.

Next, add the rest of the colors so that the design has a full clean base layer. Paint in the acorn cups in the peach color. Use the mixed Burnt Sienna color to add in the acorns and whole conkers. The rosehips are your mixed red color. Use a little of the off-white to paint the pale inside edge of the conker shell.

3a

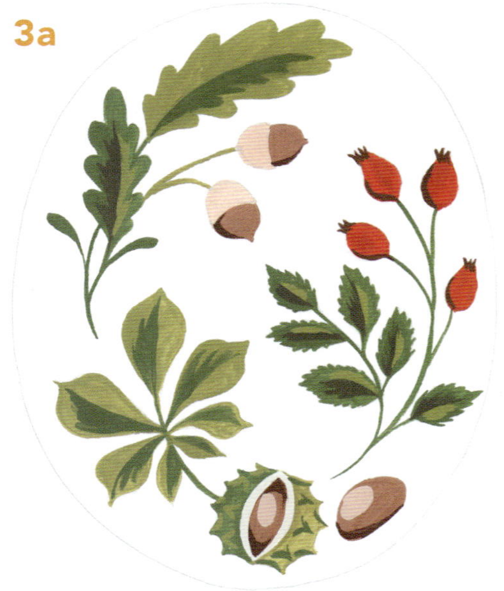

3b

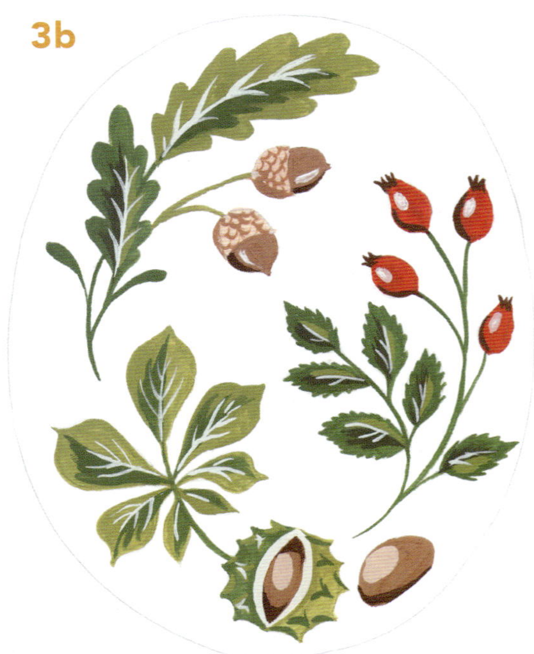

Step 3: Shadows & Highlights

Now let's really start adding some shadow and highlights on the different elements before the more detailed linework. Working methodically, we will dip in and out of the mixed colors, adding layers. Don't worry about the shading looking sketchy or flat—this just adds personality to the design.

First, use your dark green to paint in the shadow across the medium green-colored leaves. Generally, start at the base and middle of a leaf and paint up and out across one half of it.

Use a medium green to add shadow on the moss green leaves and again behind the points of the conker shells. Paint on the right side of the oak leaf and the left side of the horse chestnut leaves.

Paint tiny moss green highlights on the right side of the lower oak and rosehip leaves as well as behind the points of the conker shells.

With the brown, paint in a narrow shadow on the underside of the acorns and conker and then another shadow on the left side and the little hairy tops of the rosehips. Add a little shadow to emphasize the inside corners of the conkers and behind the points of the conker shells.

Use the peach to add the oval centers to both conkers.

Next, we will focus on adding some detailed linework on each element to bring them to life and add character. Take a look at your reference picture to remind yourself of the veins and details!

Using a fine round brush and an off-white color, draw in veins on the oak leaves, horse chestnut leaves and to the right of the rosehip leaves. Paint in the oval highlights on the rosehip berries and little shiny highlights on the acorns.

Add a few Burnt Sienna 'scale-like' patterns on the acorn cups.

4a

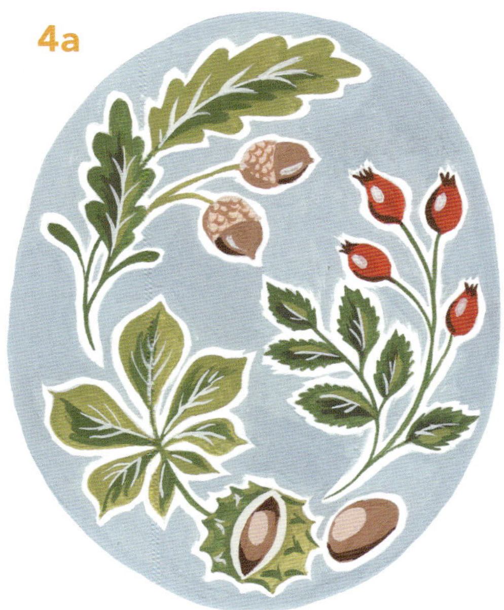

4b

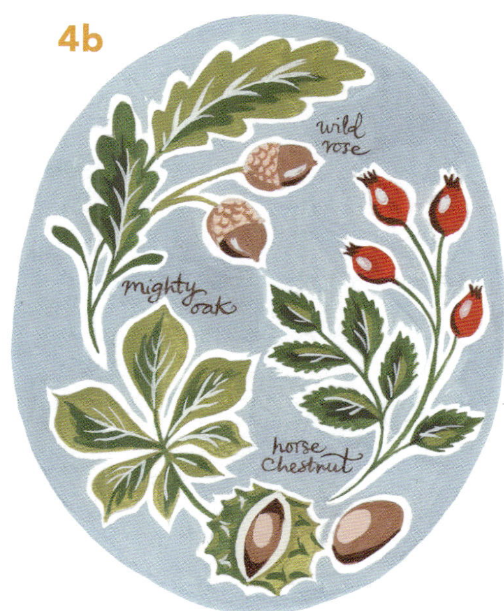

Step 4: Background & Handwritten Tags

We will be using the blue gray to paint in the background and we need the consistency to be thick and opaque but still fluid, so add a little water to your brush to loosen as you go. Using a small flat brush and leaving approximately ⅛ inch (3-mm) gap around the elements, paint in a blue outline. As with the oval edge, this will look better if it isn't too neat or precise, so don't worry about visible brush strokes and uneven spaces. Leave it to dry completely.

The last step is adding the little handwritten tags for each of the sprigs. These really tie the whole piece together. Write out the names on the blue background with a light pencil script and, with a very fine round brush, paint over them in mixed brown.

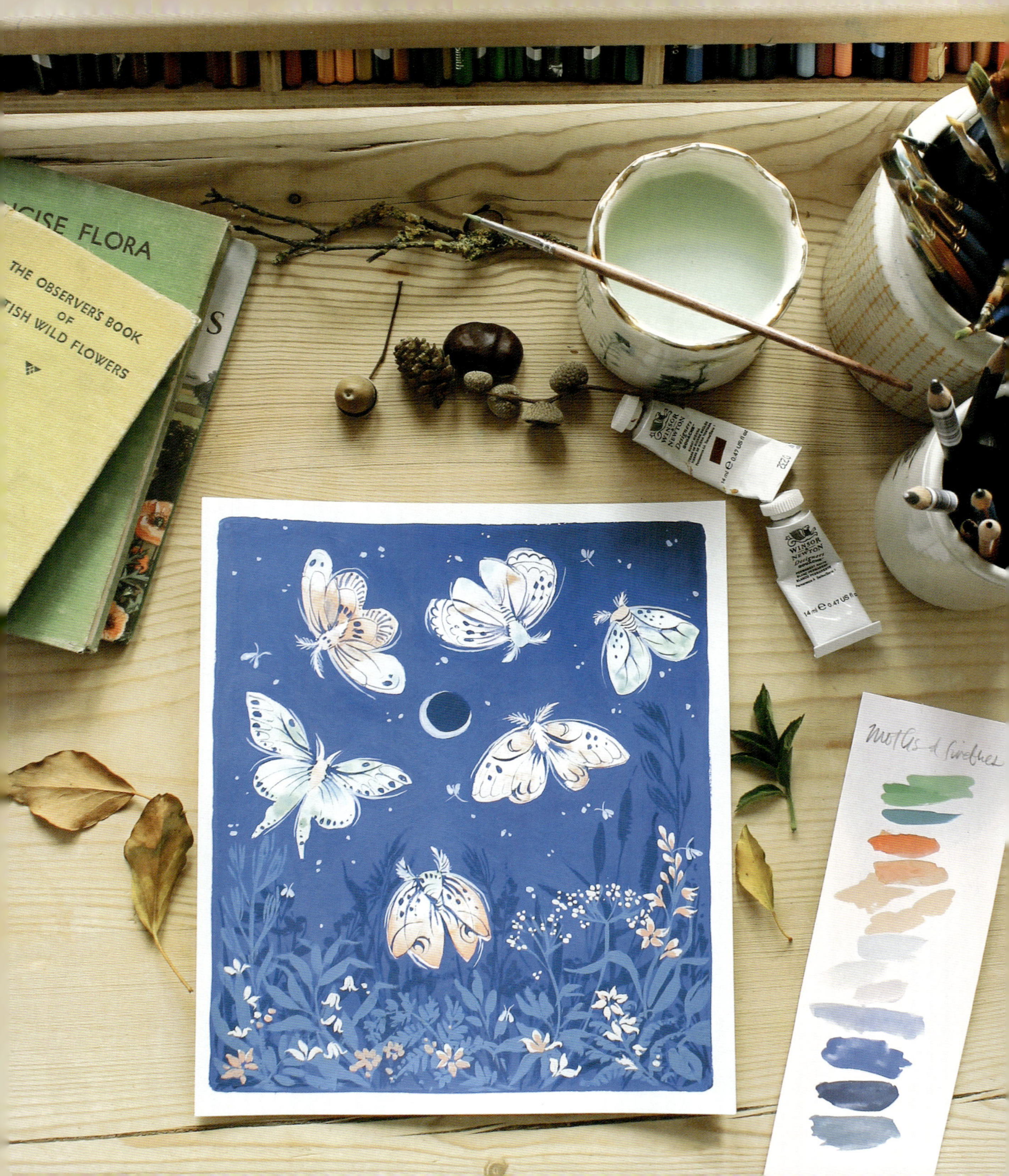

FLORA
THE OBSERVER'S BOOK
OF
WILD FLOWERS
WINSOR & NEWTON
Designers

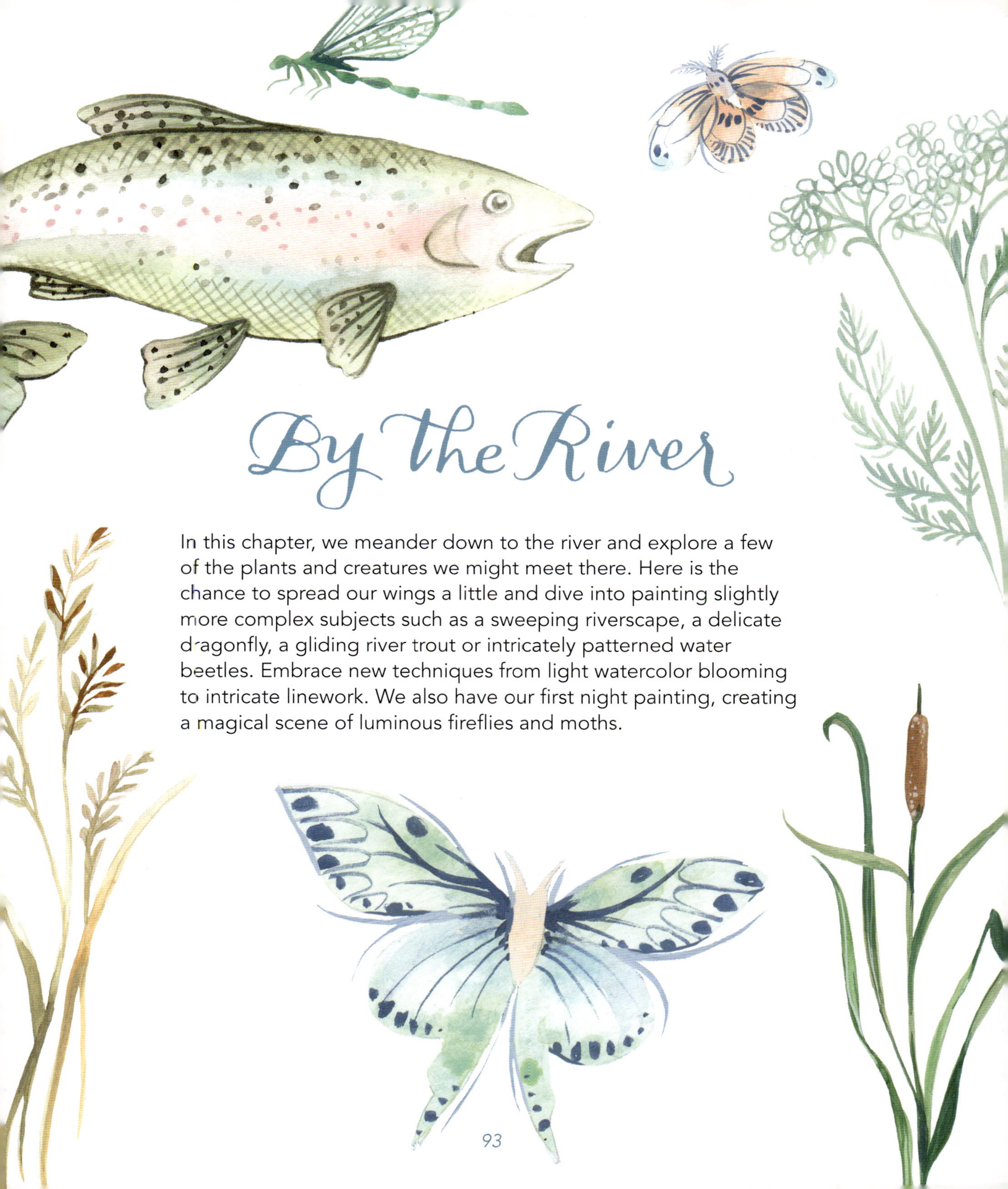

By the River

In this chapter, we meander down to the river and explore a few of the plants and creatures we might meet there. Here is the chance to spread our wings a little and dive into painting slightly more complex subjects such as a sweeping riverscape, a delicate dragonfly, a gliding river trout or intricately patterned water beetles. Embrace new techniques from light watercolor blooming to intricate linework. We also have our first night painting, creating a magical scene of luminous fireflies and moths.

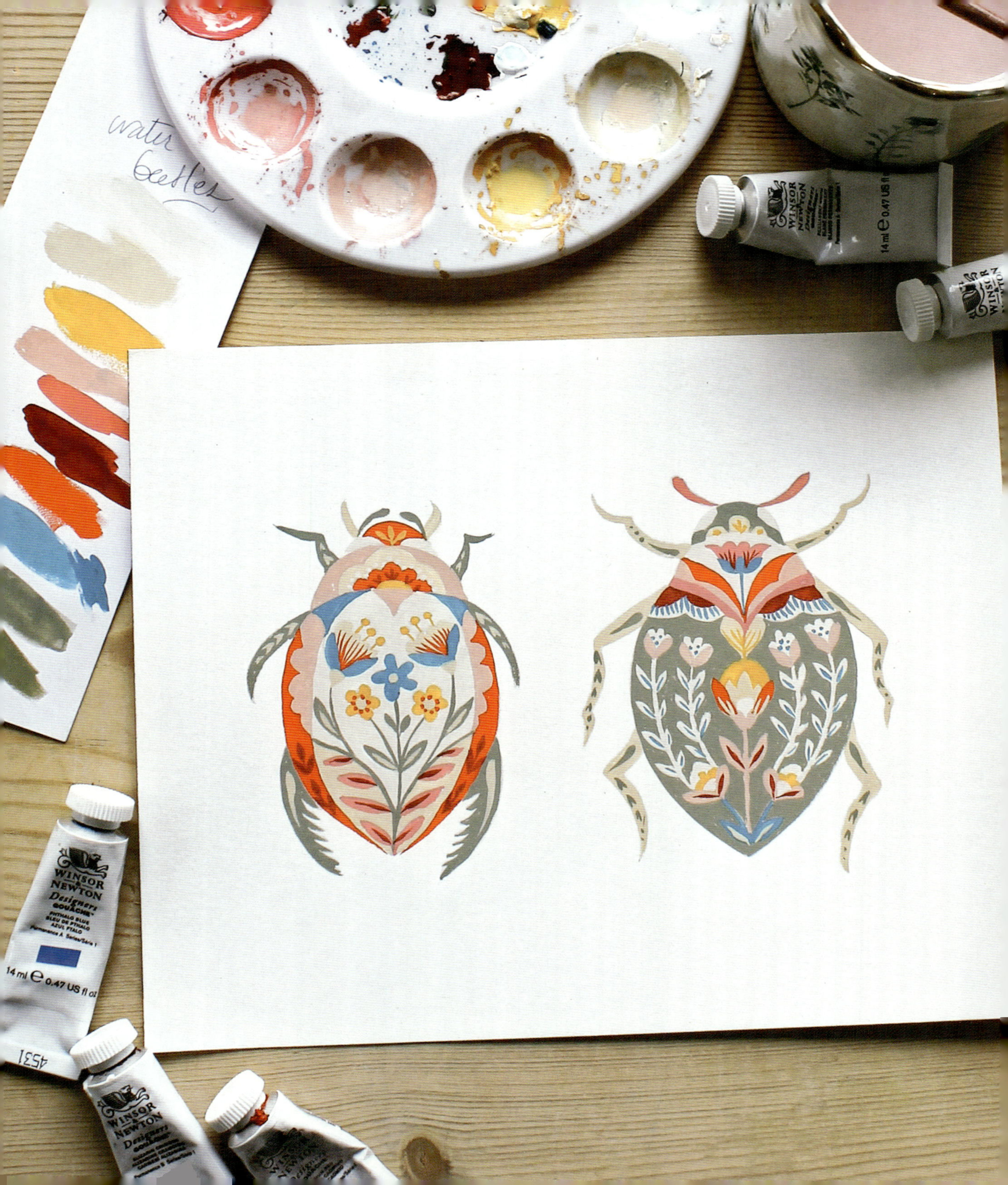
water beetles
WINSOR & NEWTON
Designers
GOUACHE
14 ml ℮ 0.47 US fl oz

Patterned Water Beetles

This warm-up project builds on the friendly creatures we tackled in the first chapter—there is something bizarrely satisfying about adding pattern to an insect or creature! Beetles particularly lend themselves to embellishment as their shells are naturally decorative. We will be working with a muted retro palette and playing with the colors—light-on-dark on one beetle and dark-on-light on the other.

COLOR MIXING

Cream: Mix the tiniest speck each of Cadmium Yellow, Cadmium Red and Ivory Black with a small blob of Permanent White.

Light Yellow: Add a large dab each of Cadmium Yellow, Cadmium Red and Ivory Black to a small blob of Permanent White.

Dark Yellow: Add three dabs of Permanent White and a dab each of Cadmium Red and Ivory Black to a small blob of Cadmium Yellow.

Light Pink: Mix a dab each of Alizarin Crimson and Cadmium Yellow with a small blob of Permanent White.

Dark Pink: Add a couple of dabs each of Cadmium Yellow and Alizarin Crimson to a small blob of Permanent White.

Orange: Add a couple of dabs each of Cadmium Yellow and Permanent White to a small blob of Cadmium Red.

Red: Mix a small blob of Alizarin Crimson, two dabs each of Permanent White and Cadmium Yellow and a small speck of Ivory Black.

Khaki Green: Add a dab each of Cadmium Yellow, Phthalo Blue, Cadmium Red and Alizarin Crimson to a couple of large dabs of Permanent White, mixing thoroughly.

Turquoise: Add a small dab each of Permanent White and Cadmium Yellow to a small blob of Phthalo Blue.

SUPPLIES

Brush: Fine round

Paint Colors: Alizarin Crimson, Cadmium Red, Cadmium Yellow, Ivory Black, Permanent White, Phthalo Blue

Other Supplies: Pencil and eraser, scratch paper

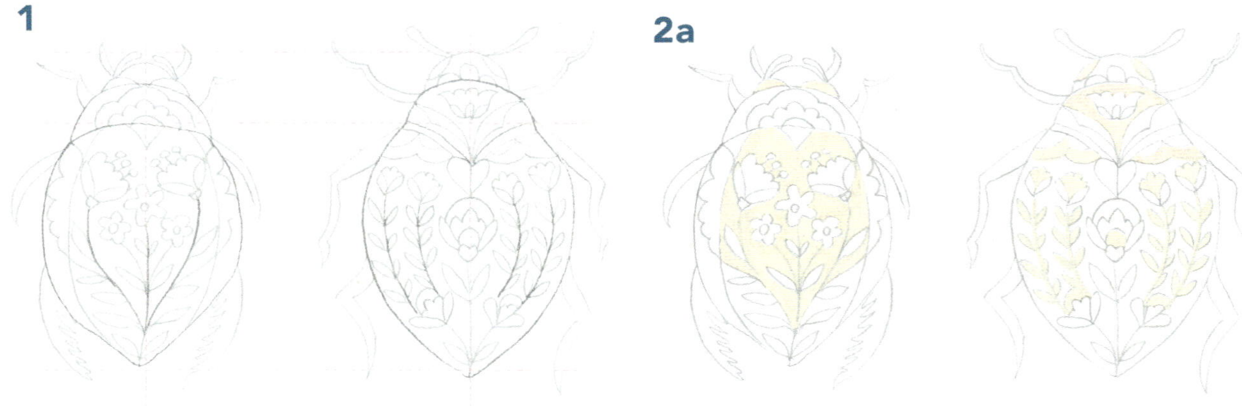

Step 1: Drawing the Water Beetles

Using my pink dashed guidelines, draw in the basic shape of the beetles' bodies, noting that the two are slightly different from one another. Add the legs and antennae, using subtly different shapes for each.

Divide both the shells in half and on each of these central lines, draw a little flower with symmetrical leaves on both sides.

You can use my slightly darker lines as a reference for the stems and details. Fill one side with a curved pattern, then carefully mirror it on the other side of the shell. Add little scalloped frills and plenty of teeny leaves and flowers. When painting, you will be relying quite heavily on the details you add here, so make it as complex as you would like the final painted design to be.

Step 2: Painting the Base Colors

Don't be daunted by all the tiny little areas of pattern. Start with the lighter colors, mixing your palette as you go and taking care to wash the brushes in between so that they do not become muddy. The consistency of the paint should be the same across all the colors, so add a little water to the mixed colors as you are loading your brush so that you have a fluid yet completely opaque line. Using a fine round brush for the whole project, we will fill areas with color and then add contrasting details on top.

Using my image as a reference, use the cream shade to carefully add in the lightest layer of color.

TIP: *It is a little tricky painting around some of the leaves and stems, so take your time and don't worry too much if you overlap colors—we can always paint over them later.*

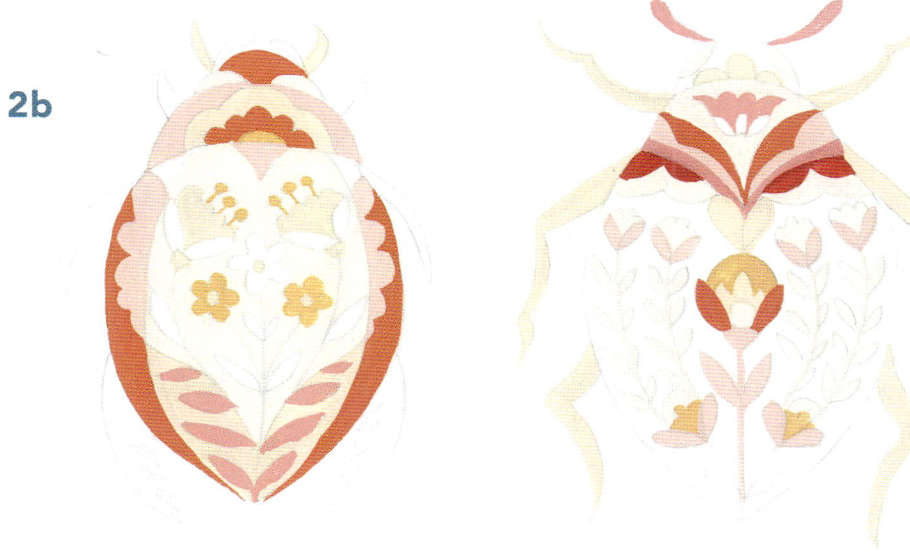

Using the image as a reference, add light yellow details across both beetles, taking particular care to paint in the legs on the right.

Use dark yellow, light pink, dark pink, orange and red evenly across the beetles as per my design.

Adding the khaki green really ties the piece together, but take your time, especially around the leaves on the beetle to the right. Add the bright pops of turquoise.

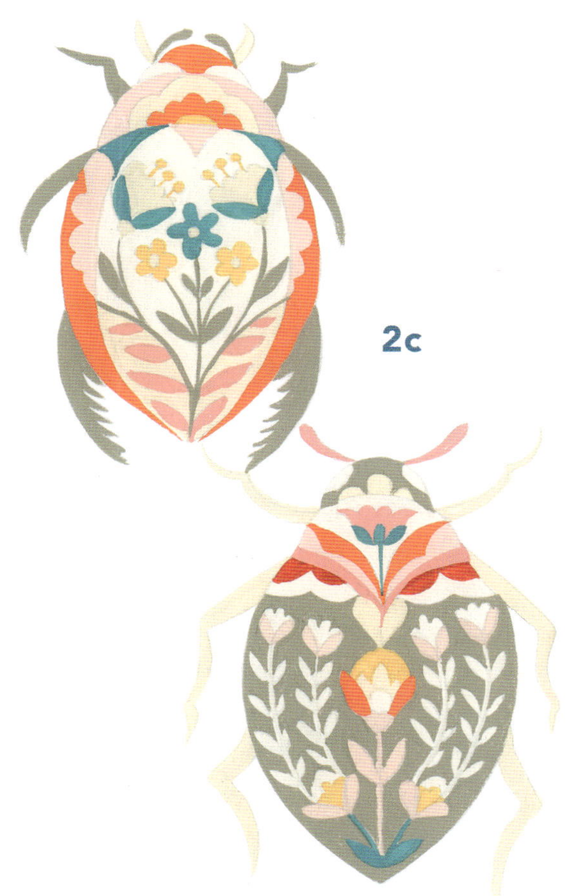

3

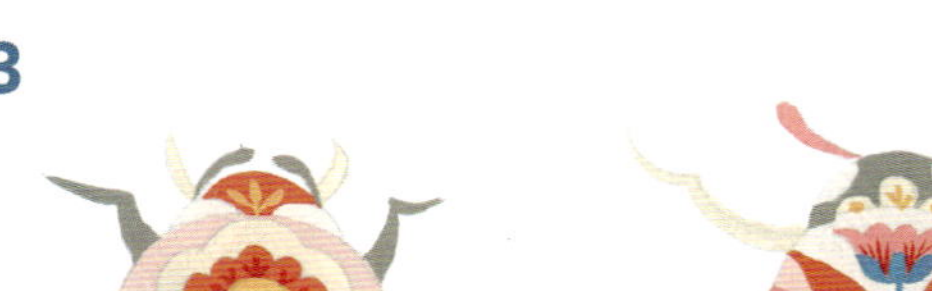

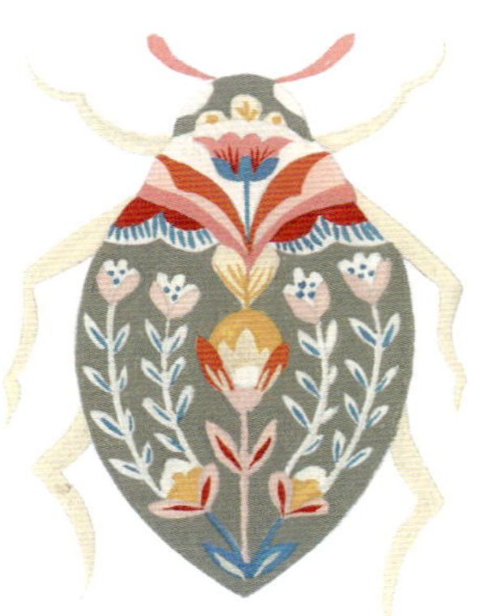

4

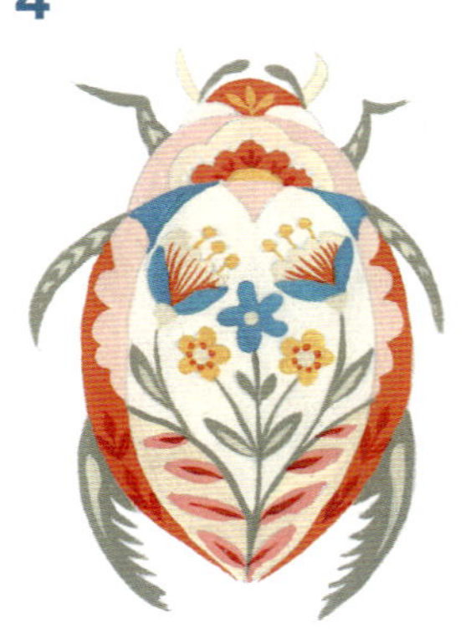

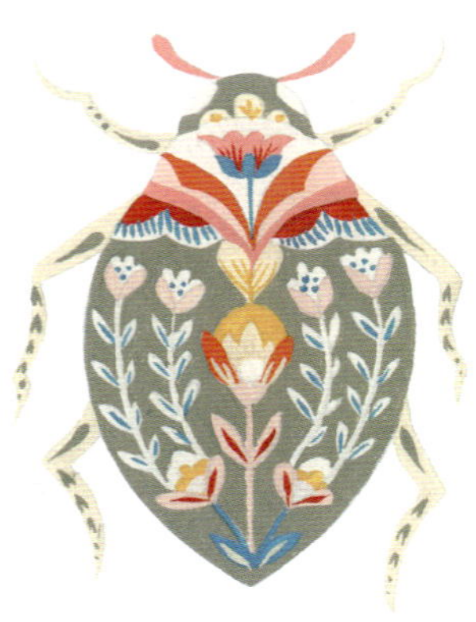

Step 3: Adding Details to the Bodies

The design should dry pleasingly flat and even and the next step is to add some contrasting dots and dashes. We will use a whole range of colors to more evenly distribute the colors across the shell.

On the beetle to the left, use the orange to paint in little line details on the petals of the large flowers and little dotty centers on the smaller ones. Use the red to paint in tiny leaf patterns on the orange areas and on the pink leaves. Add tiny dark yellow leaves to the head.

On the right beetle, paint in a few little red strokes as veins on the leaves and the petals of the top flower, cream strokes on the lower turquoise leaves and orange petals of the most central flower. Add tiny dark yellow line details on the head and center cream-colored drop shapes. Use the turquoise to add a row of little lines on the cream section of body, dots on the little flower heads and veins on all of the tiny cream stem leaves.

Step 4: Adding Details to the Legs

To finish, we paint in the patterns on the legs. These go on top of the existing layer but in opposite colors, so green on yellow and yellow on green. The design here is very simple so as not to detract from the bold pattern on the shells. Paint tiny dashes and some upside down 'v' shapes on each one, being careful to keep them symmetrical with the opposite limb.

Rainbow Trout

This project uses both wet-on-wet and wet-on-dry techniques to create a range of contrasting loose and detailed marks. We will be using gouache as if it were watercolor to create a watery ground and blend a rainbow of colors. We will also be practicing intricate linework, which will create texture and interest on the trout's body. These techniques could apply to any fish you fancy, or insects with a grassy ground, or birds in the sky for that matter!

COLOR MIXING

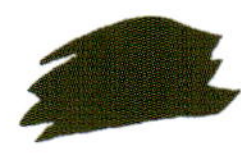
Deep Green: Add two large dabs of Lemon Yellow to one large dab of Ivory Black.

Light Blue: Add a dab of Phthalo Blue to a couple of large dabs of Permanent White and a speck of Ivory Black.

Coral Pink: Add a dab each of Lemon Yellow, Alizarin Crimson and Permanent White to a spot of Ivory Black.

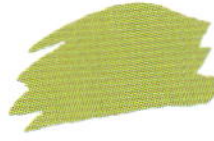
Bright Green: Mix a tiny dab each of Permanent White and Ivory Black with a small blob of Lemon Yellow.

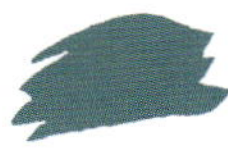
Deep Blue: Add a dab each of Lemon Yellow and Permanent White to a couple of dabs each of Phthalo Blue and Ivory Black.

Bright Pink: Add a dab of Alizarin Crimson to a couple of dabs of Permanent White and a speck of Ivory Black.

Dark Gray: Add a dab each of Ivory Black and Lemon Yellow to a couple of large dabs of Permanent White.

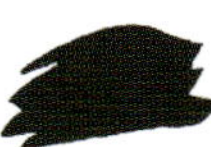
Black: Add a small spot of Permanent White to a couple of large dabs of Ivory Black.

SUPPLIES

Brushes: Fine round, small round, large filbert

Paint Colors: Alizarin Crimson, Ivory Black, Lemon Yellow, Permanent White, Phthalo Blue

Other Supplies: Pencil and eraser, scratch paper

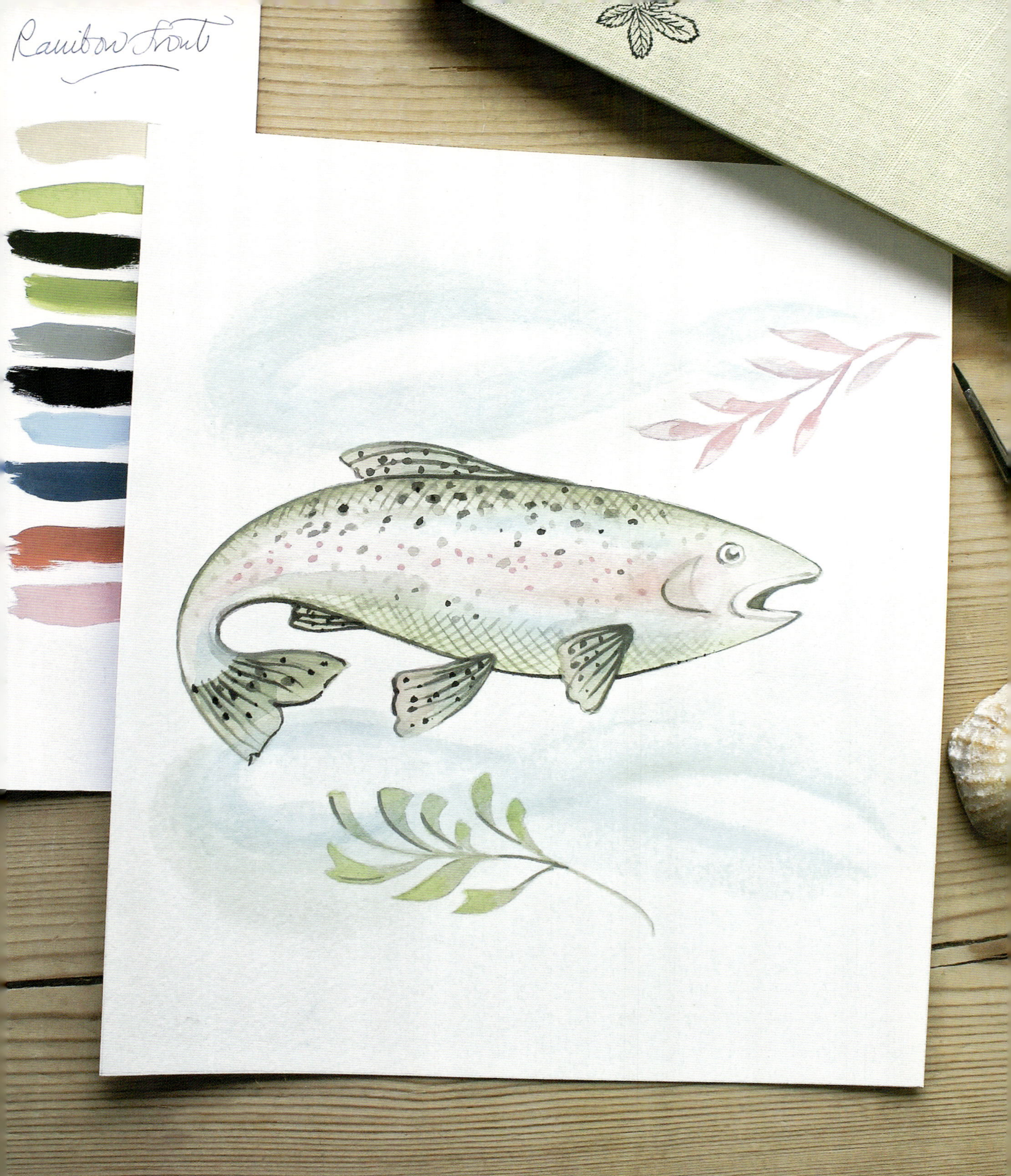
Rainbow Trout

1

2a

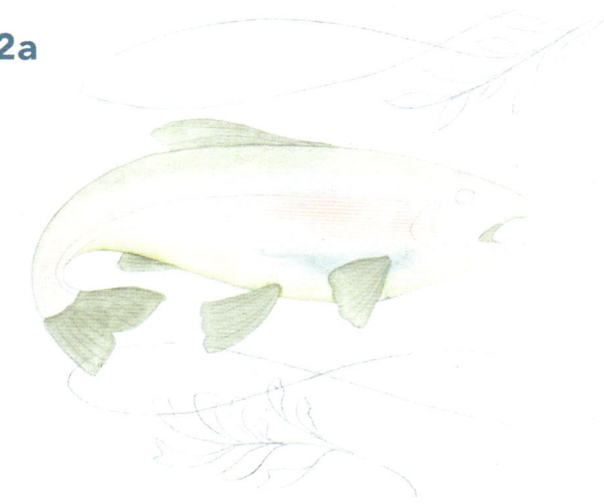

Step 1: Drawing

Draw in the trout's body first, using my guidelines as reference. Start at his head and draw in a sweeping curved line for his back. Draw his head with no mouth initially as if it were one end of an almond and carry on to his lightly rounded belly. Then add the tail, which curves back toward the belly. This could loosely be described as a triangular shape continuous with the line of his back and belly. Neaten this by adding a split in the tail and little line details.

On his head, add a crescent moon shape for the gill, a little round eye and rounded 'v' of his mouth, erasing a gap so that it appears open and adding an extra tiny perspective line so you can see inside. Add one long low triangular fin on the middle of his back and three on the underside by placing one triangle more than half set into the shape of the body, the next only overlapping the belly a small amount and the lowest not overlapping the body at all. Add short curved line details to the fins and tail.

Add two floating sprigs of river weeds, one above and to the right of the fish and the other below and to the left. Start with a curved stem, filling in little floating tendrils. In one swooping line starting in the top right, draw in a crossed loop shape to indicate some swirling movement in the water. Do the same below the fish, starting in the bottom right and overlapping the river weed and trout's fin.

Step 2: Watery Washes

The next step is mixing colors before adding them to a loose watercolor wash across the whole body of the trout. Begin by carefully painting the body of the fish—including the face but excluding the fins and tail—with a small round brush lightly loaded only with clean water.

TIP: *To see the invisible water, tilt your head low to the paper and see where the light catches the water.*

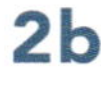

2b

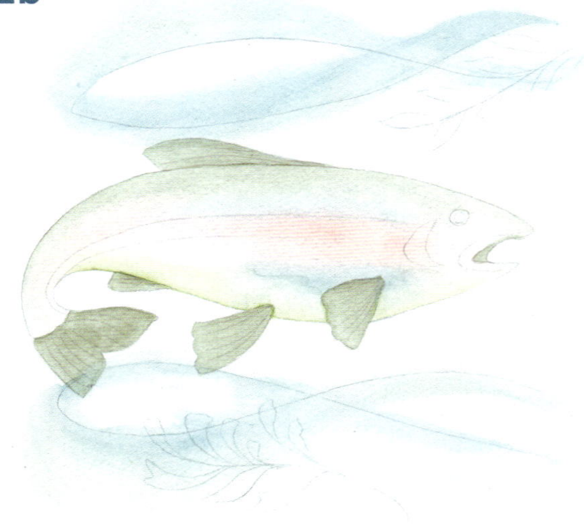

Before painting, dip your brush into a spot of the deep green and mix with a dab of water so you have a very watered-down color and then brush a thin stripe along the trout's back, blending slightly so that there is no defined edge. After cleaning your brush thoroughly, paint a slightly thinner and shorter stripe of light blue below. Next, in the center of the trout, place a thicker stripe of the coral pink, taking care to blend a little over the foremost gill, followed by a small light blue stripe and then a bright green stripe on his belly. Blend over the face and a little around the tail end and then leave everything to dry.

Using a little watered-down deep green, evenly paint in all the fins, tail and inside the mouth.

Next, we add a watery wash to the river water with the following colors and using a large flat filbert brush.

2c

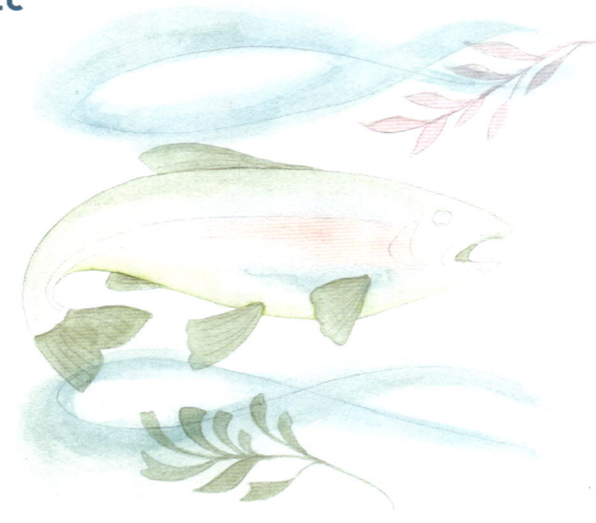

Dip the end of the brush in the deep blue color and mix with plenty of water so that you have a very faint blue consistency. Paint a wide transparent stroke over the top swirly line, blending outward a little with pure water as you go. Repeat on the line below, not worrying at all if this overlaps the fish or seaweed. Use the smallest touch of watered-down deep green to blend the blue out into the whiter areas on the page.

We will now return to the smaller round brush and paint in the river weed with a light semi-opaque wash to suggest that it is floating under water.

Use a touch of bright pink to add a semi-transparent wash to the entire top frond. Use a wash of the deep green for the lower one.

With your large filbert brush, add a tiny amount of the deep blue to add a little more intensity to the swirling water shapes and then let it dry.

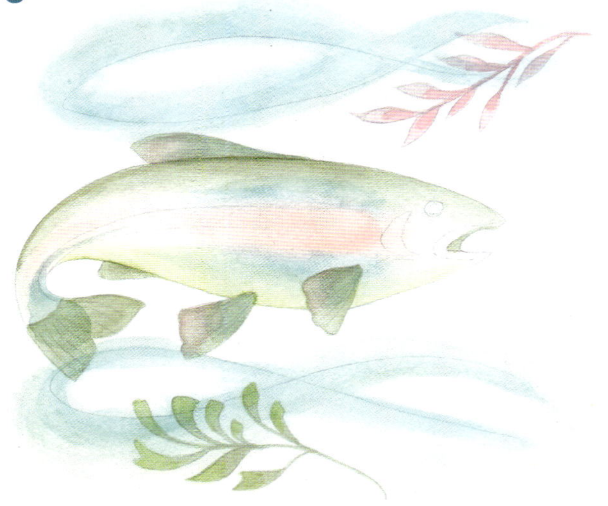

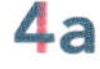

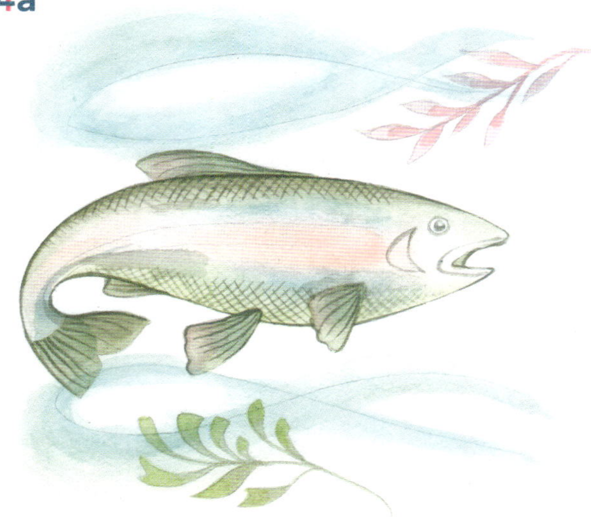

Step 3: Second Washy Layer

The next step is really to build the intensity of the trout by painting in more layers of color. Dip the end of your small round brush into a little of the deep green and mix with a dab of water so that you have a semi-opaque color to paint a long, thick stroke following the contour of his back from tail to nose. Use a little more water to blend this into the body and then repeat this process with the pale blue, coral pink, light blue and bright green.

On each of the fins, paint a little deep blue wash at the end closest to the body and at the other end, a light wash of bright pink.

Begin adding details to the river weeds. On the top weed, add a touch more of the bright pink to the reed stem and centers. On the lower one, add a touch of the bright green to the tips of the leafy tendrils. Leave everything to dry.

Step 4: Tiny Details

Now that we have the basic trout covered, we can add some of the really tiny details in gray, black and bright pink.

First, with the very tip of your brush and some transparent dark gray paint, add in the lines around the mouth, the gill and the eye. Paint around the whole fish's outline with a light stroke, adding line details over each of the fins following their curved shape.

Next, we will add textured marks in the form of cross-hatching, to give the impression of scales across the body. Cross-hatching is essentially little crossed fine parallel lines—diagonal in this case, following the curve of the trout's body—giving the illusion of shade. Use this technique right across the top of the body and then repeat for the belly. With a watery stroke, paint in a shadow to blend the edges of the cross-hatching into the pink and leave to dry.

4b

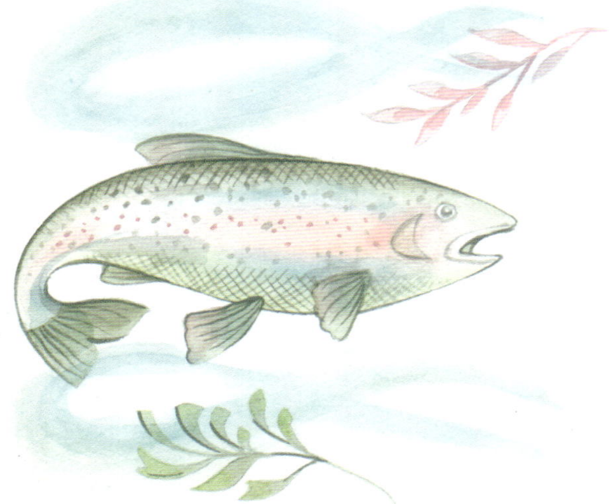

When dry, erase all the visible lines. Next, add little unevenly-shaped bright pink spots across the pink center of the body and a little shading on the face. Add a touch of transparent deep green across the gill. Use a little of the bright pink to outline the pink river weed. Repeat in dark gray for the green weed.

Add more uneven dark gray spots right across the body, including over the cross-hatching on his back.

4c

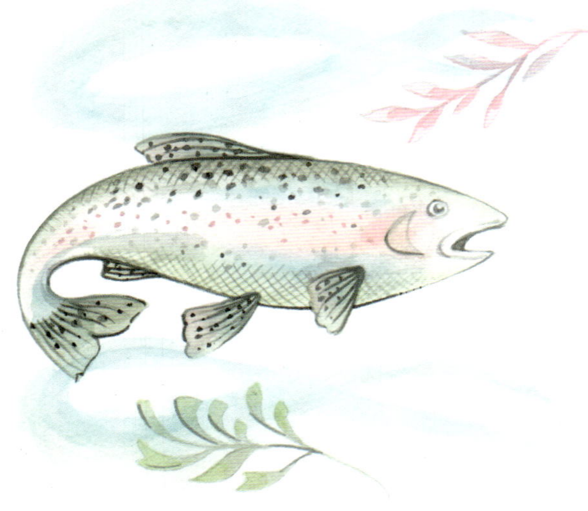

Finish the piece by adding some faint black details across the trout, such as contour lines for his underbelly and fins and black spots on his back and across all four fins. Darken the open mouth and eye a touch.

River Landscape

This project will create our first imaginary landscape, with a winding river as the focus for our little scene and a swooping red kite giving a sense of perspective. We will be working with a limited palette, really evoking that sense of late fall or early winter. The joy of this piece is in playing with brush strokes, creating texture and interest across all the hills, trees, clouds and bird feathers.

COLOR MIXING

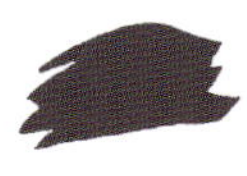
Dark Purple: Add a spot of Permanent White to a dab each of Alizarin Crimson, Phthalo Blue and Ivory Black.

Medium Gray: Mix three spots of Ivory Black and one spot of Alizarin Crimson with a large blob of Permanent White.

Light Gray: Add a dot each of Ivory Black, Yellow Ochre and Alizarin Crimson to a large blob of Permanent White and mix thoroughly.

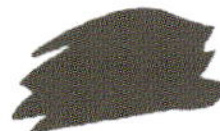
Dark Brown: Add a spot of Permanent White to a dab each of Burnt Sienna and Ivory Black.

Pale Blue: Add a dab of Phthalo Blue and a spot of Ivory Black to a large blob of Permanent White.

Pale Gold: Add a spot of Ivory Black and a dab of Permanent White to a blob of Yellow Ochre.

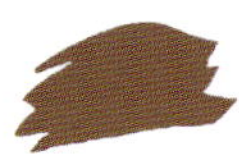
Reddish Brown: Mix a small dab each of Ivory Black and Alizarin Crimson and two dabs of Permanent White with a blob of Burnt Sienna.

Cream: Add a spot of Yellow Ochre and a speck of Ivory Black to a small blob of Permanent White.

Pink: Add a speck of Ivory Black to a spot of Alizarin Crimson and a small blob of Permanent White.

Gold: Add a spot of Ivory Black and a dab of Permanent White to a blob of Yellow Ochre.

Pure White: That's it!

SUPPLIES

Brushes: Small round, medium filbert

Paint Colors: Alizarin Crimson, Burnt Sienna, Ivory Black, Permanent White, Phthalo Blue, Yellow Ochre

Other Supplies: Ruler, pencil and eraser, scratch paper

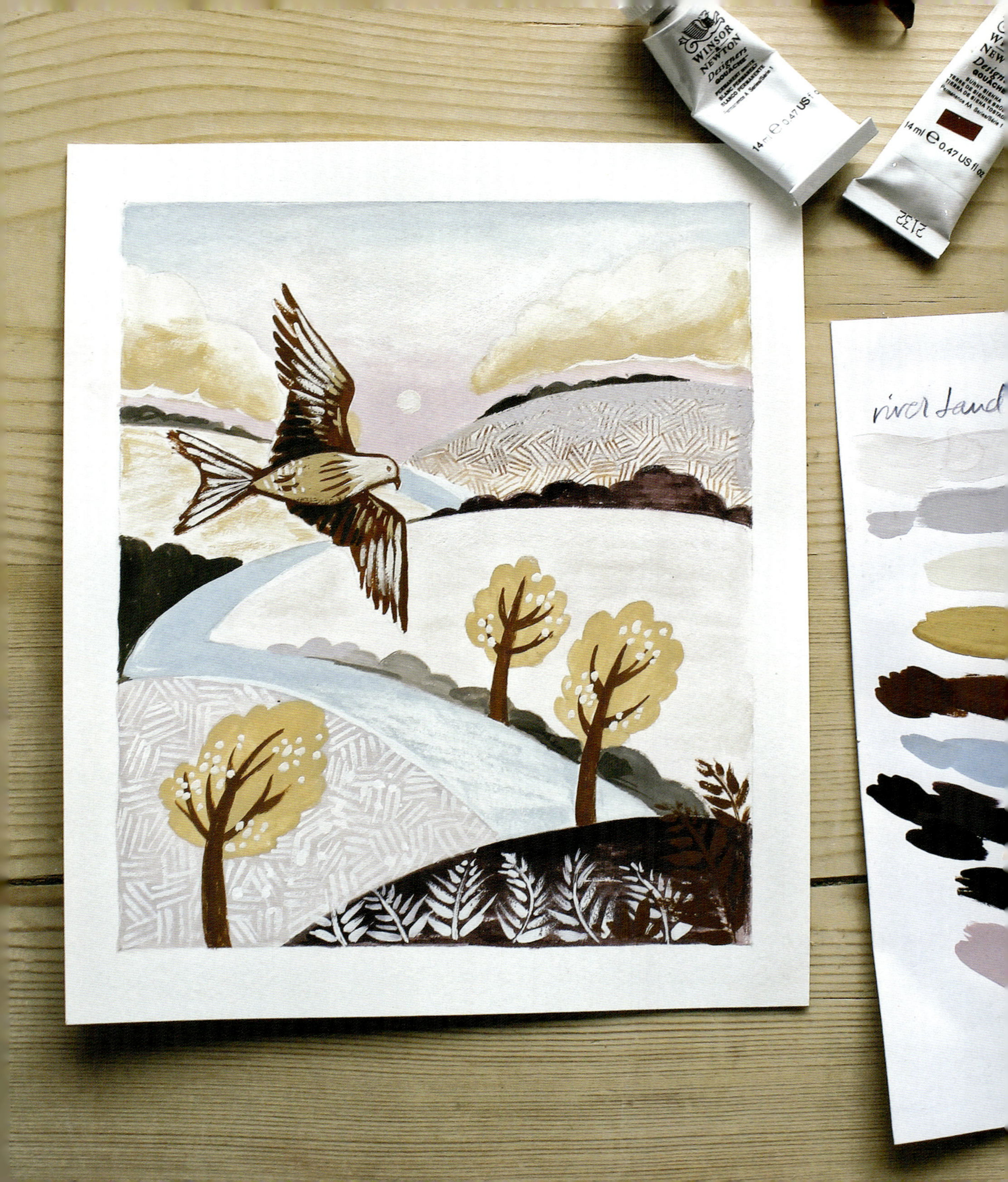

WINSOR
NEWTON
Designers
GOUACHE
14 ml ℮ 0,47 US fl oz
2132
river land

Step 1: Drawing the Scene

Draw a smallish rectangle on the page and, starting on the right side about one-fifth of the way up from the bottom, draw a curved line for the closest hill, going from right to left. Reference my slightly darker guidelines to help you place the design. In the opposite direction, draw in the next hill, followed by a third, fourth and fifth, progressively decreasing in width. The river is essentially nestled in the valley that these 'hills' make, so draw it with slightly tapered parallel lines following the curved valley, hiding it behind the third hill and peeping out again by the fourth.

Draw in three trees, with tall narrow trunks bending slightly to the right, making the trunks and branches fork and narrow to a point. Draw in an oval-like fluffy cloud shape to suggest leaves as you might in a child's drawing. Along the edges of the river and 'behind' the hills, add in some scalloped shapes to suggest hedges and trees. In the sky, draw in fluffy clouds with flattish bottoms, following the curve of the hills.

The swooping bird is a red kite with distinctive forked tail feathers. We will draw him right over the landscape drawing, erasing the lines behind afterward. About halfway up the fourth hill on the left, draw in his almond-shaped body, but with a curve on the right for his beak and head. Add a 'v'-shaped forked tail. The top wing curves almost vertically upward, then kicks up and out at an angle, curving back in and down to where the tail begins. The lower wing is slightly foreshortened, so the line comes out diagonally and then down vertically and then back to the bottom of the tail in an almost straight line.

Step 2: Painting the Background

The first step is to put down the ground colors across the whole design. We will be mixing as we go along, painting with a medium sized filbert brush. The idea is to fill the scene with a variety of textures, so remember that any varied mark making will help make your painting unique and beautiful.

1

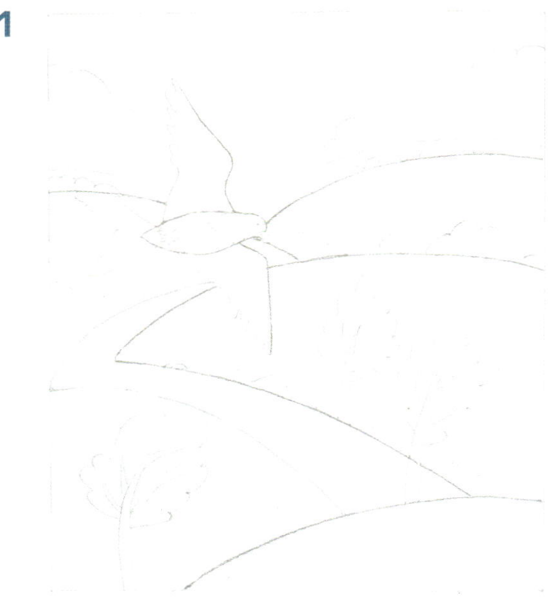

2a

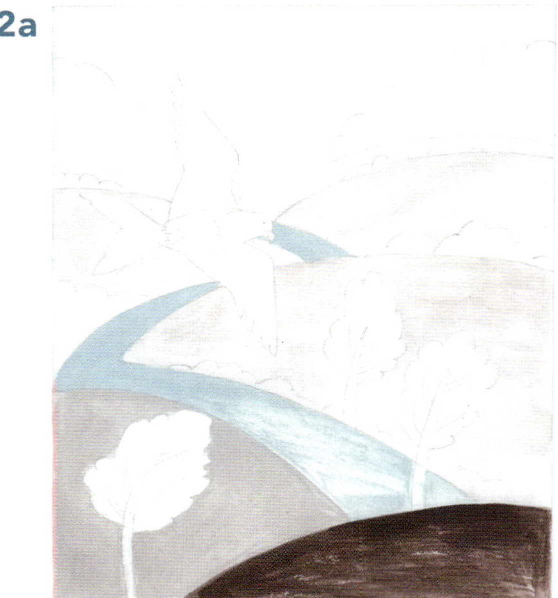

2b

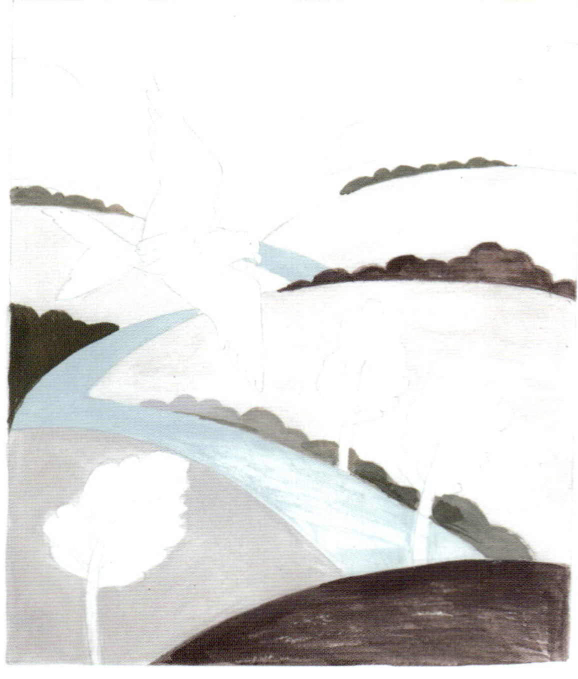

2c

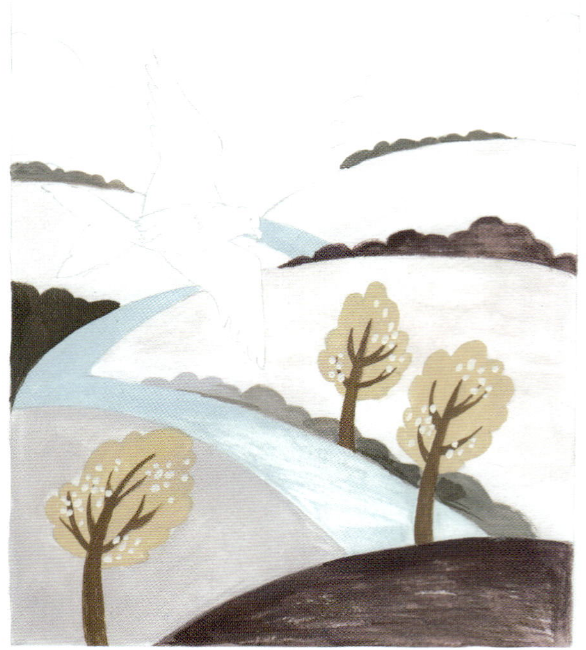

Use dark purple to paint in the closest hill with loose textured horizontal strokes.

Paint around the tree trunk and leaves, filling the second hill with an opaque, even coverage of medium gray.

Use light gray for the third hill, this time in an opaque wash of textured strokes, excluding the trees and wing. While still wet, mix a teeny speck of dark brown with some water and use this as a textured wash over the top half of the hill.

The fourth and fifth hills are also washes of light gray.

Turning to a small round brush and a dryish consistency of paint, begin painting the river with pale blue, starting at the furthest point with opaque even coverage. As you get close to the foreground, paint with horizontal textured strokes so that you can still see some of the white of the paper. Leave all these hills and the river to dry for some time and notice how they lighten considerably.

Now, we paint the hedge and woodland silhouettes using a small round brush. On the right side of the lower edge of the third hill, where it meets the river, start painting in your scallop-shaped bush silhouette in the medium gray, working from left to right. While this is still wet, work from right to left with the dark brown to form a darker, textured ombré.

Paint in the larger scallop shapes to the left of the river in the dark brown. Next, add a touch of light gray to the dark brown and paint some very narrow scalloped trees on the horizon. The final tree silhouette, on the right-hand bank of the river in the foreground, is painted with the dark purple.

Using the pale gold, paint in the fluffy heads of the trees, not worrying too much about textured edges.

Use the reddish brown to paint in the trunks and branches of the trees, using upward strokes and ending each branch in forked points.

Using a dabbing motion with a little of the cream color on the end of your brush, paint little clustered oval spots on the leaf shape, slightly overlapping the branches.

Step 3: Painting the Sky & Clouds

In this step, we will be working on the blushing wintery sky and clouds using mainly wet-on-wet blending, but also some dry-brush marks in the clouds.

Have the light gray, pale blue, pink, cream and gold colors wet and ready to paint, making sure the consistency is fluid yet opaque by adding a touch of water. Using a medium sized filbert brush and being careful to work around the wing and clouds, paint in some smooth pink from the skyline to about halfway up the sky. Clean and dab dry your brush. Then, with a little light gray, paint from the top of the piece down to meet the pink, overlapping it and blending rapidly to create a slightly fluffy and not exactly smooth ombré where the two colors meet.

Clean the brush thoroughly again, dab dry and this time paint a horizontal line of pale blue over the gray at the very top of the piece, blending into the pale gray lower down. Try to retain three distinct layered colors and be careful not to lose the light gray in the middle. If needs be, add a touch of white back on top and then leave to dry.

Use a little semi-opaque cream color to paint in the whole of the cloud shapes and working quickly while the paint is still wet, use gold to paint in the bottom of the cloud, blending the paint together in short upward strokes to give a fluffy effect. Leave it to dry.

> **TIP:** *If the clouds dry darker than you might like, dab the top of the cloud with clean water and then blot a little of the paint away. Some of the brighter white of the paper will peek through.*

Dab a little gold with a dry brush, losing the excess paint on scratch paper so only some residual paint remains. Paint in some short curved textured strokes over the ombré on the left cloud.

Using a small round brush, use a little pale gold to paint in a setting sun.

3a

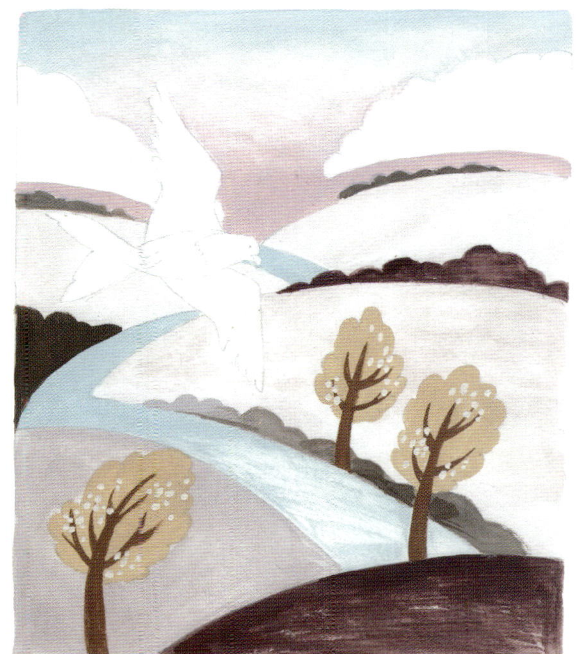

3b

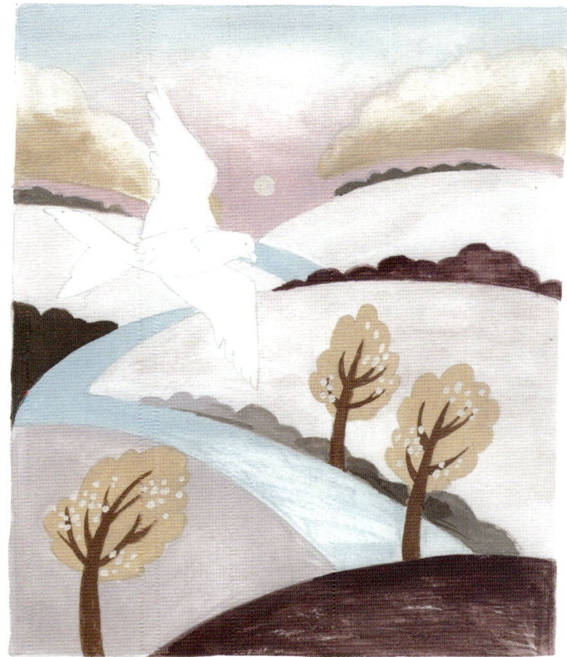

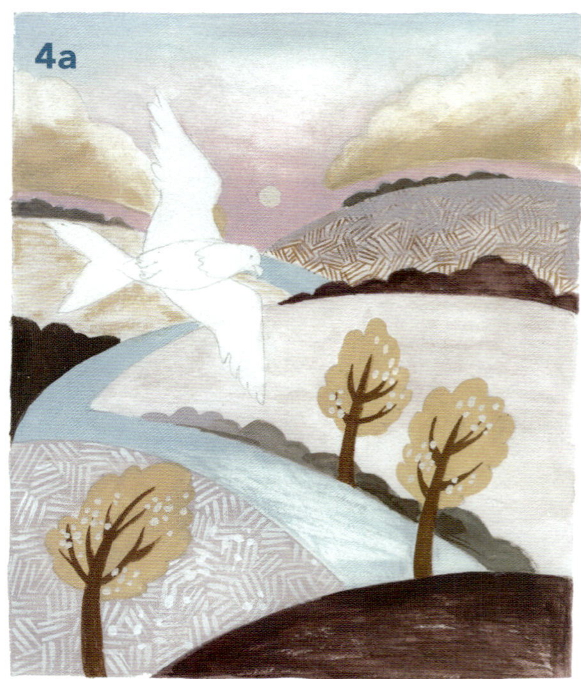

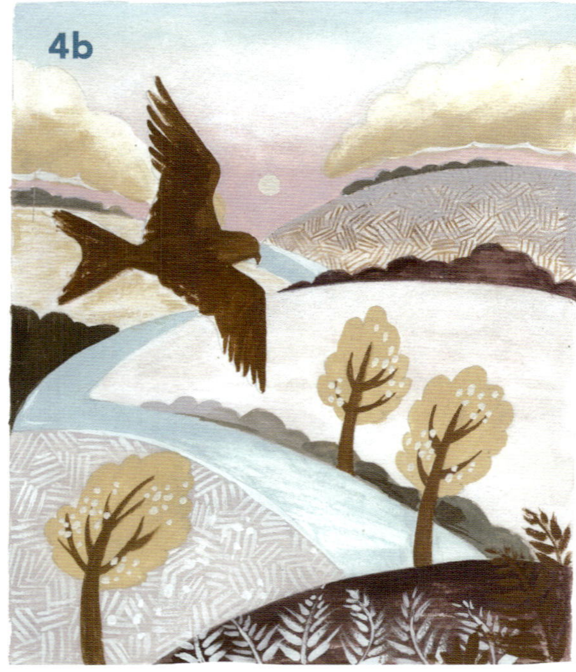

Step 4: Field Texture & Bird Silhouette

Next, we add texture to the fields that is a joyful mix of pattern and brush strokes.

Load a small round brush with fluid opaque reddish brown to create an all over pattern on the most distant field on the right. The pattern is made up of tiny hatched patches going in different directions. Start the first patch with five short parallel lines close together and repeat with another patch of lines touching the first, but this time going in a different direction. Repeat across the whole hill shape and let it dry.

Load a medium sized filbert brush with dryish medium gray and, starting on the top of the hill, cover half of the hill with loose dry textured strokes, allowing some of the pattern to peek through.

Move to hill four, the most distant field on the left. Load your brush with dry gold and then remove most of the paint, leaving a little color remaining. Use this to cover the field in loose scratchy marks so that the light gray remains visible below.

Squeeze a little pure white onto your palette and with a very clean small round brush and a dab of water, paint a slightly larger similarly hatched pattern across hill two, the nearer hill on the left. Add a few little clustered dabs to the right of the tree.

With a small round brush, use a little of the pure white to add definition and highlights. Paint small semi-opaque lines on the underside of both clouds. Using my image as reference, paint in some linear highlights on the edges of the river.

With a medium sized filbert brush, add some dry strokes to the top half of the clouds and along the top edge of the pale gray hill.

5

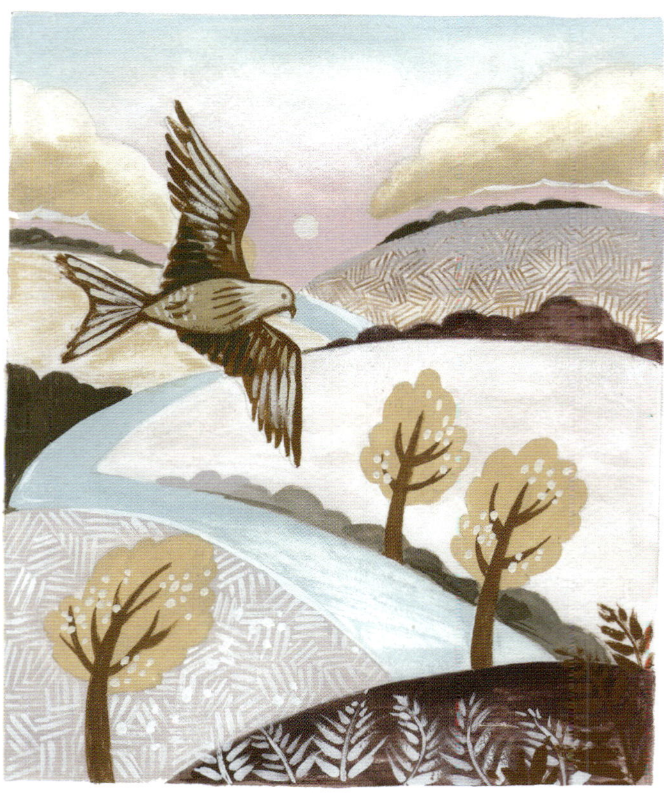

Next, we paint in a leafy pattern on hill one on top of the dark purple. Paint in about six little, evenly spaced curved stems poking up from the bottom. Start at the bottom of the stems and paint little teardrop leaves getting smaller and smaller as they reach the top of each stem.

Dip your brush in the reddish brown and paint two or three more of these stems poking in from the bottom right corner, partially covering some of the white leaves.

Lastly, we paint in our majestic red kite bird swooping over the scene. Using the reddish brown color, fill in the entire body and curved beak. When you come to the tail, start at the body and paint in joined-up individual strokes so that there is a lightly feathered effect. For the wings, I would suggest working one at a time, starting at the body, outlining the top edge first and then working down and out in separate strokes so that they look feathered. Leave to dry.

Step 5: Painting the Red Kite

Paint in the body of the kite with a little of the gold color. However, leave a very narrow edge of brown visible (especially on the beak). Leave the gold to dry. Halfway along each wing, add a few semi-opaque short strokes on top of the brown. Use a little of the dark brown to paint feathers close to the body on the trailing edge of the wings, using individual strokes and allowing the reddish brown to peep through.

Use a small amount of the cream color to fill in the head and upper chest as well as a couple of details on the lower body. Add details on the end of the wings and tail feathers. Lastly, use a small dot of the reddish brown to add some hatching strokes on the gold chest area and a little dot for the eye.

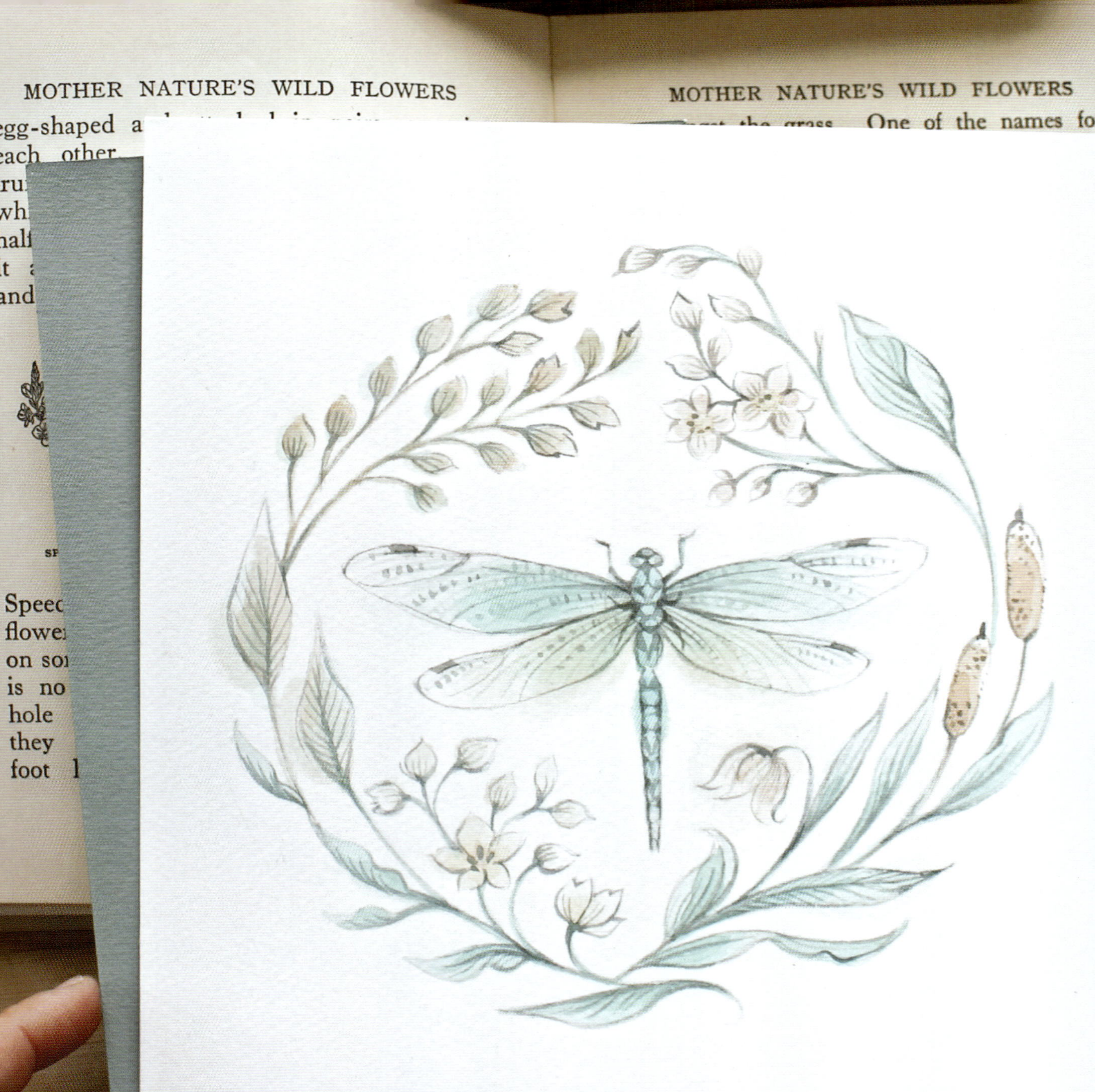
MOTHER NATURE'S WILD FLOWERS
MOTHER NATURE'S WILD FLOWERS
egg-shaped
each other
One of the names for

Reeds & Dragonfly

This project uses a light watercolor wash technique to create a delicate piece celebrating the fierce and beautiful dragonfly. I would suggest using some hot press—that is, smooth—watercolor paper to have the best chance of showing what vibrancy even the tiniest speck of gouache can achieve with water. This is a great one to practice both your paint handling and detailing with a fine brush. We will be mixing our own shade of black and using the brush to draw like a pencil to finish the piece with the tiniest detailed lines.

COLOR MIXING

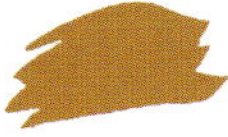

Yellow Ochre: Pure.

Pale Pink: Add a dot each of Cadmium Red and Permanent White together, mixing carefully.

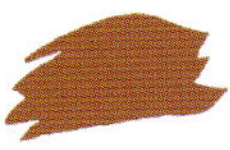

Warm Brown: Add the teeniest speck each of Burnt Umber, Cadmium Red and Permanent White together. Test on your swatch to make sure it's not too red.

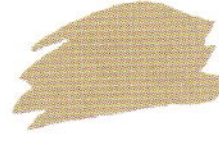

Grayish Brown: Add a speck each of Burnt Umber and Permanent White together, mixing thoroughly.

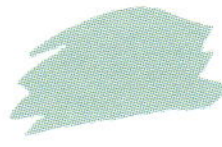

Bright Turquoise: Mix the smallest speck of Lemon Yellow with a very slightly larger speck of Phthalo Blue.

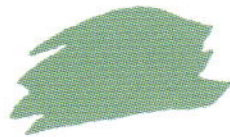

Greenish Turquoise: Add a speck of Phthalo Blue to a speck of Yellow Ochre.

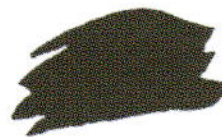

Grayish Black: Mix a speck each of Cadmium Red, Yellow Ochre, Phthalo Blue and Burnt Umber together. It should be a very dark grayish color, which you will apply watered down.

SUPPLIES

Brushes: Fine round, small round

Paint Colors: Burnt Umber, Cadmium Red, Lemon Yellow, Permanent White, Phthalo Blue, Yellow Ochre

Other Supplies: Pencil and eraser, watercolor scratch paper, gray-toned watercolor pencil

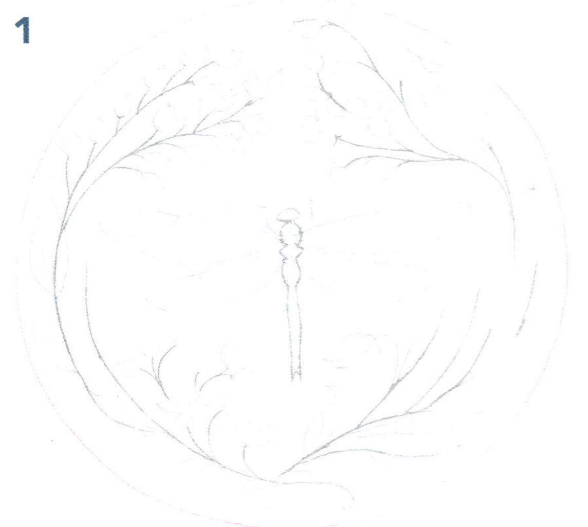

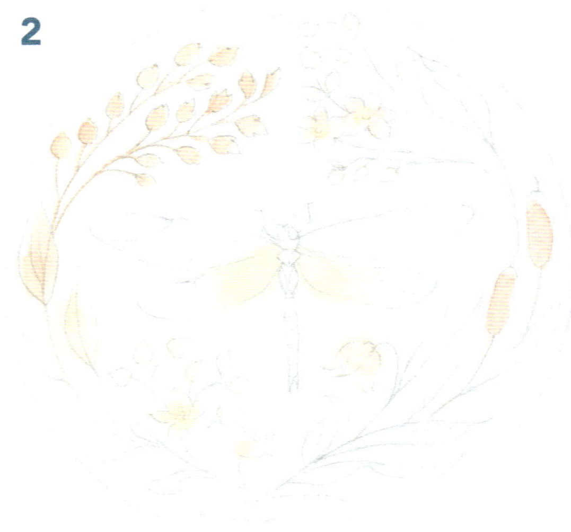

Step 1: Drawing the Design

Most of the legwork in this design is done at this early drawing stage, so really take care as you draw in your details.

Using a gray-toned watercolor pencil, draw around a pot or something else round to form a circle approximately 5 to 6 inches (13 to 15 cm) in diameter. This is the frame within which our design will sit.

Using my dragonfly shape as a reference, draw in his head and upper body, followed by the long thin abdomen. Add the outline of the four wings.

The river flowers floating around the edge of the dragonfly begin at the bottom of the circle and curve up and around to create a flowing sense of movement.

Draw the stems first, using my darker lines as a guide. Then, go on to add the leaves and flowers, from bottom to top on the right side and bottom to top on the left side.

Step 2: First Wash of Yellows & Browns

Squeeze the tiniest little amount of all these colors onto your palette: Cadmium Red, Lemon Yellow, Burnt Umber, Yellow Ochre, Phthalo Blue and Permanent White. Be sure to have a fresh pot of water handy to maintain fresh clean color. We will be dipping in and out to mix the lightest of washes.

TIP: *Less is more in this project. If a color dries to a paler shade than you are happy with you can always add another on top. It's trickier to remove light color than it is to add layers on top.*

We will begin by painting the warm Yellow Ochre and brown washes. Dip the very tip of a small round brush into Yellow Ochre and mix with several dabs of water. Test on a little swatch—it should be a bright but faint color. Paint in a circular motion on the lower wings of the dragonfly, going out below the lines.

3a

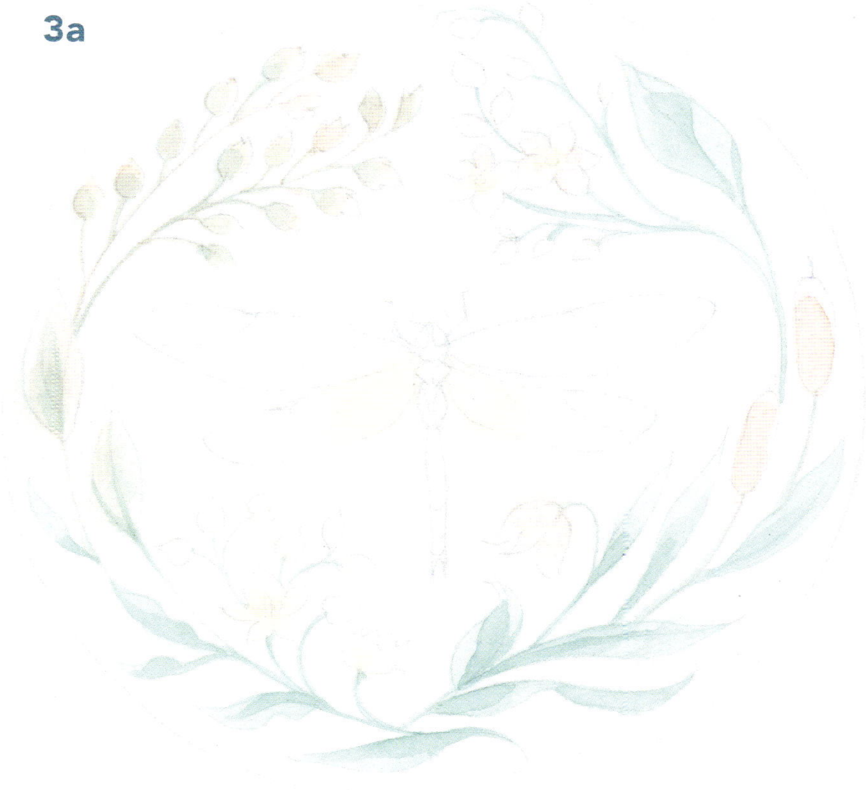

Paint in the centers and buds of the top two flowers and buds on the right-hand side, with pale pink. Paint inside the lines of the reeds on the right. Keep the color inside the lines of the reeds but allow it to go outside the lines of the droopy flowers.

With a little warm brown, add another wash over the tops of the reeds and the fine line of their stems. Add a very, very faint wash over the yellow on the wings, but keep this close to the dragonfly's body.

Carefully paint inside the lines of the detailed cluster of leaves in the top left, plus their stems, in the grayish brown. Also paint the two leaves below but allow the color to go outside the lines.

Step 3: Turquoise Wash

We will now use the bright turquoise right across the piece to give a watery feel. To create a sense of movement in the leaves, it is important to paint in the direction that they are pointing, from the base of the stem along to the tips. Start at the bottom on the right-hand side and in loose single strokes, paint in all the stems and leaves, working in a counter-clockwise direction to the top. Repeat on the other side from bottom to top. Lightly paint a layer over the leaves on the left, including the large brown ones.

3b

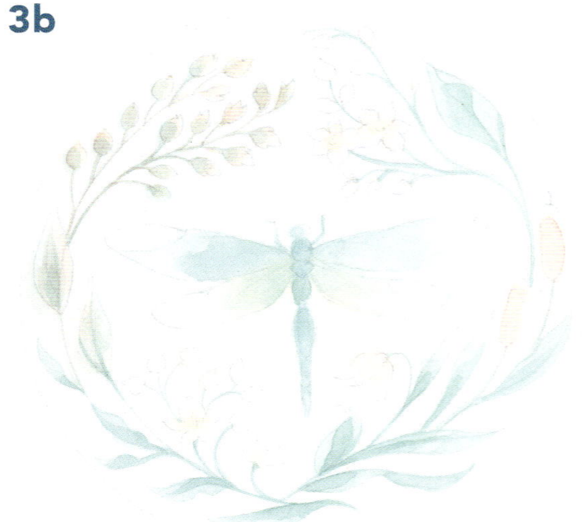

4a

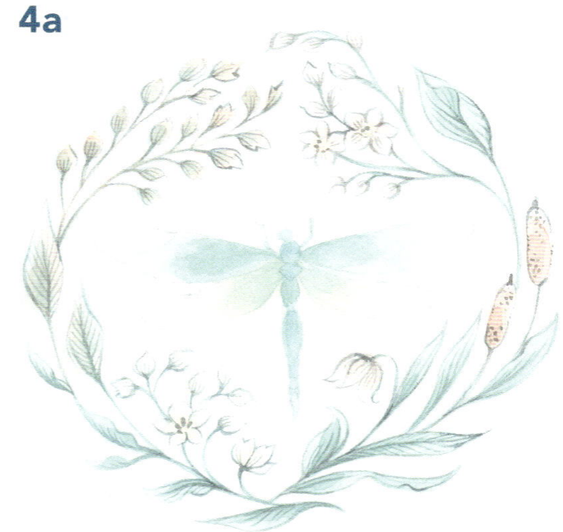

When this has dried, which shouldn't take long at all, use your greenish turquoise to add another layer to the lower leaves, not completely covering them but rather adding a loose single stroke to each.

Use a little of the bright turquoise for the body and wings of the dragonfly. Carefully fill in his body with a bright wash of color. Next, turn to the top wings, starting with slightly more color in the center and washing outward. Repeat on the lower wings and don't worry about staying inside the lines. Leave everything to dry completely.

Step 4: Fine Detailing

In the meantime, apply your grayish black color to the wings, which you will apply watered down with a fine round brush.

> **TIP:** *With darker colors, it is more difficult to remove mistakes, so go lighter rather than darker initially and add further layers if needed. Test your line on some scratch paper—having control of the consistency will give you the confidence to paint all the teeny details.*

4b

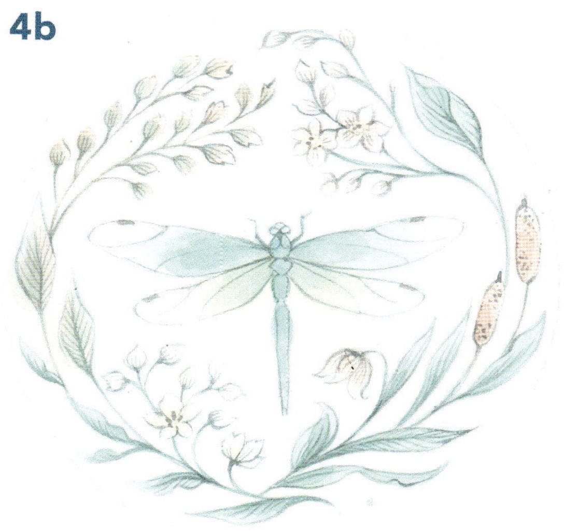

4c

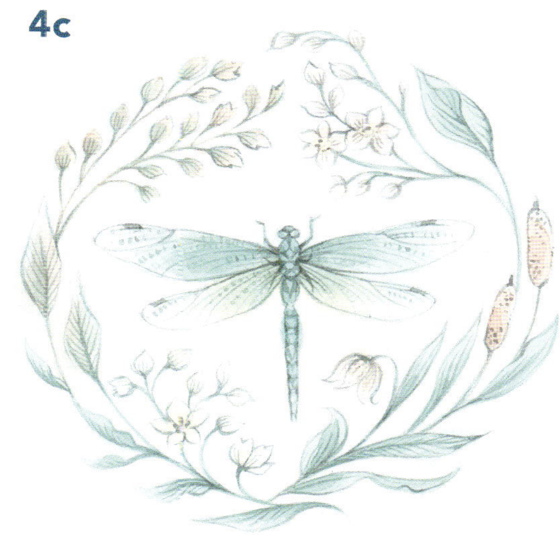

The key to retaining lightness here is to use a little of the watered-down paint while remaining controlled. Again, beginning at the bottom of the circle and working counter-clockwise, very lightly draw an outline on all the leaves and stems—you are essentially drawing with the paint. Take care to draw in the central stalk and all the little veins. When it comes to the reeds, draw in tiny little dots on both ends with the tip of your brush. When it comes to the flowers, don't forget to add a teeny, dotted circle for the center and a few little lines on the petals.

The intricate pattern on the body and wings of the dragonfly really brings it to life. Starting at the head, outline the body, adding in the six legs and the outline of the wings and main segments. Paint a slightly larger dot in the top end of each of the four wing segments.

The body pattern is a mix of tiny curves and 'v' shapes. Use my design, or a photo of a dragonfly, as a reference.

Paint the lines on each wing, keeping the lines extremely faint. These should fan out from the center in narrow, horizontal, downward-facing curves. Now using smaller strokes and a lightly delicate dabbing motion, paint little vertical dashes across some of the wings.

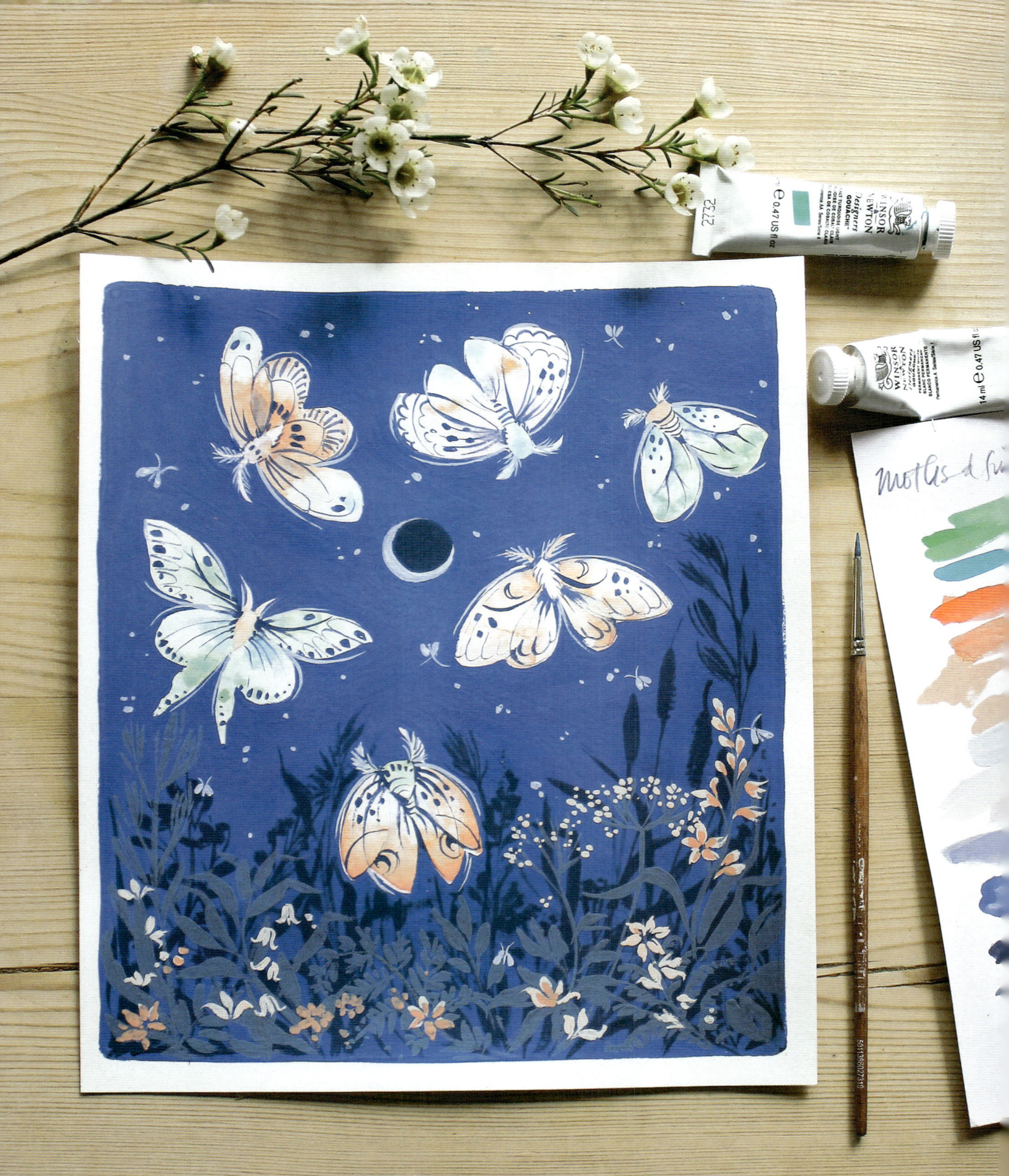
WINSOR & NEWTON
Designers
GOUACHE
2732
0.47 US fl oz

Fireflies & Moths

I believe the technical name for a group of moths is an eclipse and for fireflies it is a light posse, which just about sums up the idea for this project! We will be creating a magical and bold painting exploring the night sky—light and dark in nature. This project is a little more advanced as it pulls together several contrasting techniques—blooming, creating a dark ground and wet-on-dry and light-on-dark detailing. A challenging aspect of the project is improvising with some expressive foliage, not relying on pencil lines.

COLOR MIXING

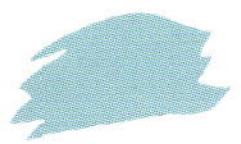

Dark Turquoise: Mix a couple of dabs of Cobalt Turquoise Light with a small dab of Ivory black.

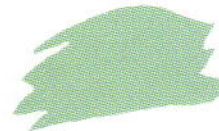

Green: Add a dab each of Cobalt Turquoise Light and Lemon Yellow to a very large dab of Permanent White.

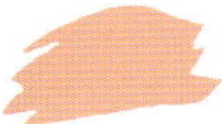

Dark Coral: Add a couple of dabs of Cadmium Red and one of Lemon Yellow to a small blob of Permanent White.

Peach: Set aside a dab of the dark coral and mix with a speck of Lemon Yellow and a couple of large dabs of Permanent White.

Light Purple: Add a couple of teeny dots of Alizarin Crimson and a teeny dot of Cobalt Turquoise Light to a large dab of Permanent White.

Dark Indigo: Add a dab each of Ultramarine and Ivory Black together to a tiny dot of Permanent White. Mix a tiny amount of this color.

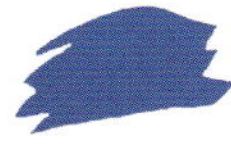

Dark Blue: Mix a very large blob of Ultramarine and two large dabs of Ivory Black together with three large dabs of Permanent White. We will need plenty of this color, probably about half a well, so that you can cover the whole background in one go.

Dark Greenish Blue: Add a dab of Lemon Yellow and a couple dabs of Permanent White to a medium-sized blob of Ultramarine.

Light Grayish Blue: Add a little a spot of the dark indigo to a dab of Permanent White.

SUPPLIES

Brushes: Fine round, small round, smallish round, medium angled

Paint Colors: Alizarin Crimson, Cadmium Red, Cobalt Turquoise Light, Ivory Black, Lemon Yellow, Permanent White, Ultramarine

Other Supplies: Ruler, eraser, tape, scratch paper

1

2

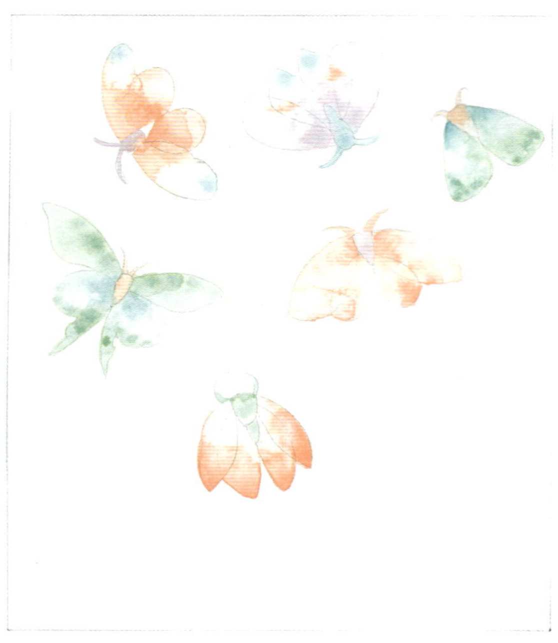

Step 1: Drawing the Scene

Begin by drawing out a rectangle with a ruler and faint graphite line, to delineate the area you will paint in.

Draw in six moths, using my design as a reference. I find it helpful to work moth by moth, thinking about varying the direction in which they are flying. For each one, draw a body in the center of the moth first. Next, draw the top wings on both sides and then the bottom wings below, ending with the little antennae.

Step 2: Blooming on the Moths' Wings

In this step, we will be using some bright, vibrant colors to paint with a blooming technique on the wings of the moths. Begin with a couple of completely fresh pots of water. Working one moth at a time and using a smallish round brush, fill in the wing shapes with pure water, excluding the body.

TIP: *If you look at the page low down and from the side, you should be able to see the water more clearly and make sure the entire shapes are covered.*

Next, using my image as a reference and working methodically, dip the very end of the brush in the teeniest bit of color—your choice of dark turquoise, green, dark coral, peach, or light purple—and then dot a speck into the area in which you would like the darkest shade. The color will bleed right off the brush and immediately begin blooming into the watered surface.

TIP: *Remember to clean the brush between each color application or you will end up with a grayish mess!*

Try to spread a little of the color across the wings with a clean dryish brush—it should move loosely. When finished, look at the piece as a whole and add any dabs of color for balance. When nearly dry, so it doesn't bleed, use a very watered-down dab of contrasting color to paint in the bodies and antennae with a light wash. Leave it to dry thoroughly.

3

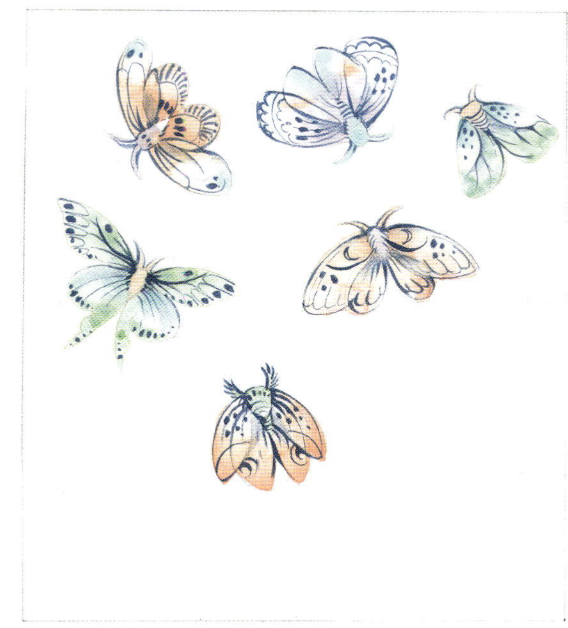

Step 3: Moth Details

The next step is to add a dark indigo pattern across the wings of the moths. Using a fine round brush, outline the moths one by one. Here you have the license to use whatever patterns you like, or use mine as a guide. I had an online picture library of moth illustrations on a screen as a reference while I worked. Try to vary each one with a range of little dots and curved lines.

When dry, water down a tiny amount of dark indigo with some water and add a smidge of a shadow on the underside of the top wing so that it appears on the lower wing.

4

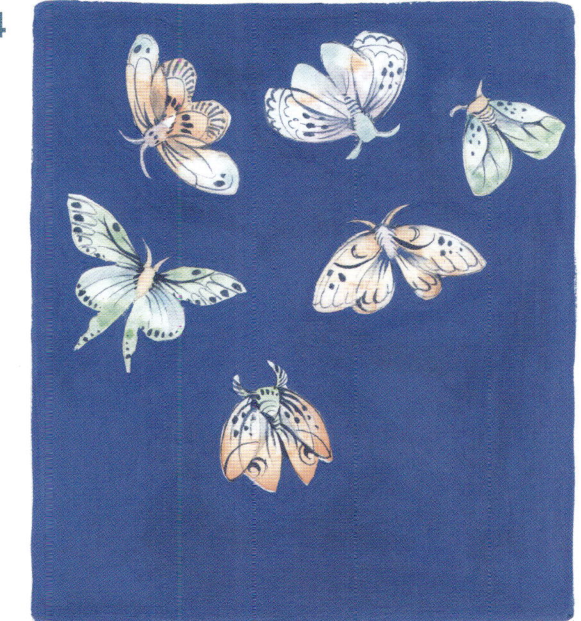

Step 4: Dark Blue Background

Next, we will be adding the rich dark blue to the whole background using a medium angled brush. We will need plenty of this color, probably about half a well, so that you can cover the whole background in one go! The consistency should be completely opaque but fluid, so be sure to test it on some scratch paper and allow it to dry before cracking on with the real painting. Load your brush and carefully paint in the rectangle with lightly rounded corners.

Paint around the moths and antennae, working left to right —or vice versa if you're a lefty—so that you don't smudge the moths. Leave to dry completely and you should have a lovely even matte coverage.

5

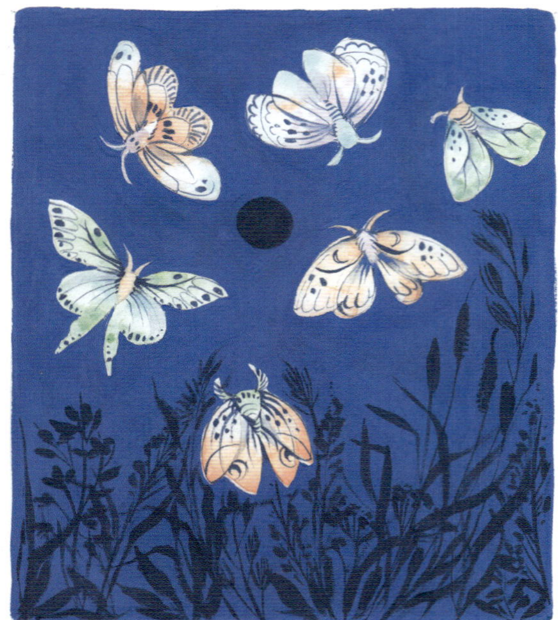

6

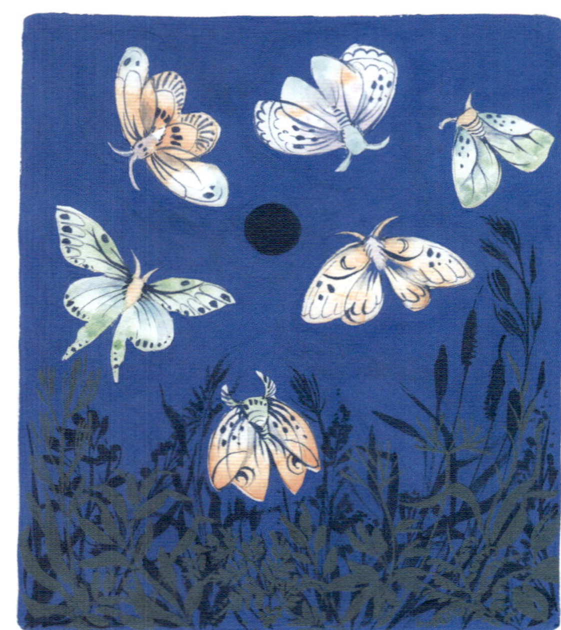

Step 5: Dark Silhouettes

Next, use the dark indigo to paint in silhouettes of riverside foliage and rushes. Load a smallish round brush with plenty of the color. Then, using my picture as a reference and starting from the bottom of the design, paint in some upward curving strokes for stems. Then add some little leafy and rounded details, varying the height and shapes and not worrying at all about neatness. Go up the page as far as the middle two moths and be sure to paint carefully around the lowest one. Leaving gaps here and there will add texture, movement and expression to the piece.

In the very center of the painting, between the middle two moths, paint a circle about three quarters of an inch in diameter. Tape all the paper edges to a table, which will help the page to remain flat and leave your piece to dry completely.

Step 6: Green Foliage

You can peel the tape off before starting on the next layer. Here, we will be using the dark greenish blue color and the same small round brush, to paint in some expressive reeds and riverside rushes on top of the indigo shadows. This time, paint in some shorter stems for the riverside foliage and some ferns and flowers in the foreground.

Try to create plants and stems of a variety of different heights so that in the final step, we can add light-colored flower heads. Work right down to the bottom of the page but let both the blue of the sky and the dark indigo shadow of the reeds show through.

Step 7: Moon & Night Sky

7

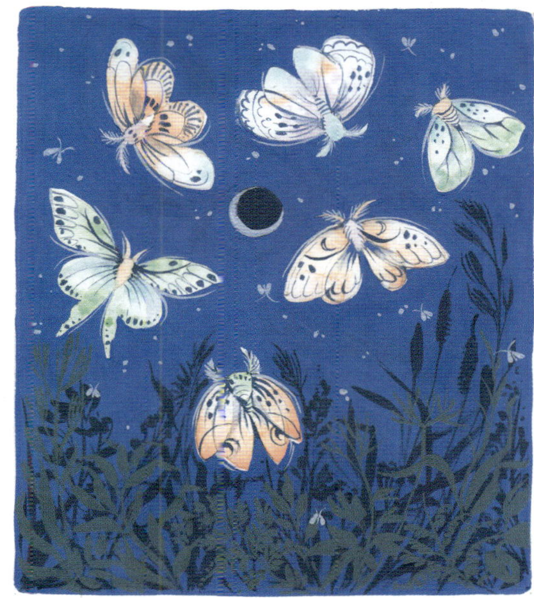

In this step, we will add in the details of the night sky. Use the light grayish blue to paint a thin slither of a crescent moon onto the central dark circle.

Above the line of the dark indigo shadows and with a fine round brush, dab in little clusters of circular dots to suggest fireflies in the night sky. Paint a handful of tiny fireflies so you can see their little wings and antennae.

Here I also use this color to add a little linear linework outlining the edges of the moths, tying them to their background and adding movement. Start where the top of each wing joins the body and draw a single thin, rounded stroke, flicking out slightly above the white of the wing. Repeat on both wings and the bottom of a couple of the moths. Also add a little painted feathered detail to the antennae.

Step 8: Light Foreground Flowers

8

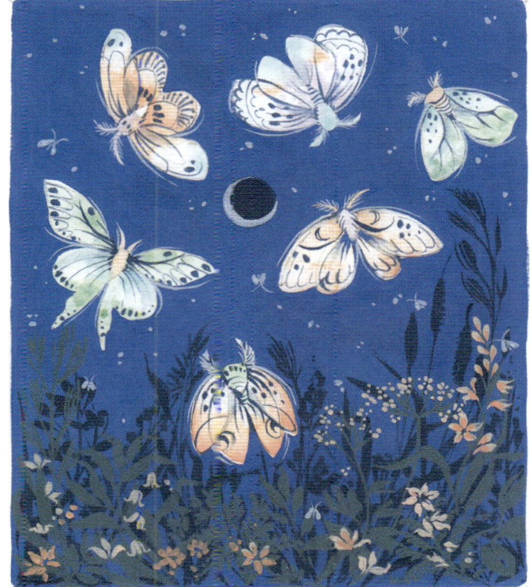

In this very last stage, we will add some light-colored riverside flowers over the shadows and leaves using some of the light and dark coral shades we mixed for the moths.

> **TIP:** *As your water and pots will probably be a bit murky at this stage, I would suggest giving them a wash and using fresh water to keep the color clean. Reactivate the paint with some clean water and brushes if need be.*

Using a small round brush, add little dotty details to suggest tiny flowers on the rounded stems. Also improvise some larger expressive flower shapes here and there, first in the peach and then the dark coral color.

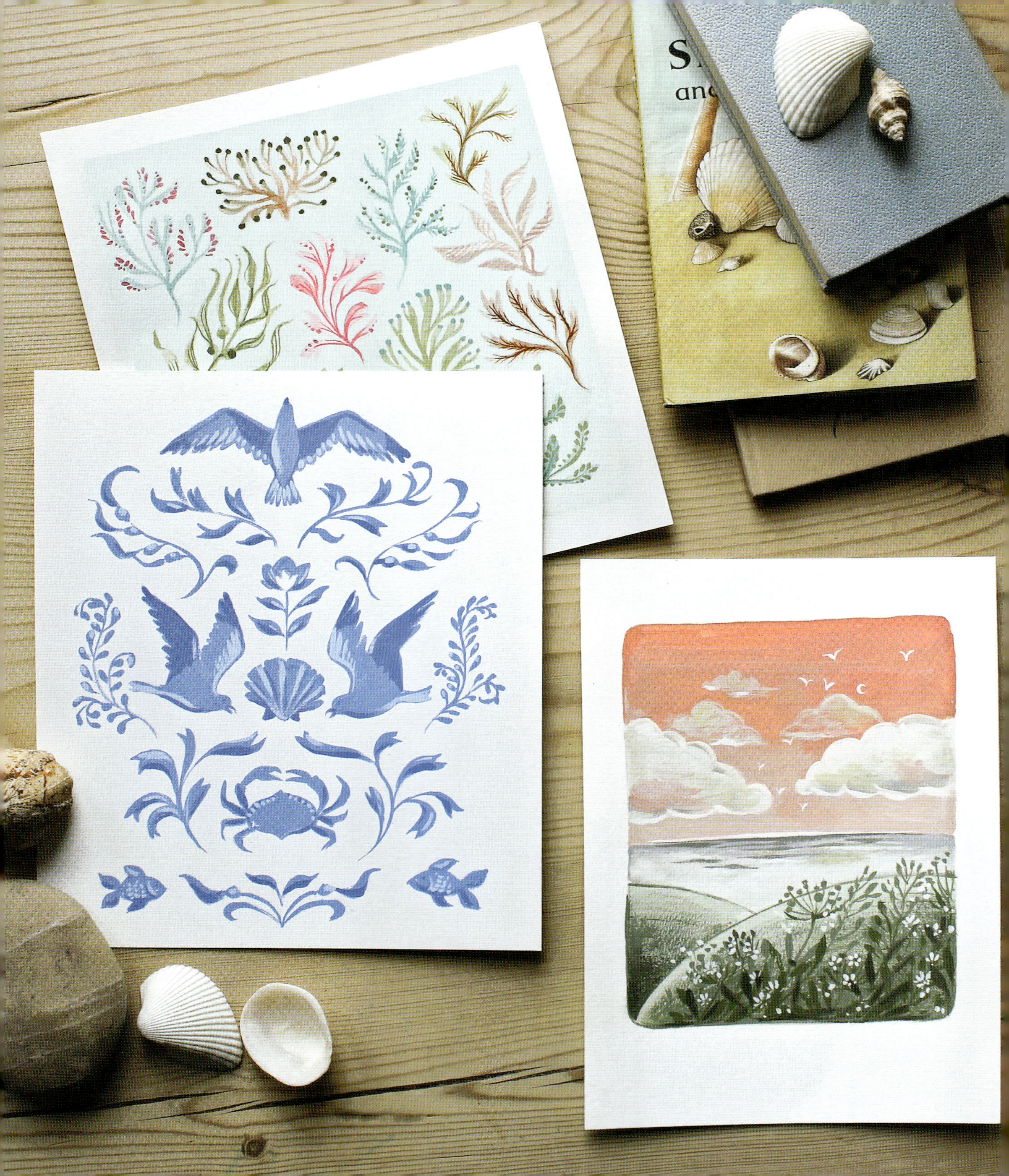

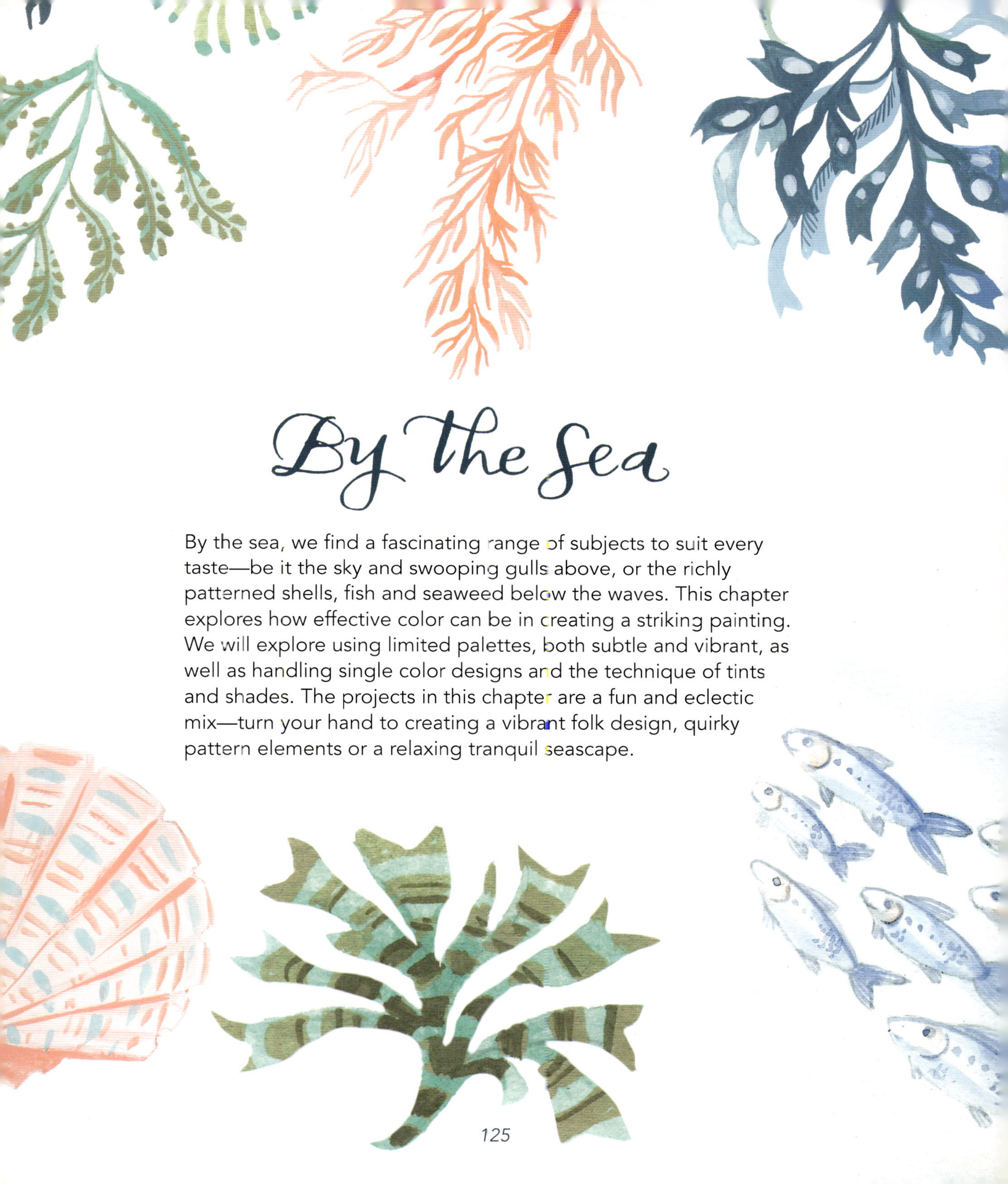

By the Sea

By the sea, we find a fascinating range of subjects to suit every taste—be it the sky and swooping gulls above, or the richly patterned shells, fish and seaweed below the waves. This chapter explores how effective color can be in creating a striking painting. We will explore using limited palettes, both subtle and vibrant, as well as handling single color designs and the technique of tints and shades. The projects in this chapter are a fun and eclectic mix—turn your hand to creating a vibrant folk design, quirky pattern elements or a relaxing tranquil seascape.

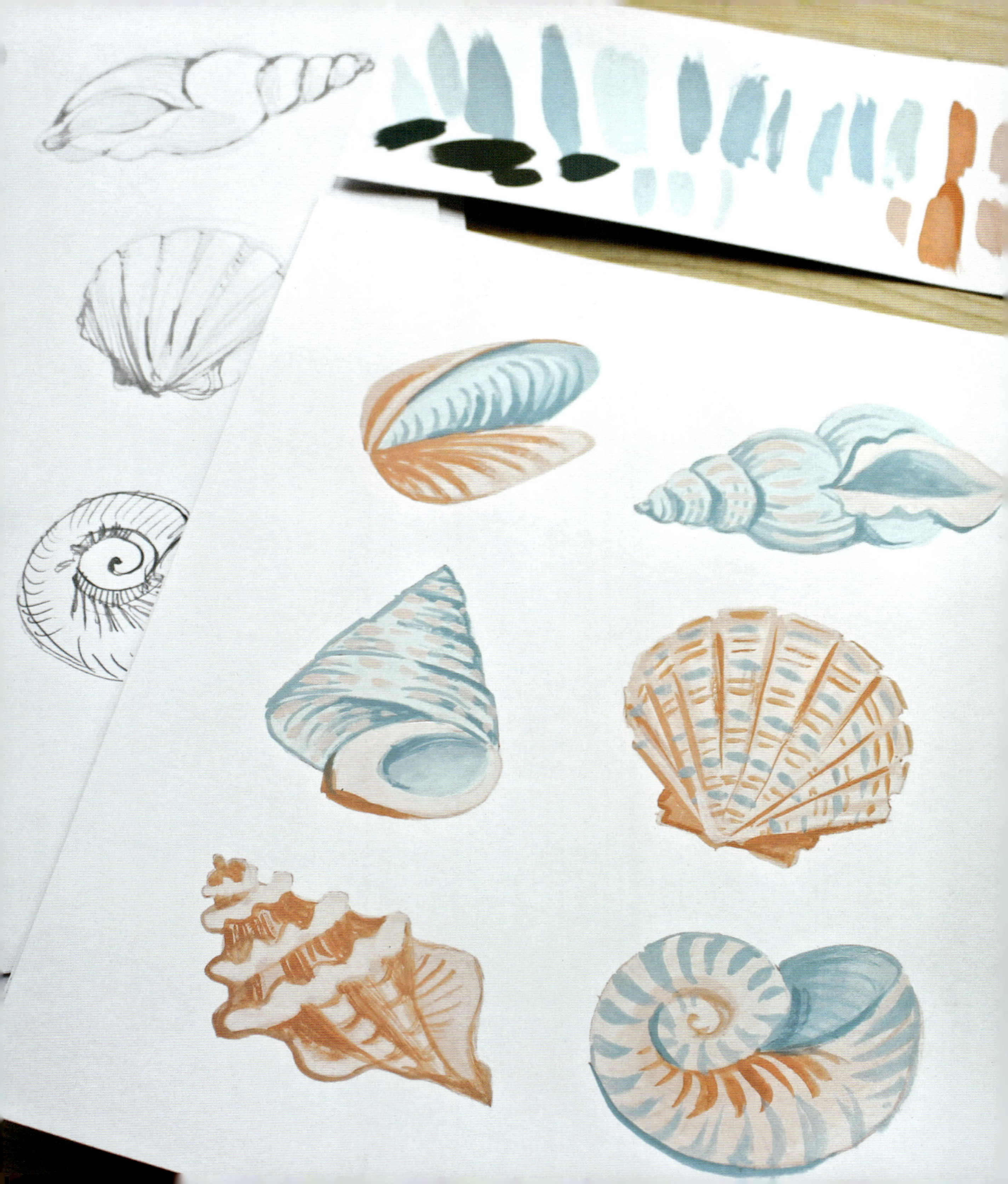

Layered Shells

This little warm-up project uses harmonious tints and shades of two of my favorite colors—coral pink and duck-egg blue—which together give a retro vibe to the design. The aim here is to experiment using a limited palette to cleverly create shadows and highlights, giving the shells a sense of fullness and three-dimensionality. It is a delight to capture in some limited way these beautiful natural patterns. This project allows us to be incredibly imaginative with a variety of strokes.

COLOR MIXING

Medium Blue: Add two dabs of Phthalo Blue and a dot of Yellow Ochre to a dab of Permanent White. Make plenty of this color as it will be used to make the tint and shade of blue. Check the color on a swatch of paper and tweak as necessary.

Light Blue: Set aside two dabs of the mixed medium blue and mix with a dab of Permanent White to create a paler tint.

Medium Pink: Add a dab of Cadmium Red and a small dab of Yellow Ochre to a blob of Permanent White. As with the blue, make plenty of this as it will be used to make the other colors.

Light Pink: Add a couple of dabs of the mixed medium pink to two large dabs of Permanent White, mixing thoroughly.

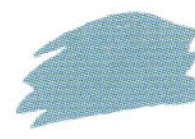

Dark Blue: Take two dabs of the mixed blue again, but this time add a dab of Phthalo Blue, a dot of Yellow Ochre and a speck of Ivory Black to create a darker shade.

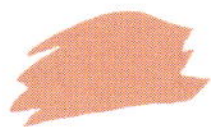

Dark Pink: Add a couple of dabs of the mixed medium pink shade to two dabs each of Cadmium Red and Yellow Ochre and then add a very small touch of Ivory Black.

SUPPLIES

Brushes: Small flat, fine round, small round

Paint Colors: Cadmium Red, Ivory Black, Permanent White, Phthalo Blue, Yellow Ochre

Other Supplies: Light brown watercolor pencil and eraser, scratch paper

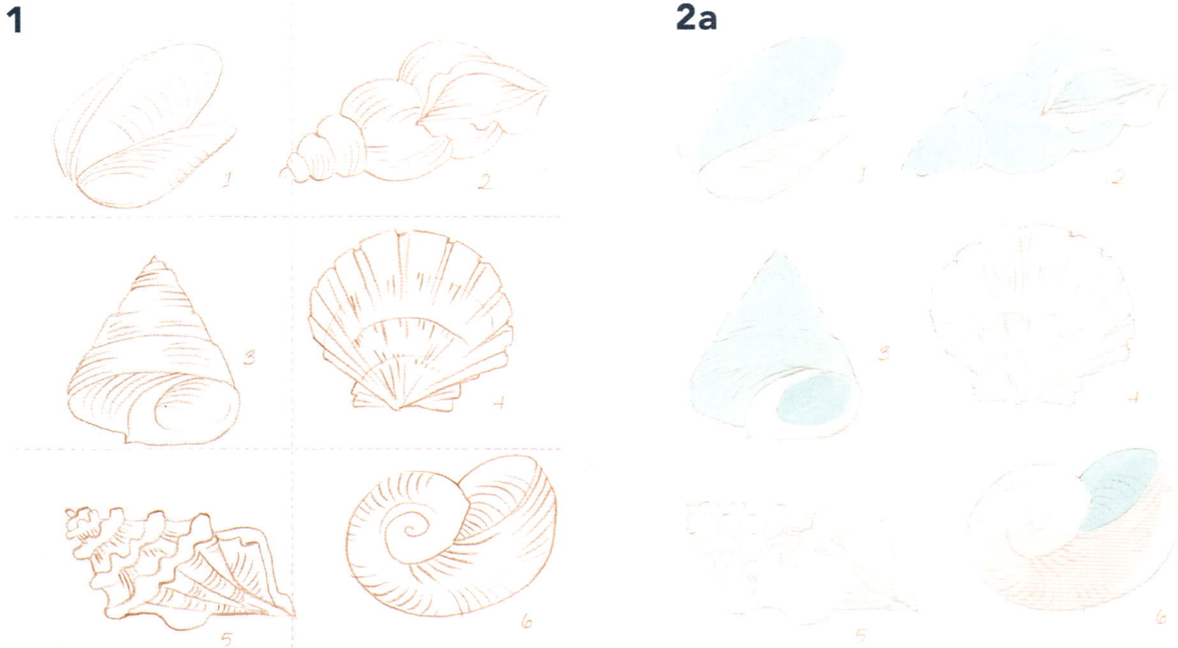

Step 1: Draw the Shells

It may help to plan your design with a faint grid, using my drawing as a reference to place your six different shells on the page. Draw the outline of the shells lightly first with a light brown watercolor pencil. Draw in as many details as you can, as these will be useful when painting in the fine details later. I have numbered them for ease of reference.

Step 2: Shading the Shells

Add a touch of water to the mixed colors and, using my guide, paint a semi-transparent pale-colored layer across all of the shells, some parts pink, some blue. Test both colors on a swatch first and note that the pencil lines should still be visible through the paint so that it will be easy to add linework later on.

> **TIP:** *If the blue and pink mix, or if your water becomes dirty, then the color can become muddy and grayish. To avoid this, I would suggest having two water pots, one for cleaning blue and the other for cleaning pink.*

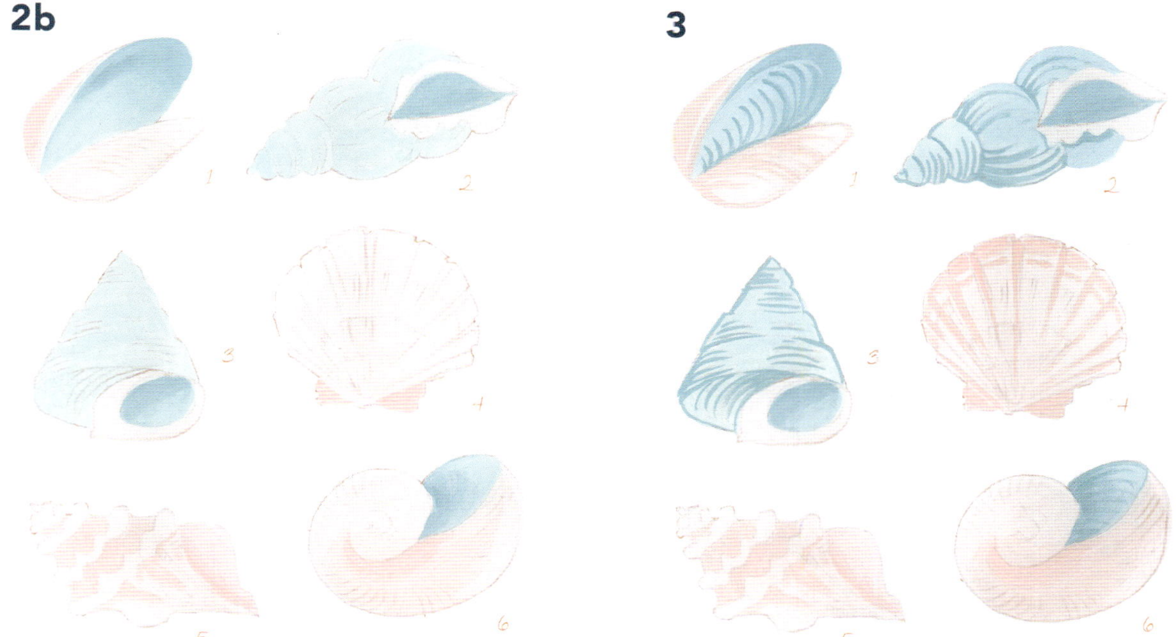

Now we will add some graduated shading to the inside of the shells, creating a sense of their volume. Start with the mussel shell—shell number 1—and use some of the medium blue color to paint the top half of the blue inner shell. While this paint is still wet, work up from the other end with the light blue tint and with light strokes, blend where they meet to create a smooth ombré.

Fill the opening of the second shell completely with medium blue and then repeat the ombré technique from the mussel on the opening of the third conical shell. With a clean brush, create a little shadow with medium pink on the top of the mussel shell, the bottom of the fourth scallop shell and add shading on the fifth shell, the spiky spiral conch shell. After cleaning your brush, paint in an ombré medium blue shadow in the opening of the sixth shell, the nautilus. Add a little shading on the nautilus shell by blending medium and light pink.

Step 3: Light Linework

In the next step, we will be using a smaller round brush and painting lines to further suggest the volume of the shells through confident dryish strokes. Using my design as a reference and the medium blue, work shell by shell to paint little line details curving around the shells' contours on the first, second, third and sixth shells.

Use the medium pink to paint a line on the edge of the top of the mussel shell and curve some lines on the bottom half. Move onto the scallop shell and add lines fanning out to suggest shadow where the grooves would be, then some thick lines running round the curve of the top of the shell.

4

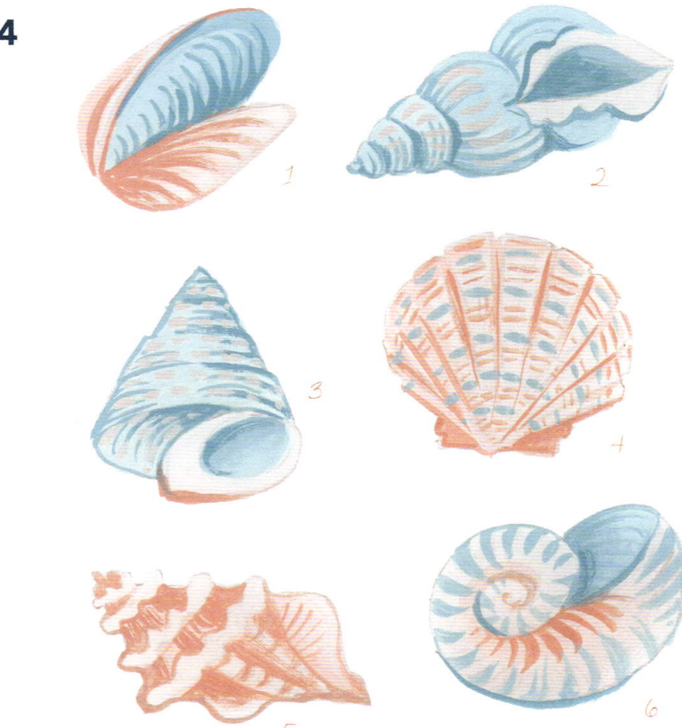

Step 4: Final Line Details

The last step of this project is adding the final fun detailed pattern to the shells, while also spreading both the colors more evenly across the design to give it balance. You can either follow my suggestions or if you prefer, add whatever patterns take your fancy!

As we start adding some darker colors, notice how this begins to draw the whole design together. Working methodically across the image, add some slightly drier dark blue curved lines, following the contours of the first, second, third and sixth shells. Test on a swatch to make sure you can see the drier strokes.

With the same technique, add dark pink across the design, to every shell except for the second shell. Pay special attention to the conch, which is a little trickier than the others.

Use the medium pink to add lots of little dashes across the whole surface of the outside of the third conical shell.

On the scallop shell, use dark pink to paint short narrow strokes forming a dashed semi-circular pattern, finishing with the similar medium blue lines.

Use your medium blue to add the striking tiger-like pattern on the nautilus shell, taking care to curve the strokes around to suggest volume. Finish with a few dark pink lines on the inside curve.

TAKING THE PROJECT FURTHER:

Try applying this technique to different shaped shells or changing the color combination. Using a dark ground will really make a light palette pop!

Folk Seagulls

This project uses a light tint and dark shade of one single color to create a striking folk-art design. It draws together a range of motifs that we might associate with the seaside into a little narrative scene that would translate wonderfully into a pattern. It's quite a straightforward piece and can be completed in four simple steps. We will use an opaque bold Ultramarine for the artwork itself, but you can use any color you like, or even try white or another light shade on a colored ground.

COLOR MIXING

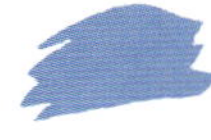

Medium Blue: Add equal amounts each of Ultramarine and Permanent White to a dot of Burnt Sienna and mix thoroughly. Mix half a well of paint to complete the first layer all in one go.

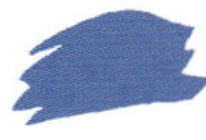

Dark Blue: Add three large dabs of Permanent White to a small blob of Ultramarine and a small dab of Burnt Sienna. When you test a swatch, it will look quite similar to the medium blue, but will dry a little darker.

Pale Blue: Mix two large dabs of Permanent White with a small dab of the mixed dark blue.

SUPPLIES

Brushes: Small round

Paint Colors: Burnt Sienna, Permanent White, Ultramarine

Other Supplies: Ruler, pencil and eraser, scratch paper

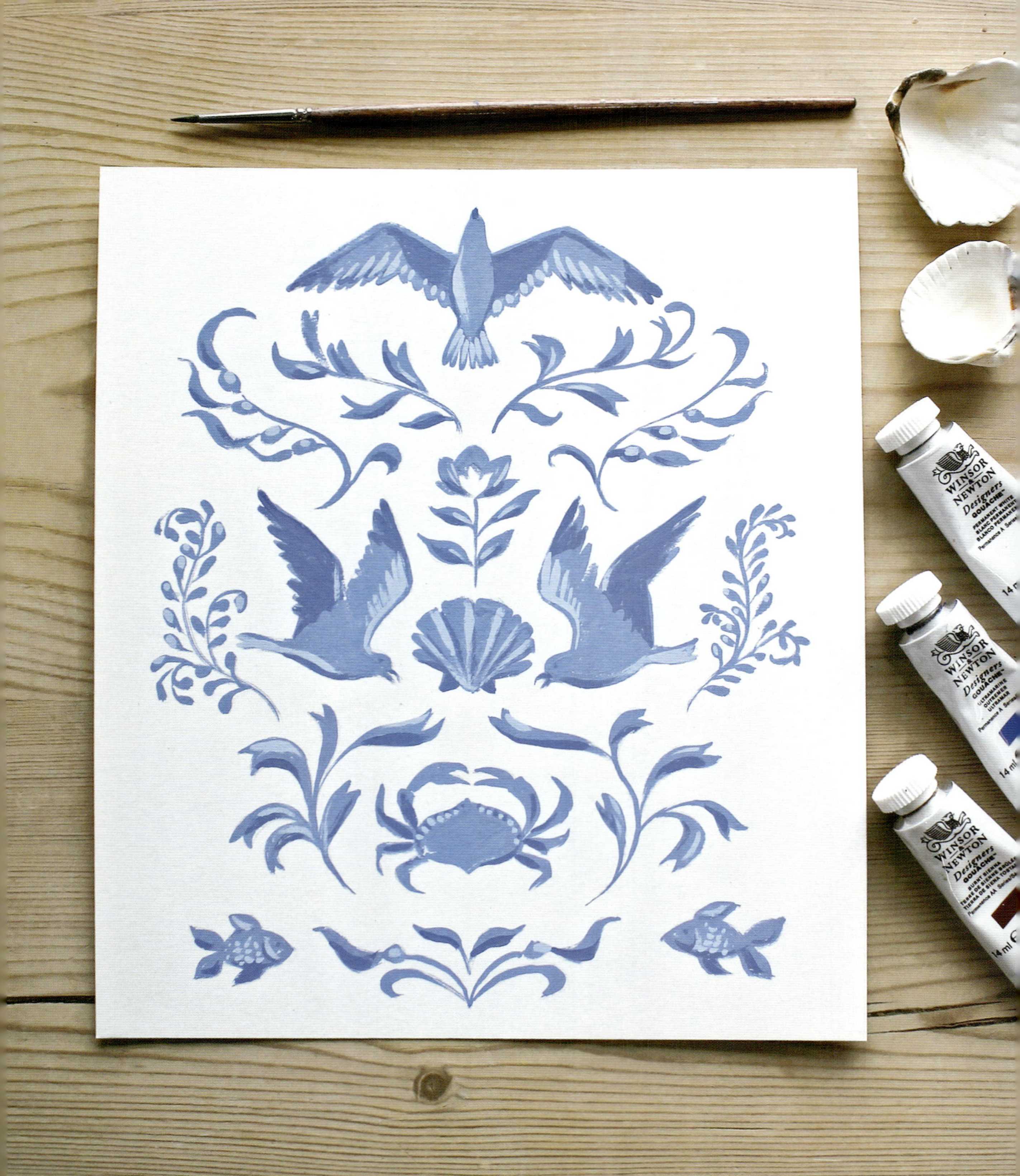
WINSOR & NEWTON
Designers
GOUACHE
WINSOR & NEWTON
Designers
GOUACHE
14 ml
WINSOR & NEWTON
Designers
GOUACHE
14 ml

Step 1: Drawing Out the Symmetrical Pattern

The drawing for this design is rather tricky, so I recommend using a graphite pencil for ease of erasing mistakes. The central elements are the two swooping seagulls and the rest of the design flows from these. I suggest using the gulls as the basis for your own design and then tweaking the other elements or types of seaweed as you please.

The drawing and planning for this piece are key to creating a successful design. Using my image as a reference, draw out a simple light grid. At the very least, use your ruler to draw very light graphite pencil lines that divide the paper into quarters.

Starting right in the center of the page, draw in the shell with the top meeting the center line. At the same height as the bottom of the shell, use my darker guideline to draw in the underside of the gull and then fill in the rest of the body and wings. Working down the middle vertical line, draw in the crab and then the seaweed below. Move up to draw in the straight flower stem above the shell and then the top gull with outstretched wings.

The design is symmetrical and I would suggest drawing each element on both sides as you go. All the other motifs fan out from the central line of elements, curving to frame them. Fill in the gaps with little fish, shells or curved fronds of seaweed. Take care to use a light touch with your pencil lines throughout.

Step 2: Main Blue Layer

We will use our medium blue to complete the first layer all in one go. The consistency should be opaque but fluid, so add a touch of water when loading your brush. Test your mixed color on scratch paper and let it dry so you can check that you are completely happy with it before you begin painting.

1

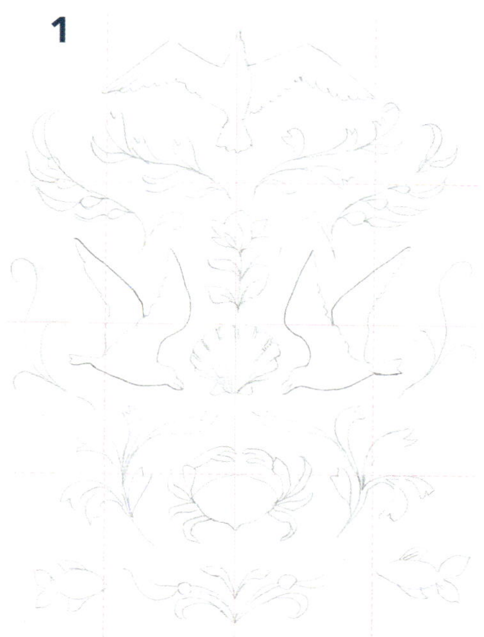

2

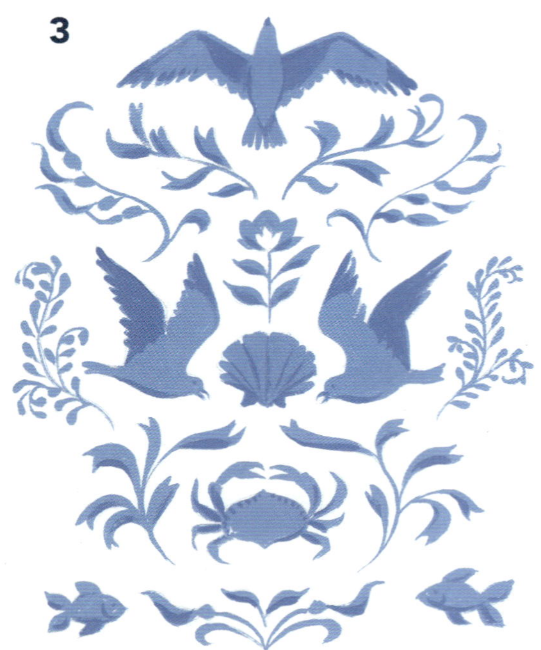

Use your small round brush for the whole design, utilizing the brush tip for fine details. Adding more pressure to the brush creates a wider stroke that you can use to fill in the larger areas such as the gull wings and crab's body. Start with the top gull and work downward methodically. To avoid smudging the paint and to make it comfortable to hold the brush through all the fine details, I like to rotate the paper as I work—sometimes even painting upside down!

The effect we are trying to create is a silhouette, but by using loose strokes and leaving any textures visible. I would suggest outlining elements first before filling them in. Use a light touch when painting over the seaweed stems so that they are fine and delicate.

Step 3: Darker Shade

Next, we add details in a little dark blue shade. Work methodically down the design as before, but this time add details rather than fill in whole shapes. Add a little shadow on the underside of the top gull's wings, then on the underside of the seaweed tendrils. Paint in the shadow and details on the two swooping gulls' wings, shell ridges and the underside of seaweed, crab legs and body and fish bodies.

Step 4: Lighter Tint

We finish the design by adding a few teeny details in the pale blue color. Working downward once again, paint little feathered details on the top gull's wings, tail and a stroke on the body. Add a few little dots here and there on the seaweed.

Moving down, add little details on the seagull wings and stripes creating shell ridges. Finally, add dots to the edges of the crab shells and the body of the fish for scales.

Seaweed Pattern

Seaweed is a fun and useful little motif to practice painting and there is a lovely range of patterns you can make with different shapes and varieties. This is a great project if you are feeling a bit stuck and need loosening up. The technique we will be using here is staining, which is essentially mimicking watercolor to create a light, soft, washy ground. We will also practice a range of strokes and patterns on each frond, tying the design together with a relatively limited palette.

COLOR MIXING

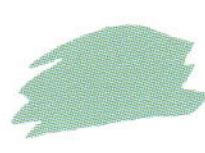

Aqua: Mix four dabs each of Cobalt Turquoise Light and Permanent White together, then add a couple dabs of Burnt Umber and a dab of Yellow Ochre.

Warm Sand: Add a dab each of Burnt Umber and Yellow Ochre to a small blob of Permanent White.

Medium Bright Pink: Add a couple of dabs each of Opera Pink and Permanent White together with a small dab of Burnt Umber.

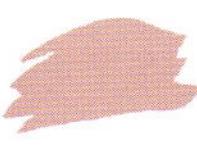

Mauve Pink: Add a couple of dabs each of Opera Pink and Permanent White together with a small dab each of Burnt Umber, Yellow Ochre and Cobalt Turquoise Light.

Olive: Add a dab each of Yellow Ochre and Cobalt Turquoise Light together with two dabs of Permanent White.

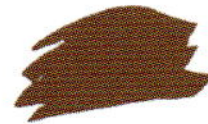

Dark Brown: Add a dab each of Permanent White and Opera Pink to a little blob of Burnt Umber.

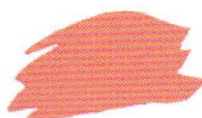

Dark Pink: Add a small dab each of Opera Pink and Burnt Umber to a dot of Permanent White.

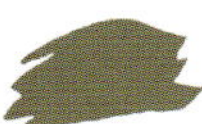

Dark Olive: Mix a dab each of the mixed olive green, Cobalt Turquoise Light and Burnt Umber.

SUPPLIES

Brushes: Fine round, small round (or small spot if you have one), large filbert

Paint Colors: Burnt Umber, Cobalt Turquoise Light, Opera Pink, Permanent White, Yellow Ochre

Other Supplies: Masking tape, ruler, pencil and eraser, scratch paper

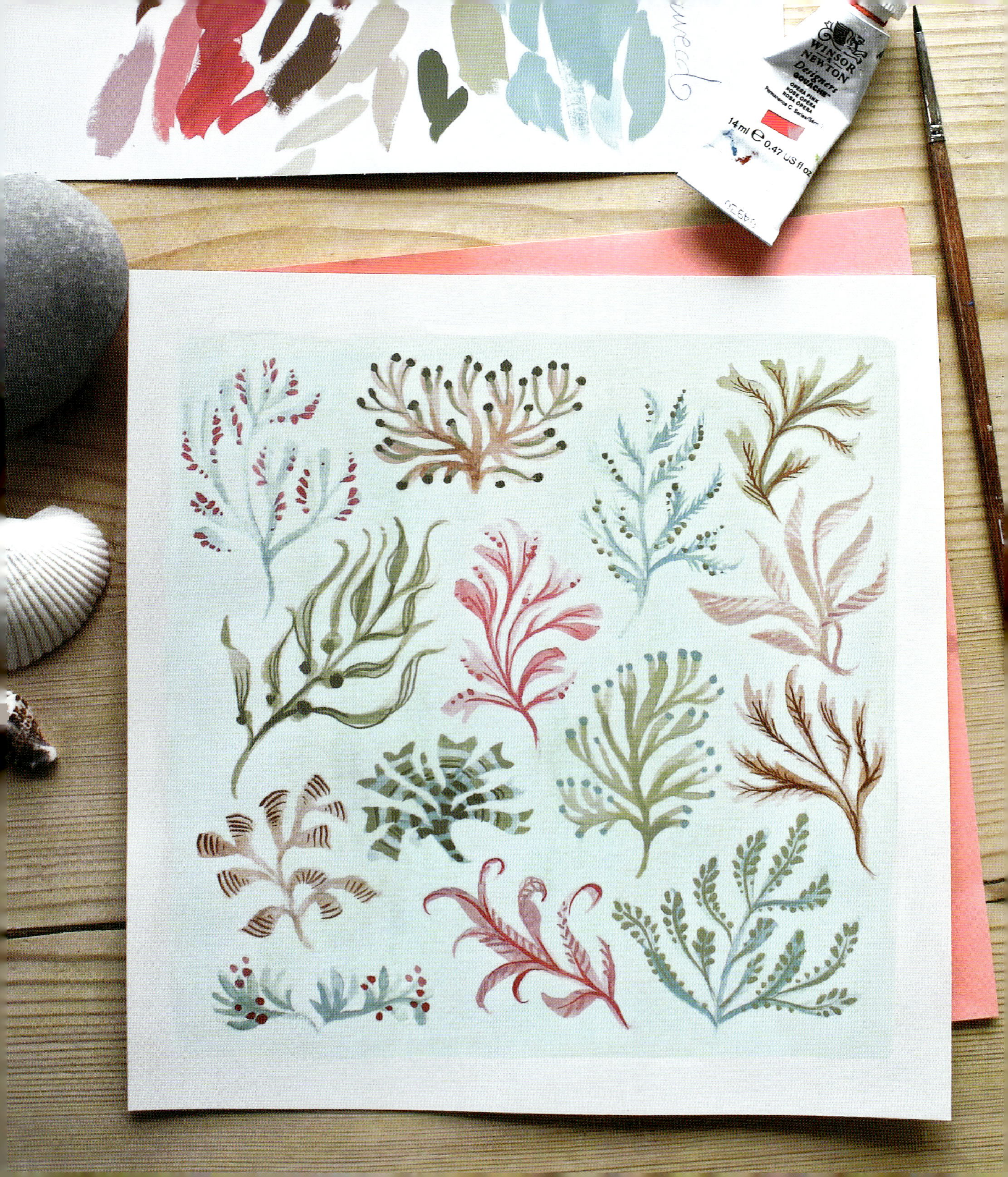

WINSOR
NEWTON
Designers
GOUACHE
14 ml ℮ 0.47 US fl oz

1

2

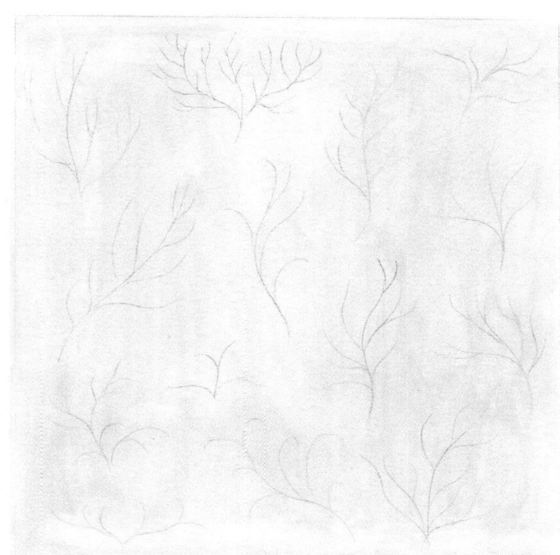

Step 1: Drawing the Seaweed Lines

If you look at an online picture library, you will come across literally hundreds of different varieties of seaweed and ways of painting them. With this in mind, feel free to use my examples as the basis of your sketches, or to make up your own!

First, choose the size of your pattern elements and either cut the paper to a suitable size or draw in a rectangle to fill. Using a graphite pencil, draw in a range of lines branching upward and curving out to the left and right—these will be your seaweed shapes. Don't worry about adding any further detail at this stage, as we will do this all freehand. Leave a little space between each, but also try to fill gaps with tendrils of varying lengths.

Step 2: Background Stain

As the piece is quite watery, I would recommend taping your paper to some spare board or your desk for this stage so that the paper doesn't warp and go wrinkly. Leave it taped like this until it has dried completely. We will use aqua to stain the washy ground as you might in a watercolor painting. Using a large filbert brush, pop a dab of the color in a clean well with plenty of water—be sure to test a swatch and leave it to dry before starting on the real piece. The color should be lovely and light.

Paint in the ground with wide washy strokes, not worrying too much about even coverage but aiming instead for a very pale transparent color. When it comes to the edges of the piece, apply a little more water to the brush and blend lightly into the white paper. Leave it to dry completely.

3a

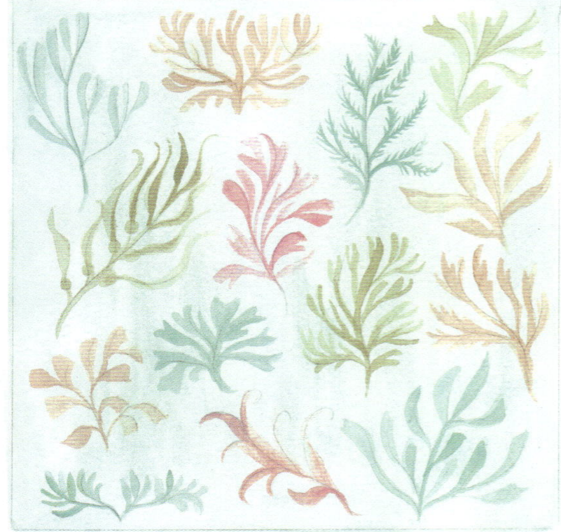

3b

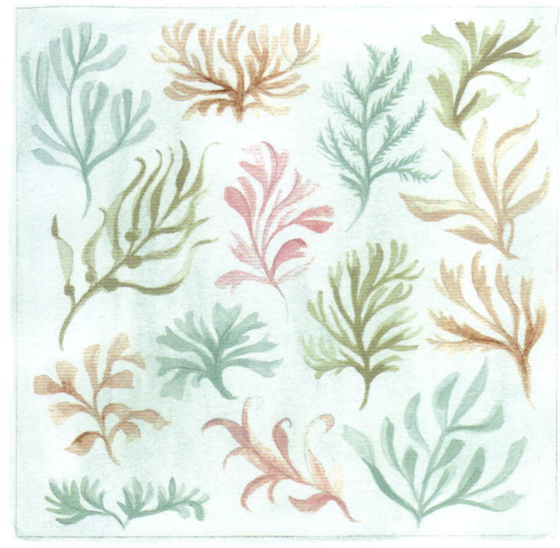

Step 3: Painting the Seaweed

When applying paint across the design, it is important to try to balance similar amounts of each color. This first step is a watery wash, so all the colors will be painted in with a fine round brush and a dab of the color mixed with a little water so that the paint is semi-transparent without being too watery.

Both greens will look quite similar, as will the pinks, so only use the lighter tint of each in this step. I would suggest working color by color, working by eye, adding the colors where you feel they sit happily.

Choosing your first color, in my case aqua, paint a narrow line over the drawn stipe—their stems—and then thicken slightly to form thick blades, which look like swirly twirly fronds. Add plenty of little extra blades, as you might on the branches of a tree. Space the following colors as evenly as you can—warm sand, medium bright pink, mauve pink, olive and dark brown. Work color by color and wash your brushes thoroughly between each so they do not become muddy.

We will be trying to make each of the shapes unique and beautiful, so the more carefully you paint them, the more complex and stunning the final design will look. Think about varying the thickness of the blades and adding a few bulbous floats—the little round bubbly bits—here and there.

Add a second semi-transparent layer on top of the first for each piece of seaweed, using exactly the same color to add depth and three-dimensionality. Paint from the base of the stipe on about half of the shapes, blending from dark to light—that is, applying less paint the further you go from the base—out into the blades.

Across some of the thicker fronds, do the opposite. Add color from the edges into the center, which will give the feeling of movement, as if each one is twisting in the water. Leave it to dry completely.

Step 4: Painting the Patterned Details

The last step is the most fun! Here, we add details to all the seaweed and can enjoy our palette. Use a spot brush if you have one, as we will be painting in lots of little dots and dashes. It's a good idea to have as much control as possible when creating this opaque bright layer.

In all honesty, there is no particular logic to the way in which the color details have been applied. I would suggest adding the colors one by one, so first I have added the dark pink, then the medium bright pink, the mauve pink and finally the dark brown. Carefully spread them evenly across the design and try to make each seaweed unique. In some of the wider fronds, you will be ab e to add two colors in both line and dotted details. Others will look effective with a single contrasting bright color at the tips. Try varying the size of dots to suggest movement.

Next, I have added the olive, dark olive and aqua. Be sure to erase all the pencil lines when the paint is completely dry.

TIP: *Some of the detail you paint may get lost in the staining, especially with the lighter colors. In this case, simply apply a second coat so that they are complete.y opaque.*

TAKING THE PROJECT FURTHER:

These are quite loose and watery little seaweed designs, but they would also be wonderfully effective painted with a more opaque technique. Try painting three small clumps of seaweed floating upward from a central point. Use leftover paint from the palette that you have already mixed, but use far less water and make sure that when applied, each seaweed is a flat color. Leave layers to dry before going on to the next and finish by adding little fine-lined opaque patterns on top.

4a

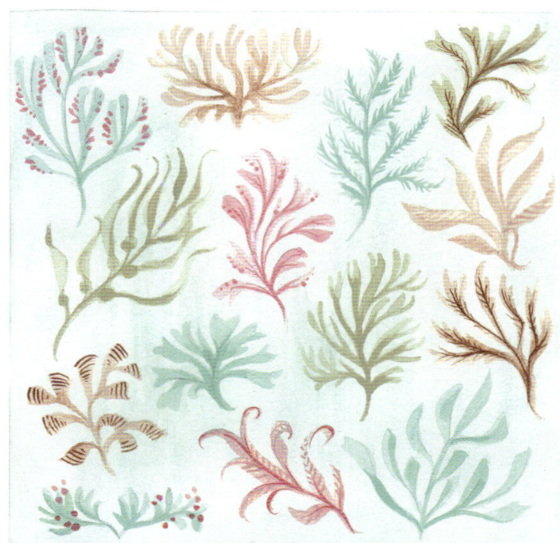

4b

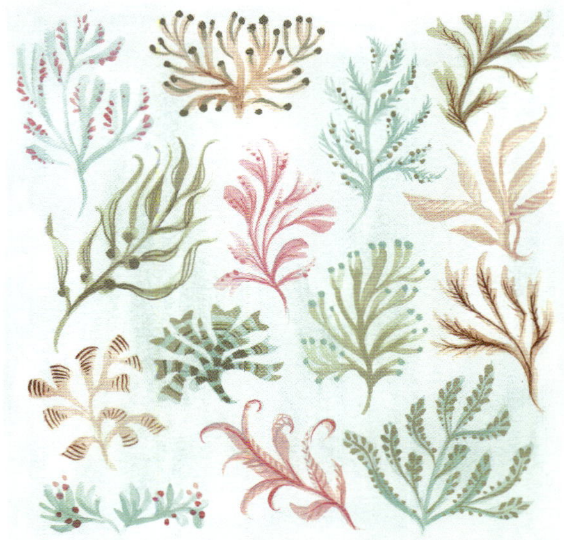

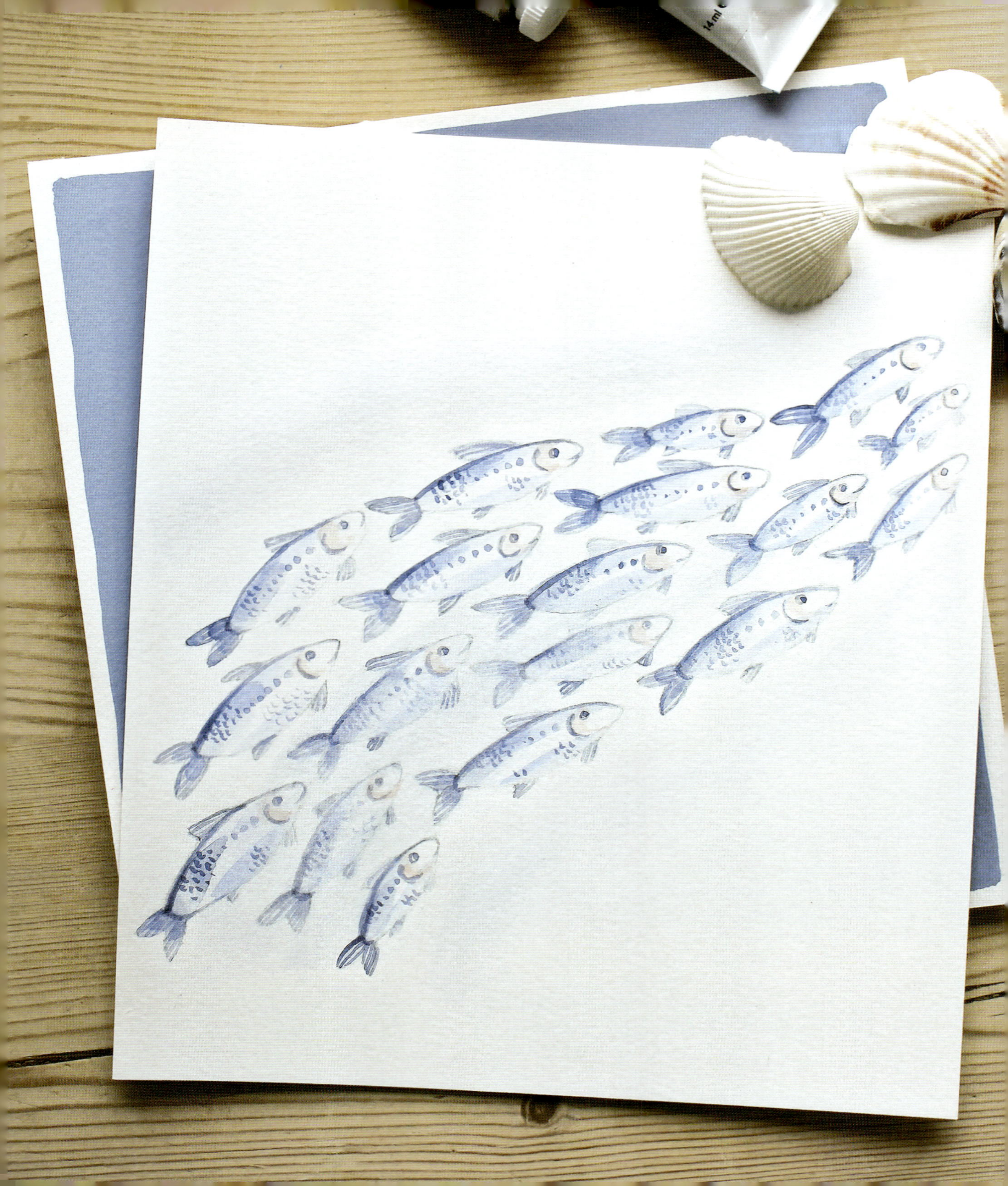

Shoal of Sardines

This project uses a range of light wet-on-wet techniques, building up color as you might with watercolor painting, which means that we won't be using white. Although the finished painting may look complex, you are essentially repeating each little step eighteen times so it is quite a speedy, loose one to complete, as well as the repetition being very relaxing! This project primarily uses two colors: Ultramarine and black, with the addition of the tiniest pop of orange mixed straight from the tube. The key is careful layering.

COLOR MIXING

Pure Ultramarine: A nice little blob and that's all.

Grayish Blue: Mix two tiny spots of Ivory Black and four spots of Ultramarine.

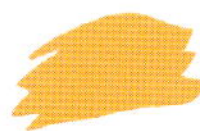

Orange: Take a tiny speck of Cadmium Red and a small dot of Cadmium Yellow straight out of the tube and mix in carefully. It should have a nice reddish tone.

Dark Ultramarine: Mix a little Ultramarine with a speck of Ivory Black.

SUPPLIES

Brushes: Very fine round, small flat, large angled

Paint Colors: Cadmium Red, Cadmium Yellow, Ivory Black, Ultramarine

Other Supplies: Masking tape, ruler, graphite pencil and eraser, grayish-colored watercolor pencil, scratch paper

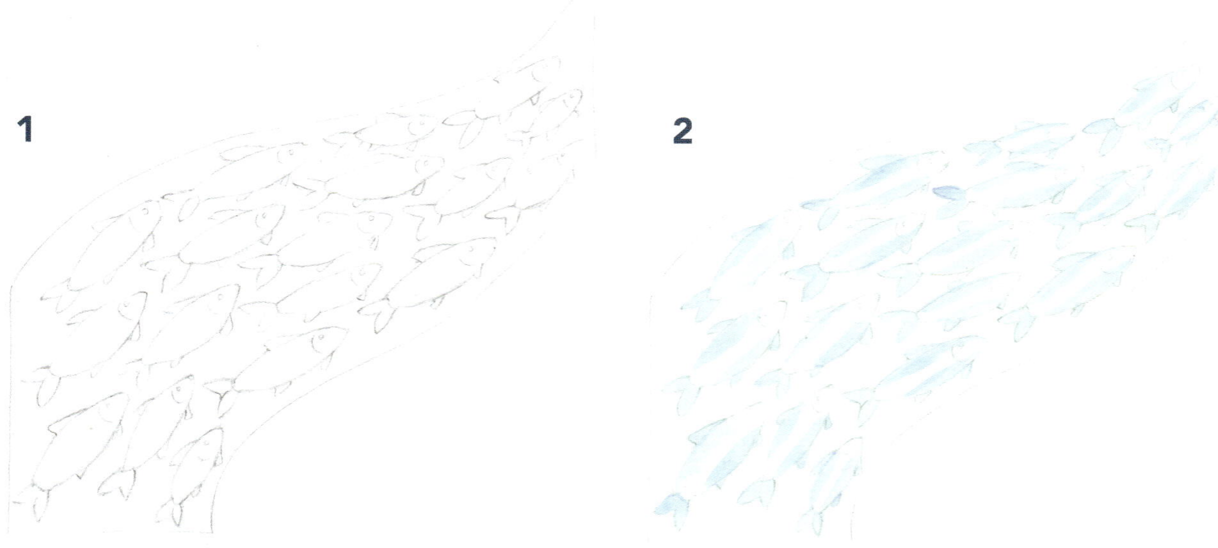

Step 1: Drawing the Shoal

Using a light graphite pencil, draw your first curved line from the top right corner, swooping back and down to a point about halfway up the left side of the page. Leaving a gap that widens slightly like a funnel, draw in the second curved line, also from left to right, ending up a third of the way across the bottom of the page.

With a grayish watercolor pencil, start drawing in the fish, again working right to left. Be sure to make their bellies slightly more curved than their backs. We are trying to fit them in as closely and as evenly as we can so we will draw the basic shape—just bodies and tails—of them all first, then add the fins for them all before detailing all the faces together at the end.

Start at the front of the shoal with a small fish midway between the two lines and the two adjacent ones set back slightly on each side and then work backward using my design for reference.

Step 2: Light Shading

The next step is adding light shading on the back and belly of the sardines with pure watered-down Ultramarine with a small flat brush. Put a dot of paint in a well with plenty of water. Load your brush so that when you test a swatch you can create a controlled, bright but transparent stroke of color. Paint two parallel strokes on the body of each fish, following the curves of their backs and bellies. Next, paint in the fins and tails of all the fish.

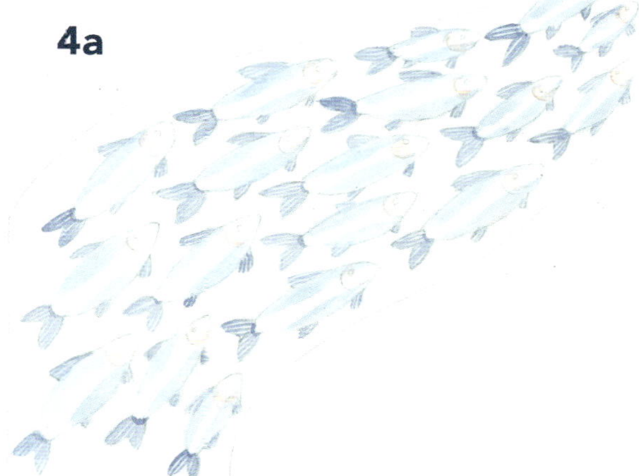

Step 3: Fine Line Details on Fins & Tails

Swap to a very fine round brush so that you have plenty of control for the fine details. As you go along, test lines on your scratch paper, making sure that the color is semi-transparent and not watery.

We will be painting tiny lines across all of the tails in grayish blue, trying to get in as many you can, as well as a little curved 'c' where the tail meets the body. You will only be able to get in three or four tiny lines on the fins fanning out from the body of the fish. Notice how some will be slightly darker or lighter than others depending on when you dip into the palette for more paint—this is fine.

Step 4: Pops of Orange & More Intense Color

> **TIP:** *As we are mixing with plenty of water, have a little kitchen towel handy to dab any rogue blots, very dark lines or blobs of color.*

Next, we will add some more intense color including our tiny little pop of orange. I would suggest using a separate, clean pot of water to avoid an unintentional gray mess. With a small flat brush, paint a little orange 'c' shape just in front of the line of the face fin.

4b

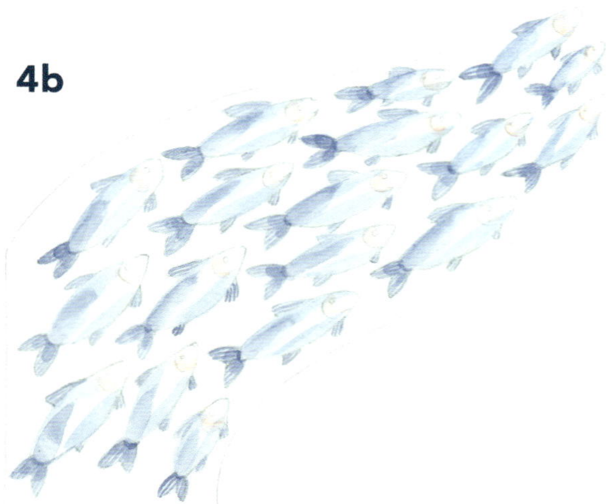

5

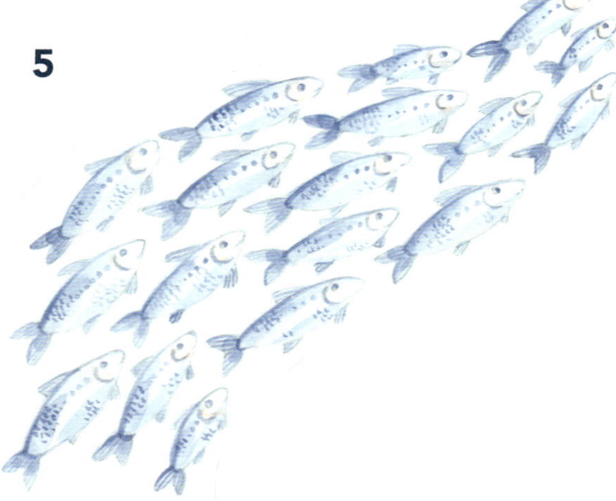

The next step will be to add a little more vivid dark Ultramarine on the body of the fish using a single stroke. Paint your stroke from the left where the tail meets the body, forward and up over the back. Add two little rounded strokes on the part of the tail closest to the body.

Step 5: Bright Linework & Details

This step ties together the whole shoal with some stronger colored linework and little details on the face and scales.

Using your very fine round brush, use a touch of the semi-transparent grayish blue and with a single stroke, paint one outline from the tail right over the top of the fish and curving round the nose to create a little mouth on each sardine.

Paint in all the little 'c's for the gills. Add a circle for the eyes with a dot in the circle to the right of center. Add a series of little dots from the face gill back to the middle of the bodies.

Lastly, add the scales, which are created by painting minuscule, curved 'c' shapes, in two or three patches over the body of the fish.

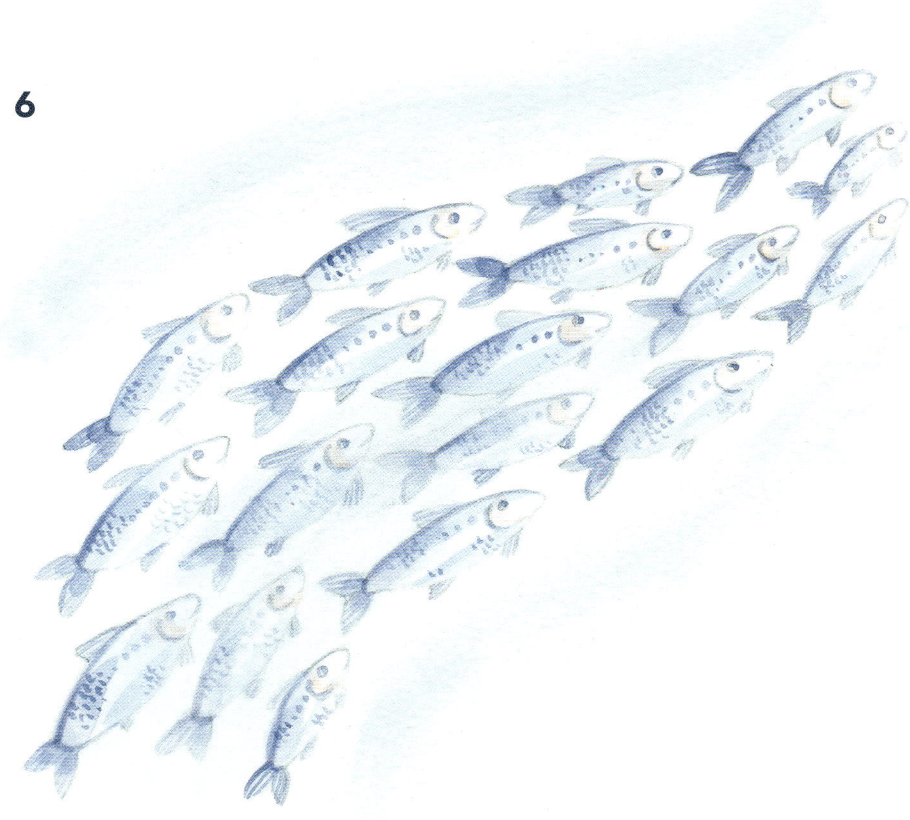

Step 6: Washy Water Strokes

The very last step is a loose wash with a large flat brush to emphasize the water the shoal is in. I would suggest taping all four edges of the paper to your desk or a bit of board for this step so that it doesn't warp with the watery wash.

Use a touch of the dark Ultramarine and a large angled brush and, working right to left, paint a single curved flat line above the shoal to suggest the flowing water, lightly blending outward into the white paper. Repeat below the bottom of the shoal. If you are feeling brave, add a wide curved stroke up through the middle of the shoal!

Leave it to dry completely and then erase all visible lines.

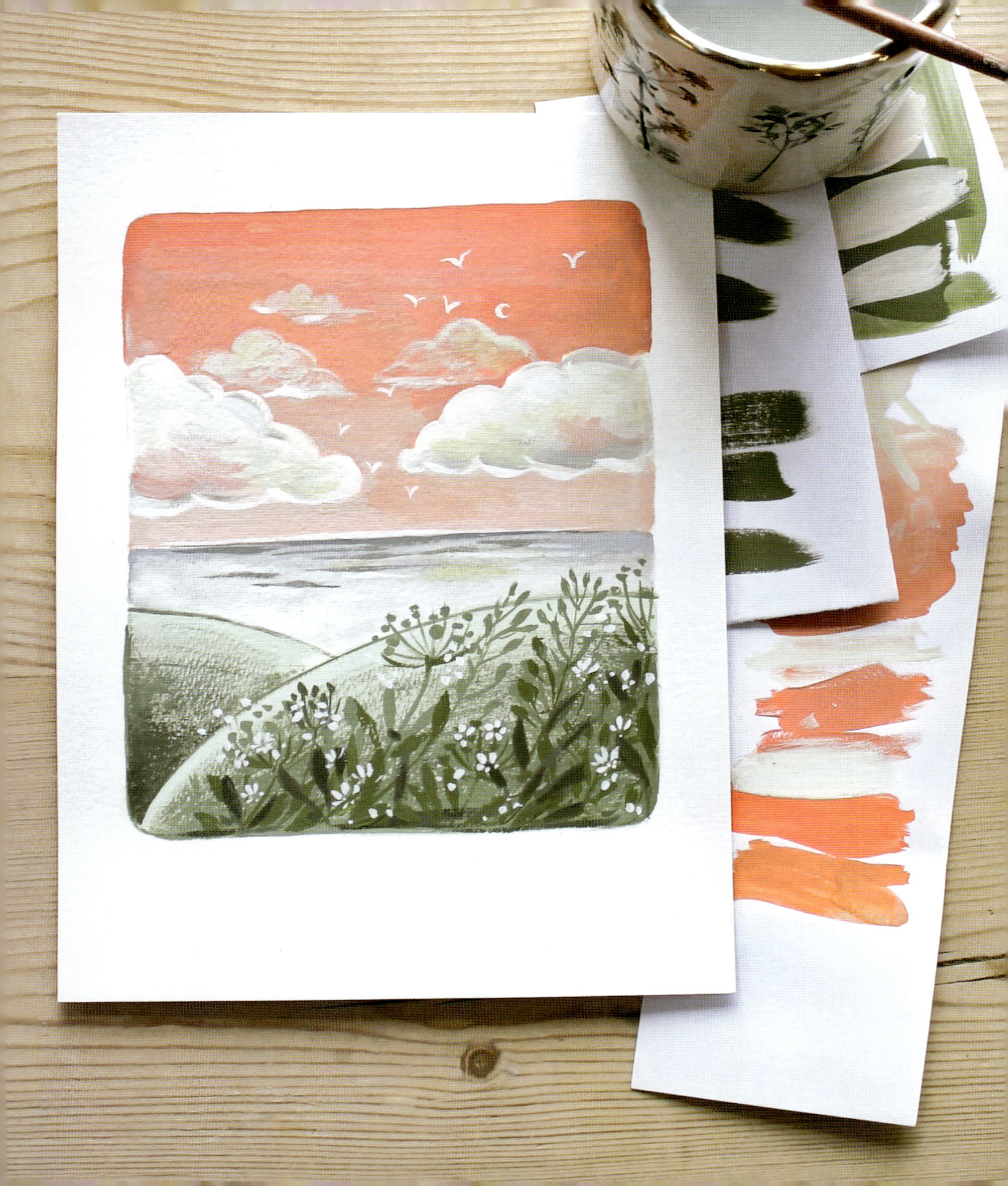

Tranquil Seascape

This is an evocative moody scene of land, sea and sky at dusk. Here we draw together lots of the techniques we have been learning throughout the book, such as blending wet-on-wet ombrés, layering dryish shades on top of one another to create texture and using a fine brush to create beautiful details. Believe it or not, we will only use a really limited palette of black, white, Opera Pink and Lemon Yellow. White is used to great effect with details on the clouds, moon, waves and foreground flowers.

COLOR MIXING

Pale Khaki: Mix a large dab of Ivory Black and a slightly larger dab of Lemon Yellow with a medium sized blob of Permanent White.

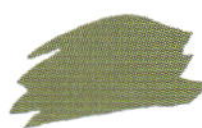

Khaki: Add equal sized blobs each of Lemon Yellow, Ivory Black and Permanent White.

Medium Gray: Add a speck of Ivory Black to a small dab of Permanent White.

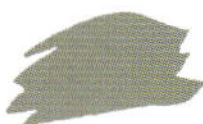

Dark Gray: Mix a dab each of Ivory Black and Permanent White and a speck of Lemon Yellow.

Deep Yellow: Add a small dab each of Lemon Yellow and Opera Pink and a speck of Ivory Black, to a small blob of Permanent White.

Deep Coral Pink: Mix a small blob each of Opera Pink, Lemon Yellow and Permanent White together with a dab of Ivory Black. Create plenty of this color for the sky.

Pale Yellow: Add a teeny dab each of Opera Pink and Lemon Yellow and a small speck of Ivory Black, to a small blob of Permanent White. You only need a little of this.

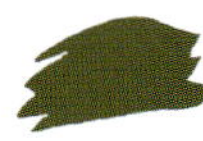

Greenish Khaki: Add equal sized blobs each of Ivory Black and Permanent White to a slightly larger blob of Lemon Yellow.

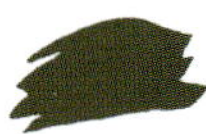

Dark Khaki: Set aside a little of the khaki and mix with a dab of Ivory Black. This should have a grayish tone.

Pure White: That's all.

SUPPLIES

Brushes: Fine or very fine round, small round, small flat, medium filbert, large filbert

Paint Colors: Ivory Black, Lemon Yellow, Opera Pink, Permanent White

Other Supplies: Pencil and eraser, scratch paper

1

Step 1: Simple Drawing

The drawing for this scene is minimal. Begin by penciling out a smallish portrait rectangle. Using my design as a reference, draw two simple curved lines to place the hills and one horizontal line for the skyline over the sea. Draw in two slightly offset clouds, one coming in from each side of the page. Next, draw in two smaller clouds peeking out from behind with fluffy tops and flattish bottoms.

2

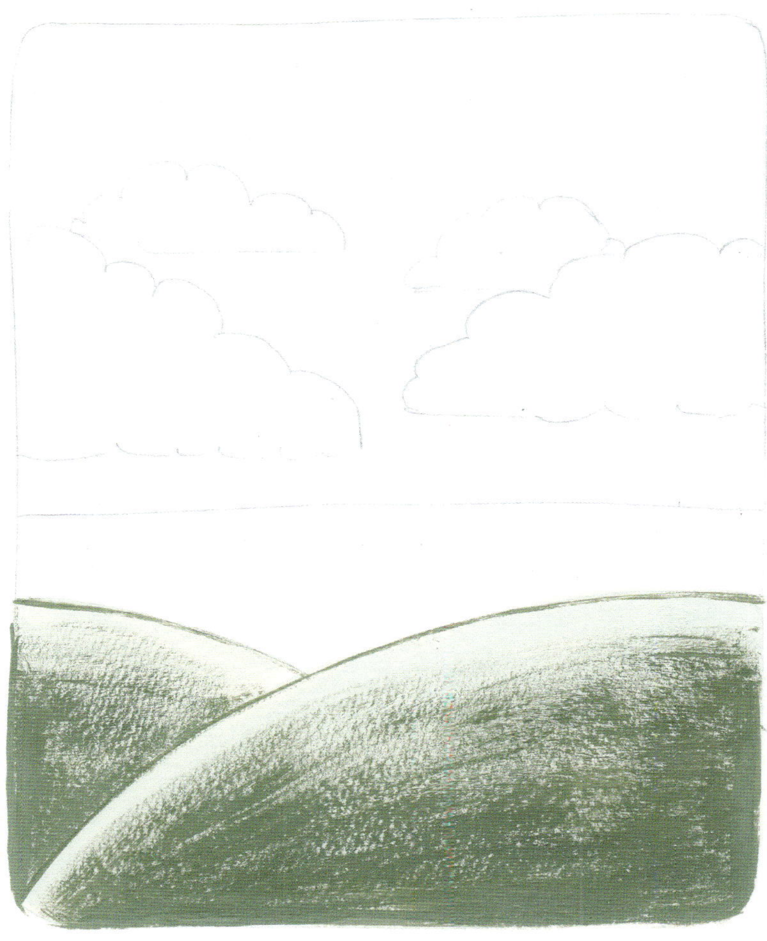

Step 2: The Hills

Use your pale khaki color as the underpainting for the two hills and add a touch of water so that the paint is opaque and only just fluid. Paint the front hill in first, then the one behind, following the curve of each hill.

Now use the khaki for the foreground. Outline both of the hills lightly with a fine round brush before switching to a small flat one and use a dry-brush technique to apply the bulk of the color. Use only a tiny amount of water so that the paint isn't too thick but is still pretty dry. Load your brush and then use your scratch paper or paper towel to remove excess paint to the point where you are only creating textured brush strokes. Working quickly, as the paint will be drying by the second, work from the bottom of the design in wide curved strokes to about three-quarters of the way up both of the hills.

Be careful to leave some of the pale khaki completely unpainted along the tops of the hills.

3

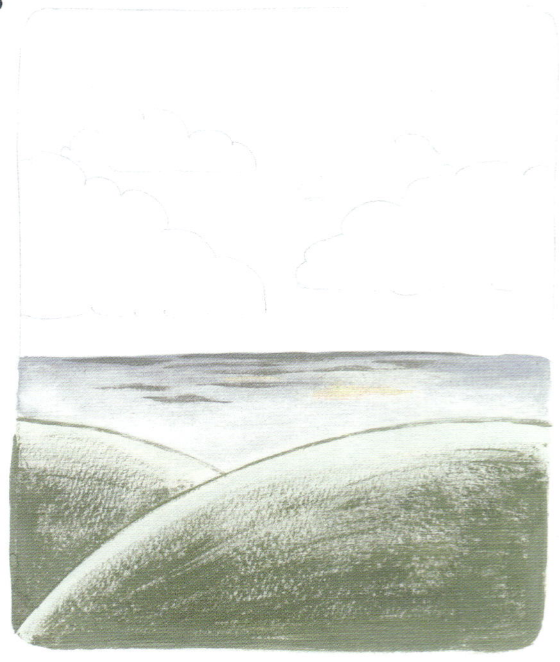

4a

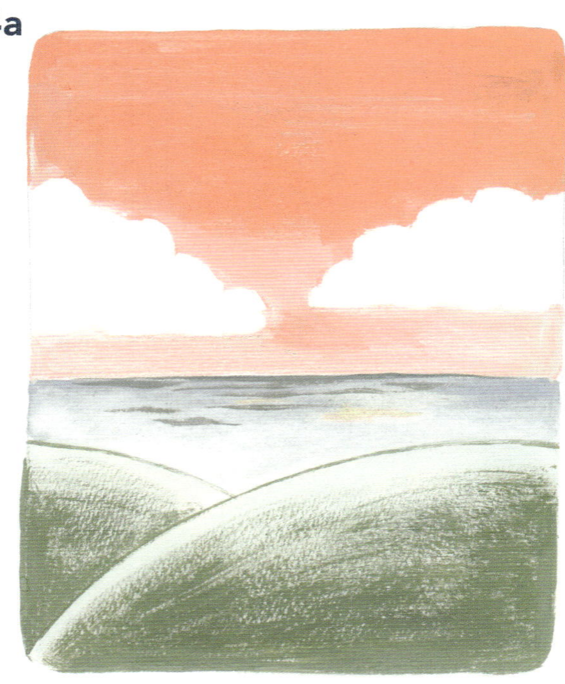

Step 3: The Sea

Moving on, we will use a wash technique for the sea with a small flat brush. Paint a thick medium gray line below the skyline with the widest edge of the brush and an opaque consistency. With plain water, blend this color downward with horizontal strokes so that the color lightens to the white of the paper where it meets the land and then leave it to dry.

Using a fine round brush, paint in the horizontal dark gray line of the sky and several horizontal lines below to indicate distant waves.

With a tiny watered-down speck of deep yellow color on the tip of a small flat brush, paint a little wash to suggest sunlight on the water.

Step 4: The Sky & Clouds

Next, we will be using a wet-on-wet technique to blend a deep coral pink with a lighter yellow, creating an ombré effect in the sky.

Load your medium sized filbert brush with deep coral pink, mixed with just a touch of water. Start at the top of the design and, applying your paint so that the color is pure and intense, work downward in opaque horizontal strokes, leaving the two large clouds unpainted. As you work lower, add a little water so that the color is not quite as deep and continue right down to where the sky meets the sea. Working quickly, while the paint is still wet and starting at the skyline, use a brush loaded with opaque pale yellow to blend upward and toward the middle of the sky. Blend as much as you can to create an even ombré.

4b

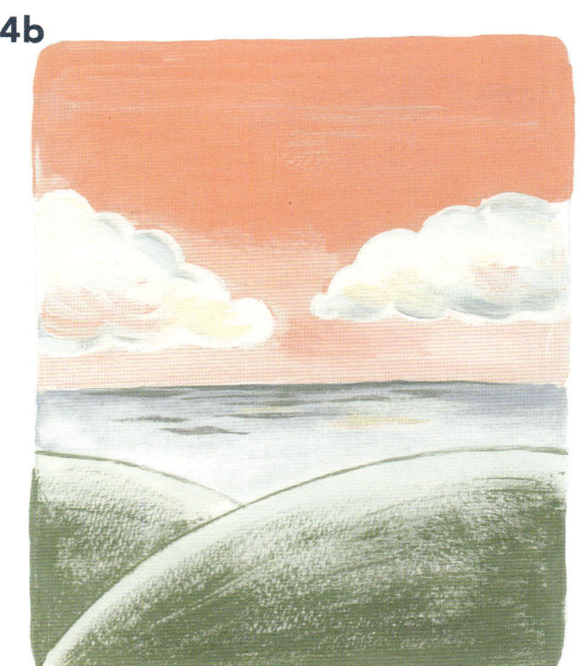

4c

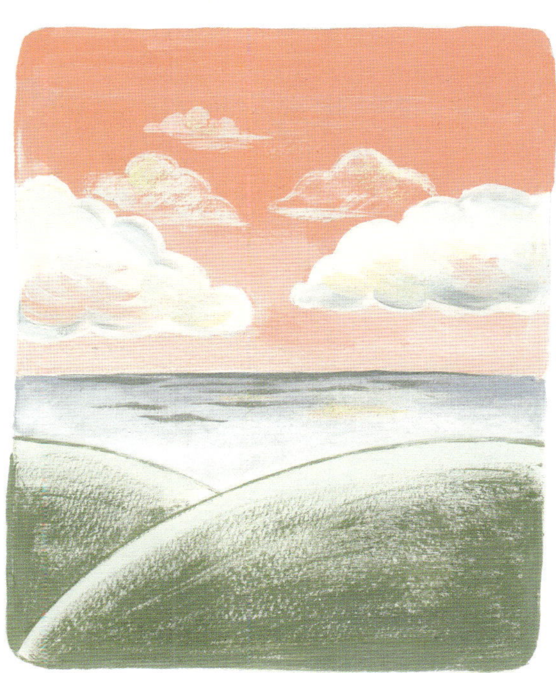

Next, we turn to developing volume and depth in the clouds, beginning with the pale yellow tone. Adding a touch of water, use a large filbert brush to fill in all the clouds with loose opaque strokes and rounded edges, overlapping slightly into the pink sky. While they are still wet, dab a touch of the mixed dark gray and with a small flat brush, use curved strokes to add texture and give the sense of fluffiness to the bottom of the clouds.

With a touch of the deep coral pink and a touch of water, add a few curved brush strokes in the middle of the clouds to give them weight as if they are about to burst open!

When dry, use a little watered-down wash of the dark yellow shade and place some rounded, rolling strokes on both the top and underside of the clouds. Add a dab of the pale yellow here and there to blend in the different colors.

Load your brush with the pale yellow and remove most of the excess on some scratch paper or a paper towel so you can paint with a dry textured stroke. With circular strokes, paint your two extra clouds back in and then another smaller one between and above these. Add a dry touch of the darker yellow to the top of these clouds.

5a

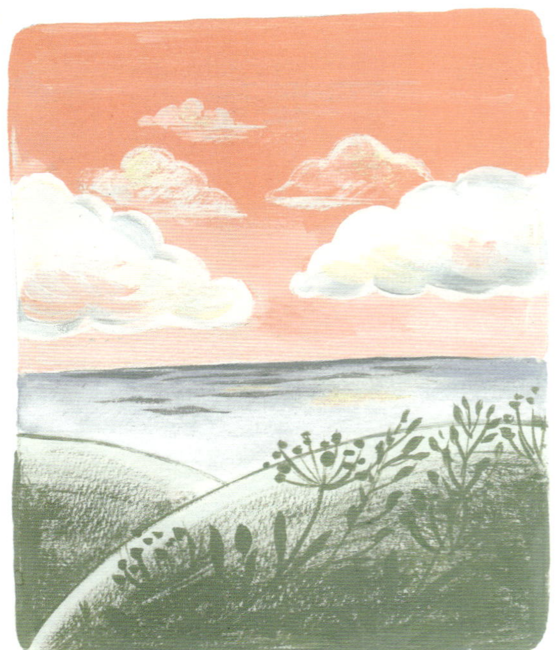

5b

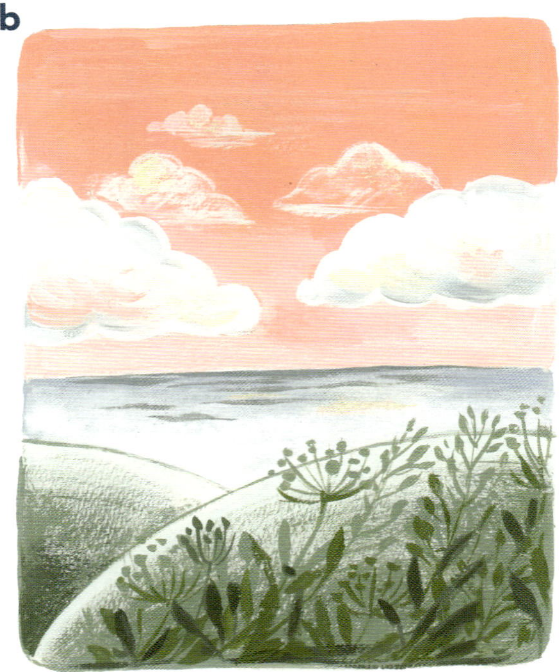

Step 5: Wildflower Silhouettes

Now return to the foreground and with the mixed khaki, create a wild meadow blowing slightly to the right. Using a fine round brush paint in a range of curved lines of slightly differing heights coming up from the bottom of the design. Use a loose variety of strokes to add heads and textured marks to suggest stems, grasses and leaves. As these are the same color as the initial shading, some of the lower details will not be completely visible.

Use your greenish khaki to add more foreground details slightly lower down on the wildflower silhouettes. Don't be afraid of overlapping, dotting or using the side of the brush to create textured marks. Using a dry brush, add a little more shading low down on the left hill.

Use your dark khaki to paint even more leafy marks right along the bottom of the design.

6

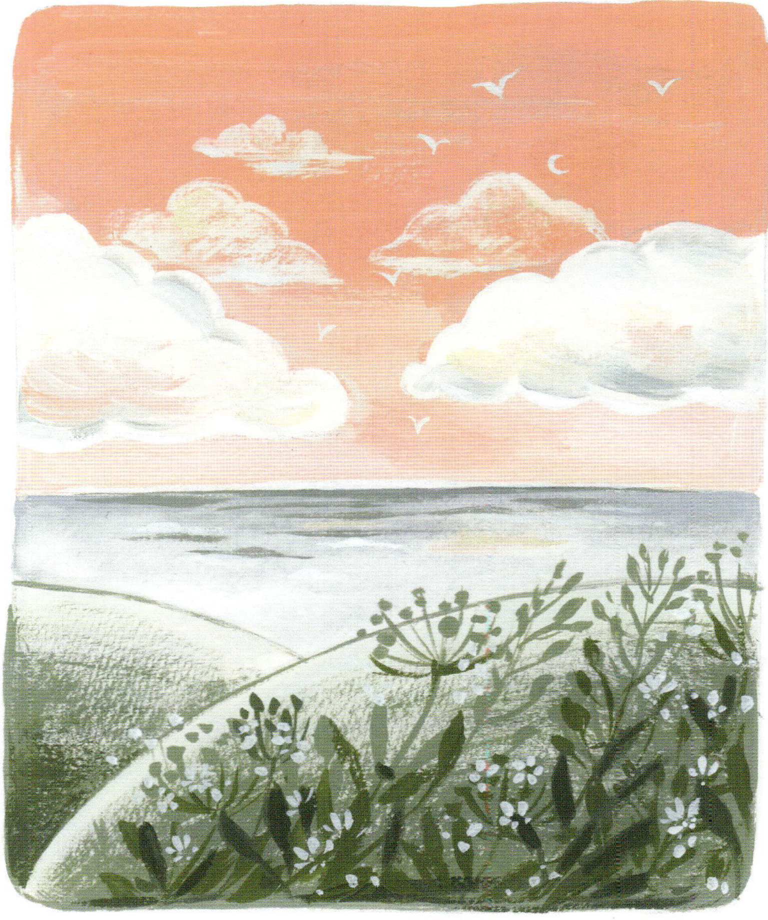

Step 6: White Highlights

Finish the piece by adding some pure white details. With a fine round brush and in the center of the sky just below the cloud line, paint in tiny curved 'v' shapes to suggest gulls in flight. Just above the cloud on the right, paint in a tiny crescent for the moon.

Moving down the piece, paint in a faint white line just above the darker line of the sea. Paint some very fine, slightly waved horizontal strokes in the sea to suggest waves.

In the foreground and on top of the wildflower meadow, use the tip of your brush loaded with opaque white to dot tiny petals, creating the suggestion of small, blowing flowers.

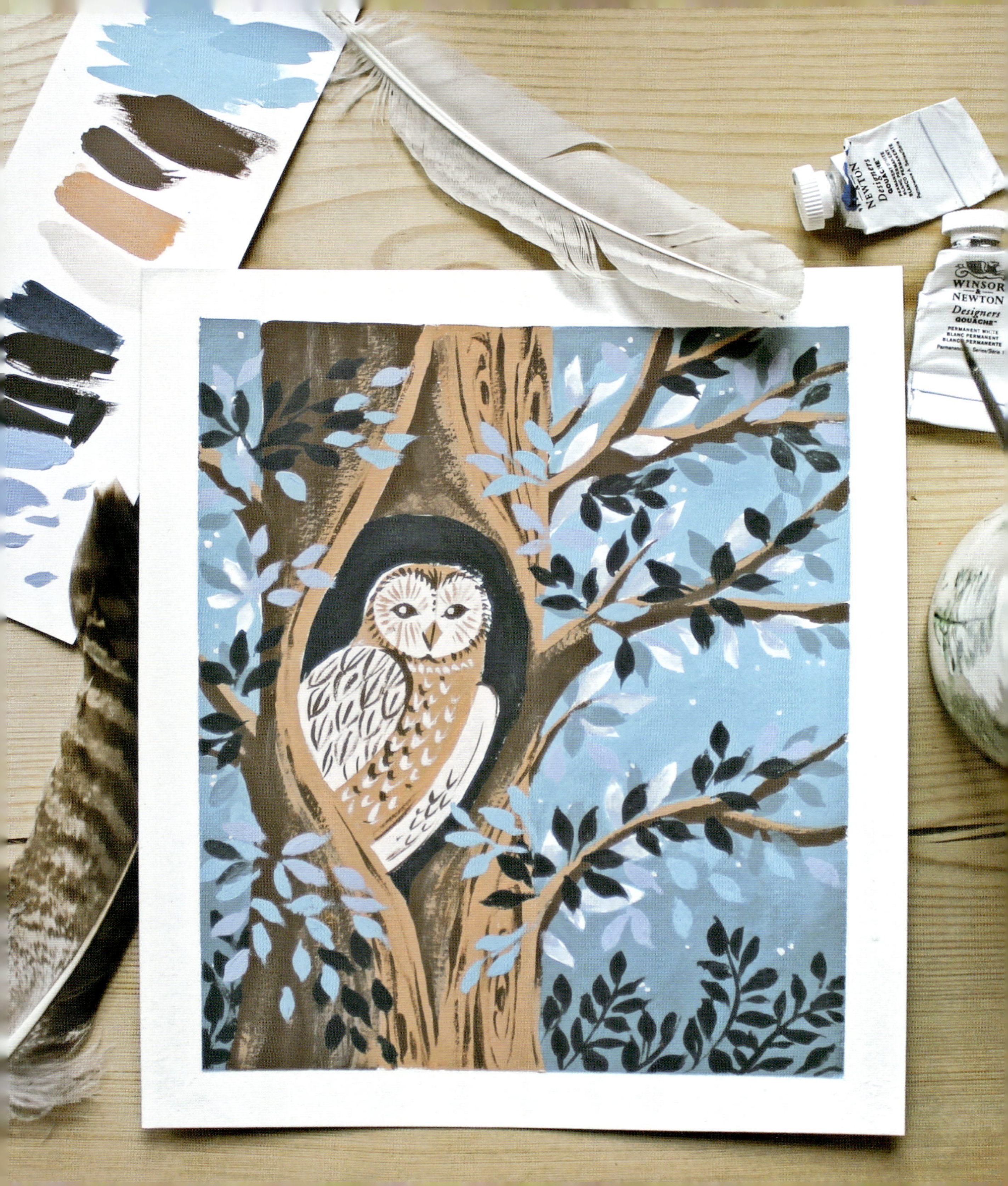
NEWTON
Designers
GOUACHE
WINSOR & NEWTON
Designers
GOUACHE
PERMANENT WHITE
BLANC PERMANENT

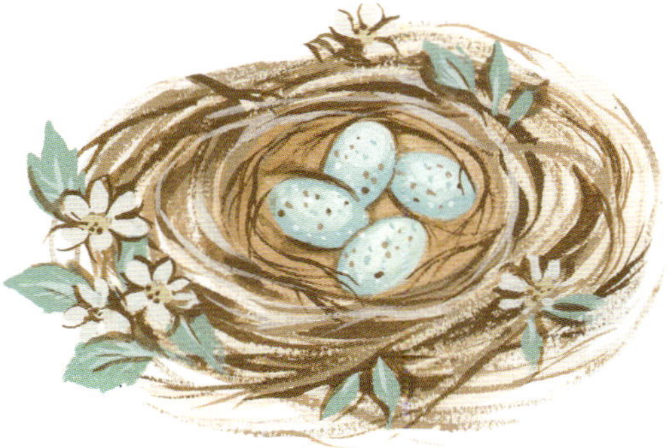

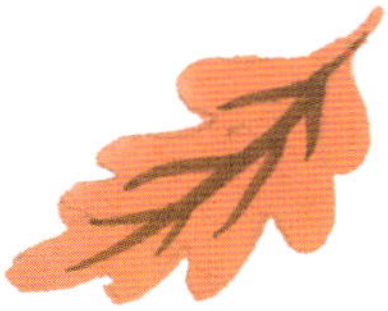

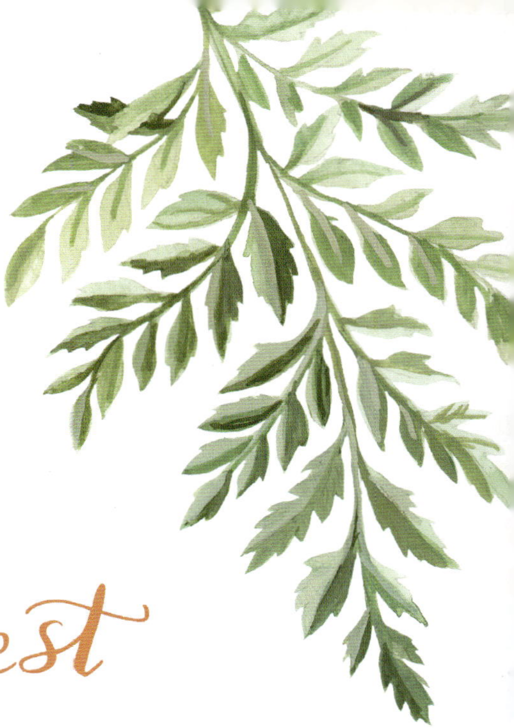

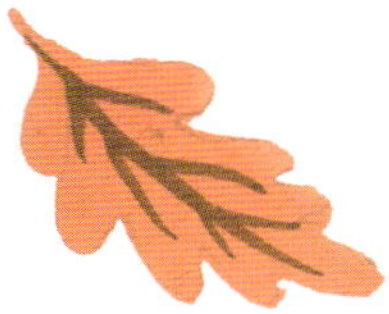

In the Forest

In our last chapter, we wander into the forest and embrace all that this wonderful habitat has to offer us, naturally developing both learned and new techniques. No forest scene of mine would be complete without a layer of fallen leaves, clusters of mushrooms or whimsical woodland birds and creatures. This is probably our most diverse range of projects. We will create an intricate border of ferns, a classic songbird with her nest of eggs and we will finish with an atmospheric night portrait of a majestic owl nestled in a leafy tree.

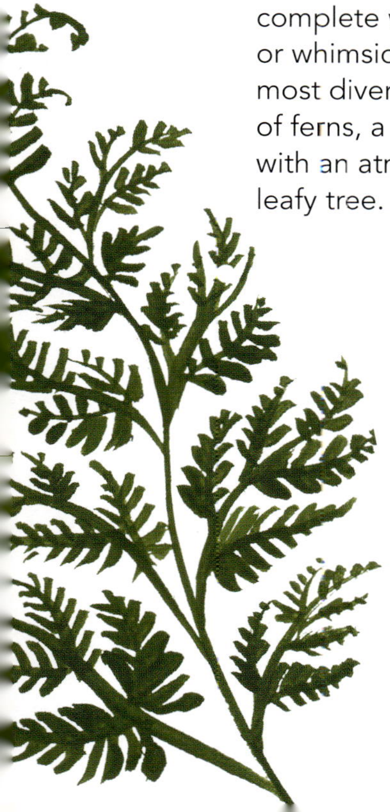

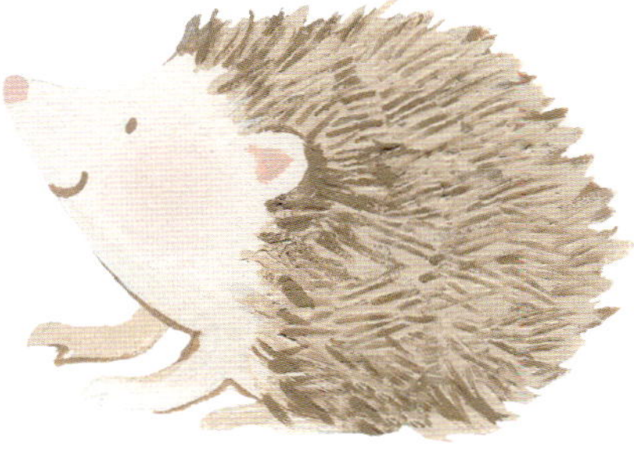

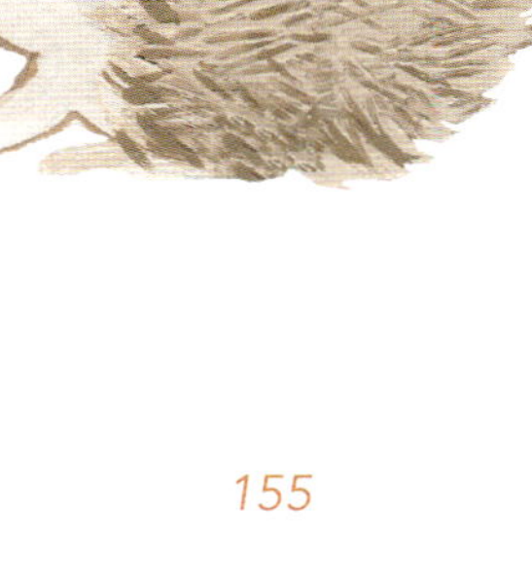

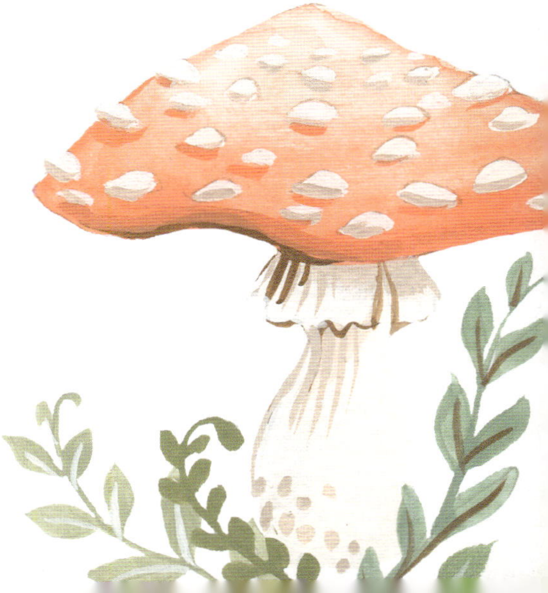

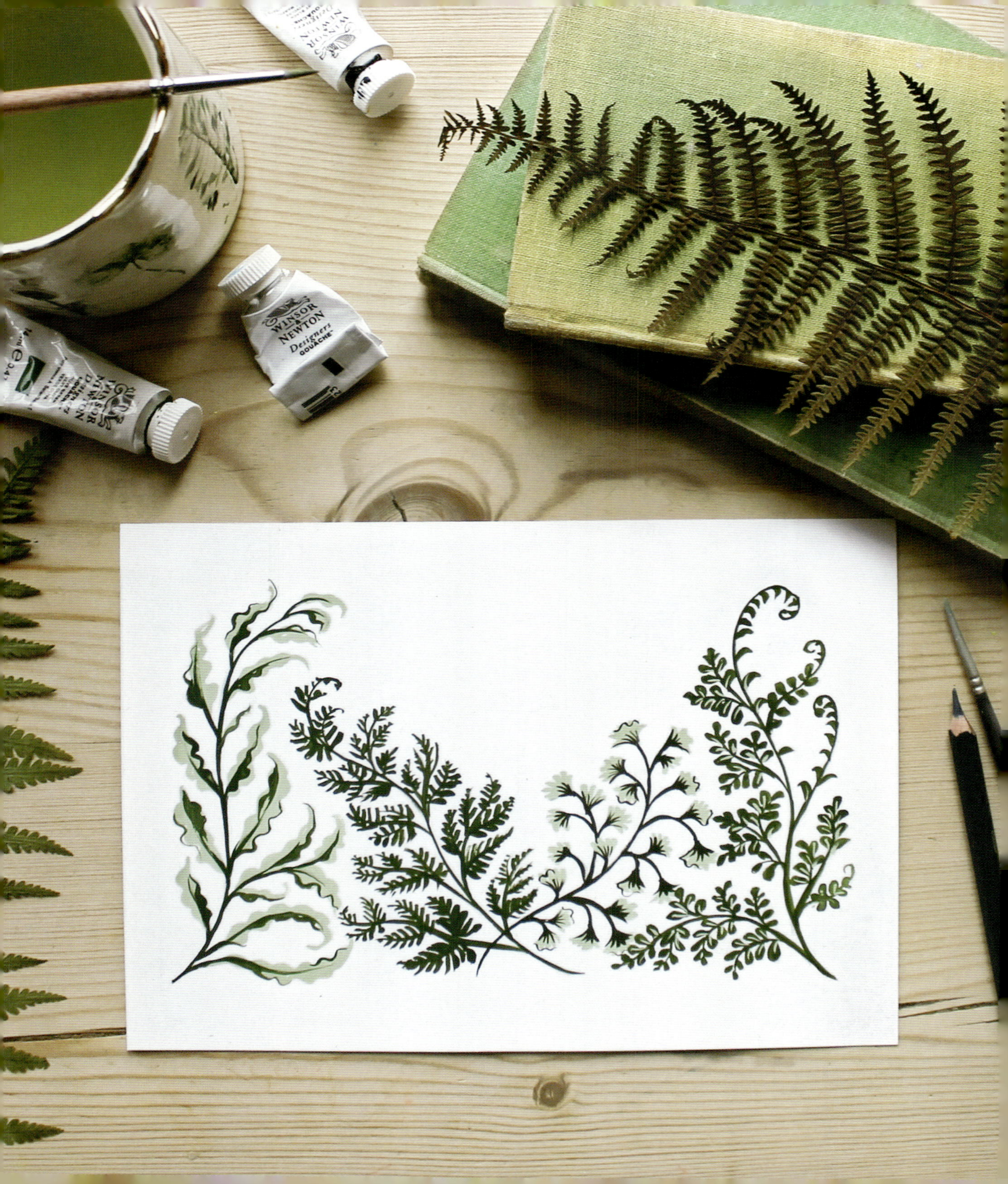
WINSOR & NEWTON
Designers
GOUACHE

Fern Border

This project is a simple way into painting one of the most beautiful and complex leaf structures in nature. Our painting will aim to give a loose impression of the plants rather than a botanical study. Ferns are a wonderfully versatile element in both patterns and other graphic and illustrative projects. Once you have the hang of painting the first couple of leaves, the others follow suit in exactly the same format—indulging in the repetition can be wonderfully relaxing.

COLOR MIXING

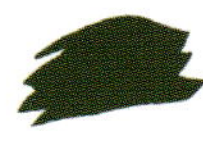

Olive Green: Pure from the tube. If you don't have this color, you can use any medium or dark green, or mix a large amount by adding even amounts of Ultramarine and Cadmium Yellow together, adding white to create a lighter tint and black for a darker shade.

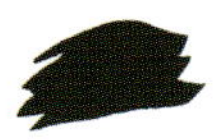

Dark Green: Add a tiny dot of Ivory Black to a dab of pure Olive Green to make a darker shade.

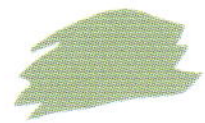

Light Green: Mix a small dab of Permanent White with a large dab of pure Olive Green.

SUPPLIES

Brushes: Very fine round, fine round, small round

Paint Colors: Ivory Black, Olive Green, Permanent White

Other Supplies: Green or gray watercolor pencil, graphite pencil, scratch paper

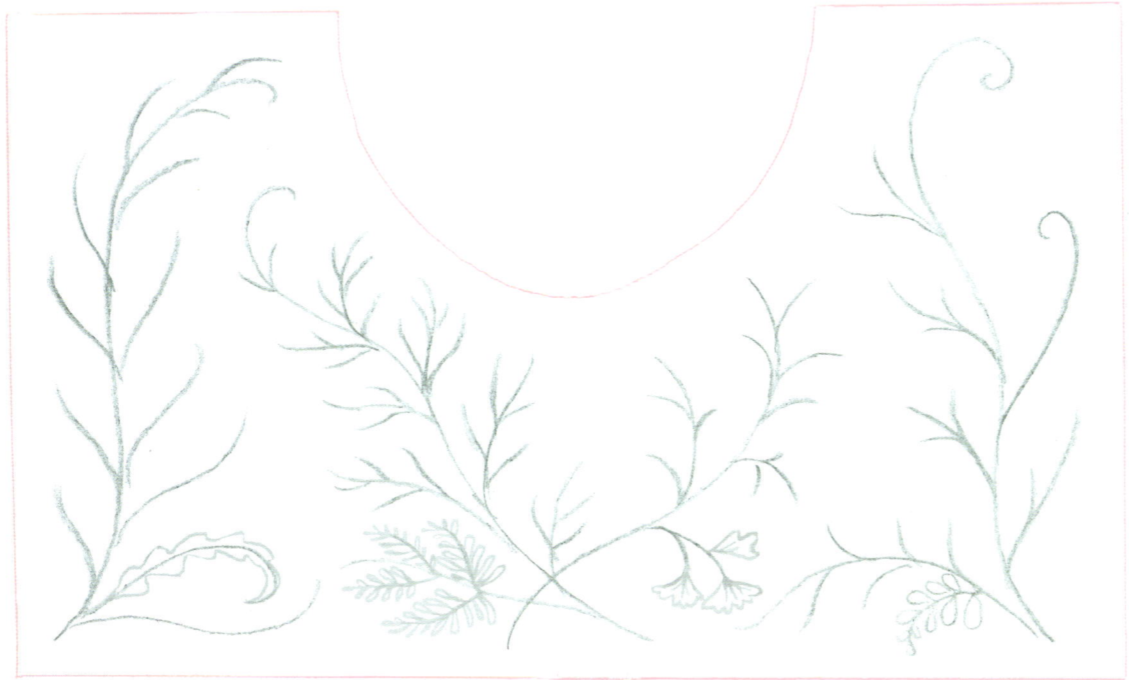

Step 1: Fern Guidelines

Using my drawing as a reference, use a light graphite pencil to place your own guidelines and outline the basic shape of the border before you begin. I have never found it helpful to draw out a precise preliminary drawing of a fern before painting it, partly because I am rather impatient, but also because I feel you can get just the same results with limited linework.

I have used a simple 'skeleton' sketch for four little ferns, which you can use as a reference to draw in four of your own curling stems. The whole leaf is called the frond and within this, I have drawn in the spine, or midrib as it is called, the smaller pinnae and the smallest pinnules. For each of the different types of ferns I have drawn in one guide pinna. We will paint in all the rest freehand!

To create an even and balanced composition, begin by drawing in the two ferns that overlap in the center and then two more curling in and up, one from the bottom left and one from the bottom right. I would suggest using a light grayish or green watercolor pencil.

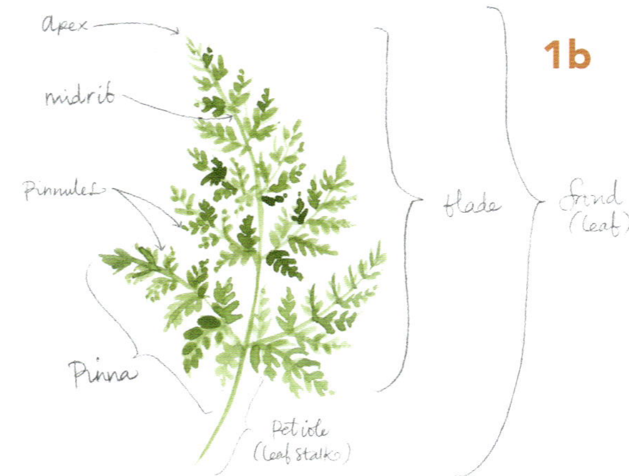

2a

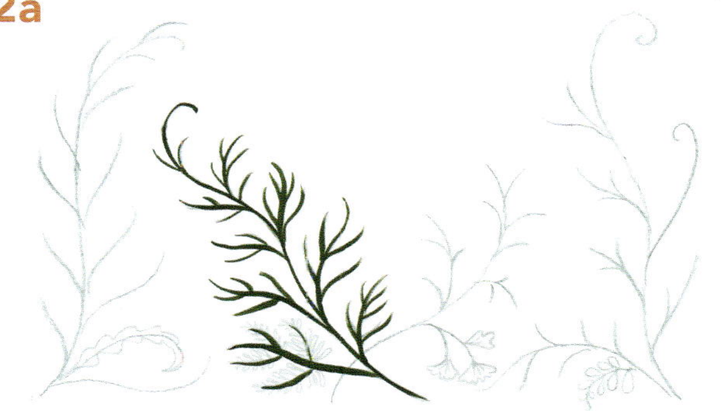

2b

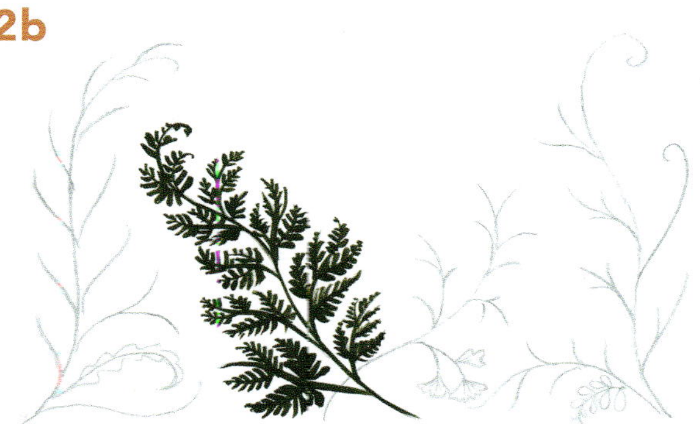

Step 2: First Fern, Center Left

To minimize mixing and allow us to really concentrate on the shapes we are painting, we will use tints and shades of pure Olive Green. A very fine round brush will give us good control for all the fine details. Mix the paint with a touch of water to create an opaque but fluid consistency. Begin with the most complex of the four, the second blade from the left, a common fern with lots of intricate detail.

Starting at the base of the stem, paint a line upward and then out over all of the visible drawn lines using a steady hand.

The structure of this fern means that its widest point is at the base and that it tapers up into a point like a triangle. Each of the tiny pinnae also follows this pattern, as do the pinnules covering each pinna.

With this in mind, begin painting the lowest pinna. Paint tiny little lines radiating out and down, getting smaller toward the tip. Repeat on both sides of the pinna and then move up your pinnules, getting smaller as you go so that we are essentially creating little leaves within leaves.

Move up one side of the fern, repeating this process on each new line, working from large to small, with lots of tiny little rounded strokes. Fill in the other side of the frond, again working from large to small.

3a

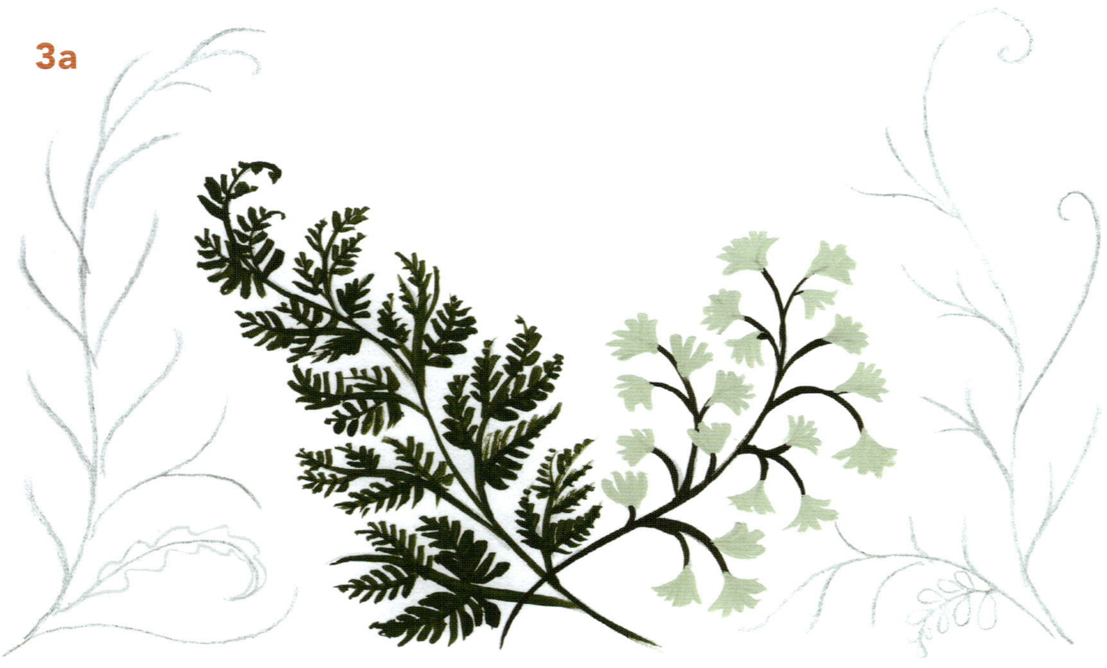

3b

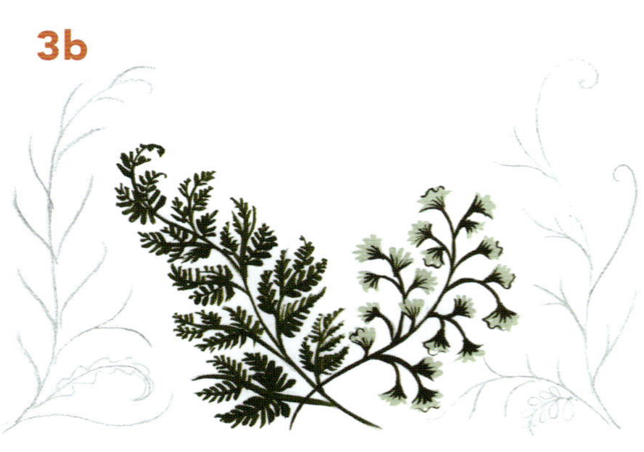

Step 3: Second Fern, Center Right

Ferns come in all different shapes and sizes and the structure of the next one is such that the pinnules sit at the end of the stalks like little fans.

Paint over all of the stalk parts of the fern with the dark green shade. Using my drawn guide as a reference, paint in pinnules at the ends of the stalks with the light green tint, echoing a fan shape with a wavy top.

When completely dry, use a fine brush to paint in tiny little darker-colored details on each of the light green pinnules, the details radiating from the point where the pinnule is joined to the darker green stem point. Also add a few little wavy lines on some, but not all, of these pinnules.

4a

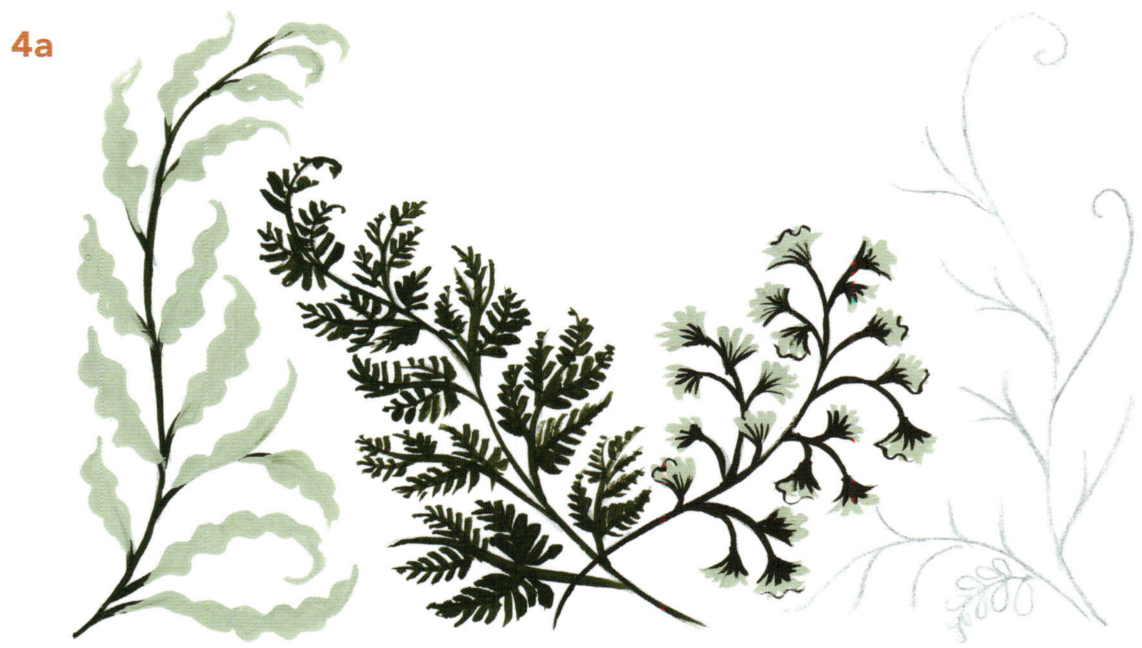

Step 4: Third Fern, Far Left

The fern on the left has long narrow pinnae coming off the main midrib and we will paint it with two colors to really highlight its wavy nature and create a sense of three-dimensionality.

Paint in the drawn stems with the pure Olive Green. Then, beginning at the bottom of the frond, use the light green shade to paint the individual pinnae with a slightly wavy line on each side. Carry on throughout the whole frond, slightly decreasing the size of the pinnae as you approach the top.

When thoroughly dry, with one single curved and tapering stroke, paint in the central vein of each pinna in the pure Olive Green. Sketchily, with no uniform pattern, add some shading and small wavy outlines to one side of some of the leaves.

4b

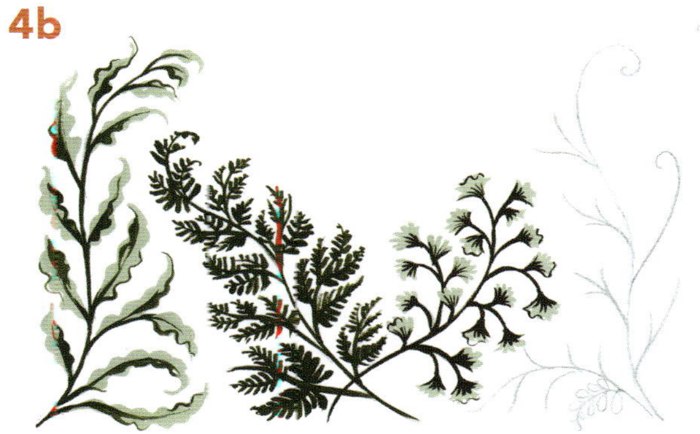

5a

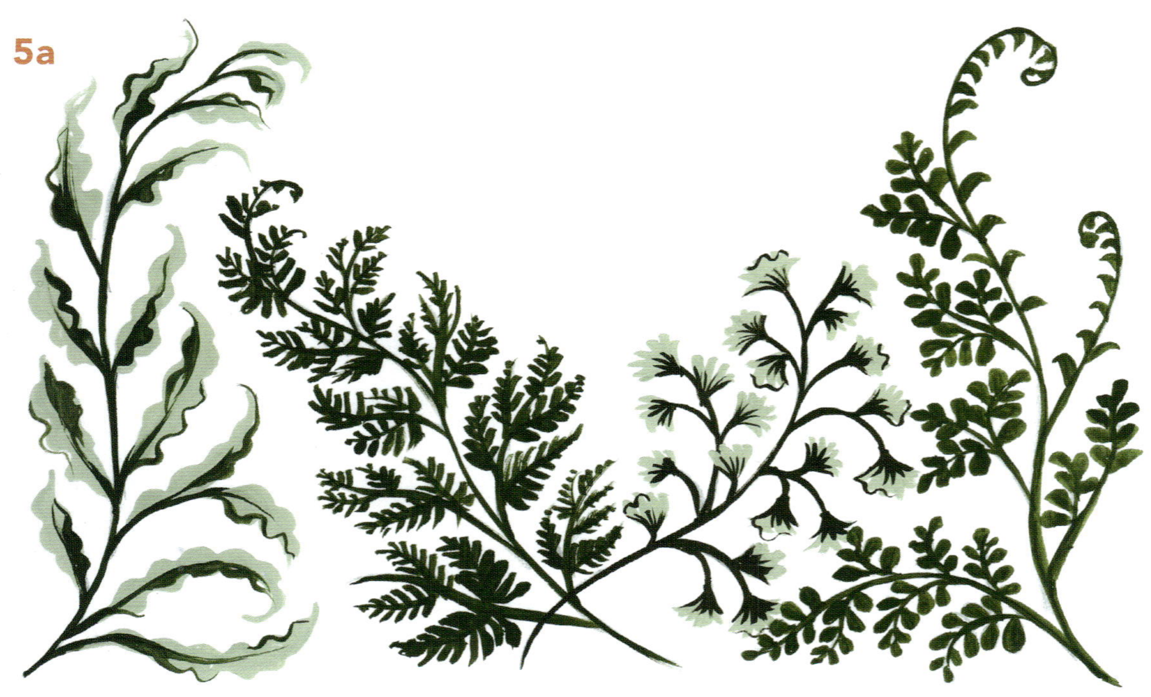

5b

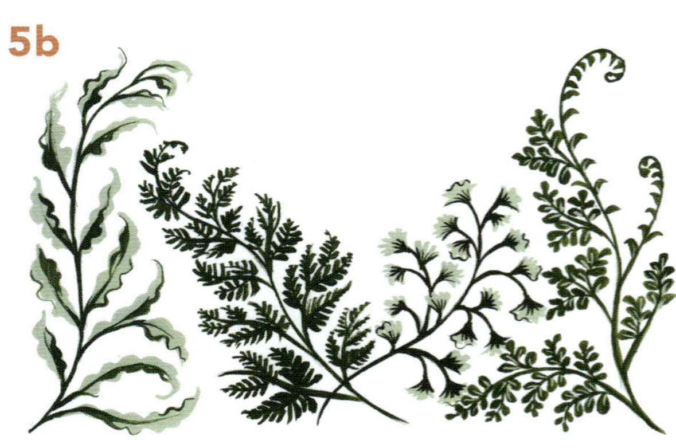

Step 5: Final Fern, Far Right

Our last fern on the right is similar to our first but with a slightly simpler leaf structure, rounded pinnules and two separate lovely curly fronds.

Paint in the stem with the pure Olive Green and, using my guide leaf as a reference, imitate your painting of the first fern, except this time make each tiny pinnule the shape of a teardrop. Fill the main two stems again, reducing their size as you reach the top.

The curly stems of the pinnae need to be approached slightly differently. Work from the middle of the spiral and on the inside of the curl, paint in tiny little curled pinnules, the gaps between them widening as you reach the main stalk.

When dry, add tiny light green vein details to most of the teardrop pinnules.

6

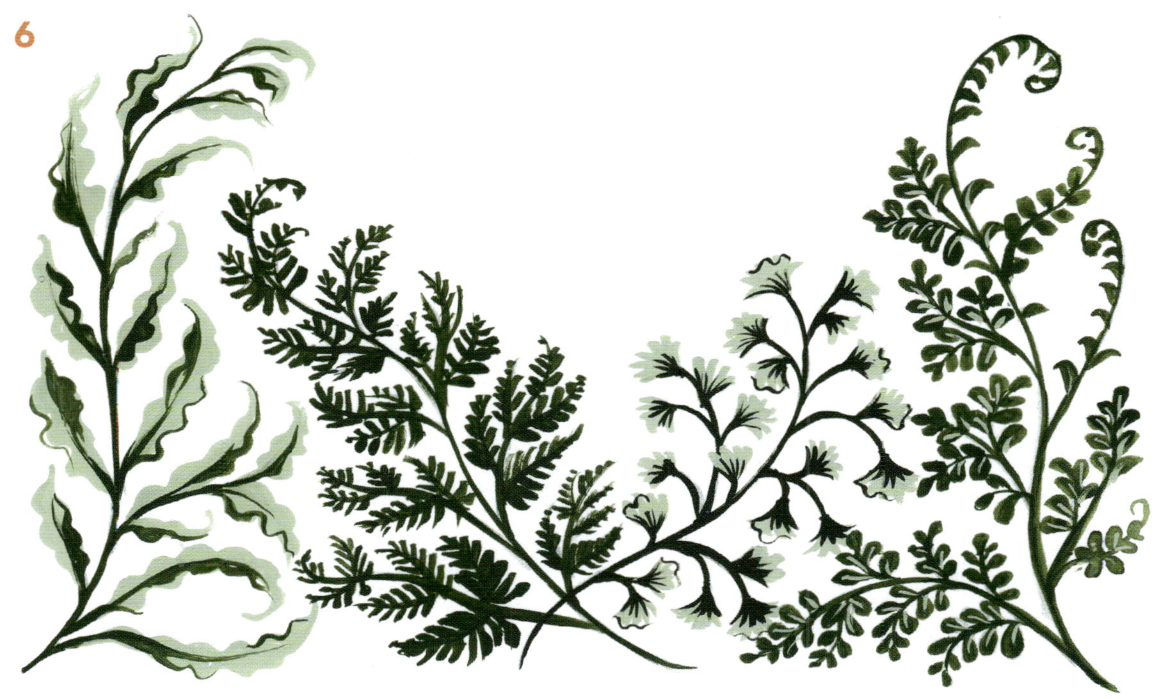

Step 6: Filling in the Gaps

The reality of painting in this loose way is that when you have 'finished' the design, you will often notice that there are a few gaps in the design or unbalanced areas that need tweaking.

When it comes to this piece, I feel that the first fern we painted could be extended to fill the slight gap to its left and that the other three ferns could do with some 'bushing' out. Using your instinctive creative eye, paint in whatever you need to, adding and overlapping until you are completely happy! When all is dry, don't forget to erase the original graphite pencil guidelines.

TAKING THE PROJECT FURTHER:

Research 'botanical ferns' online and choose some different shaped plants to draw using the same techniques as above. Try drawing out the same or a similar drawing again and painting it in with a more watery and transparent paint. Do you prefer it?

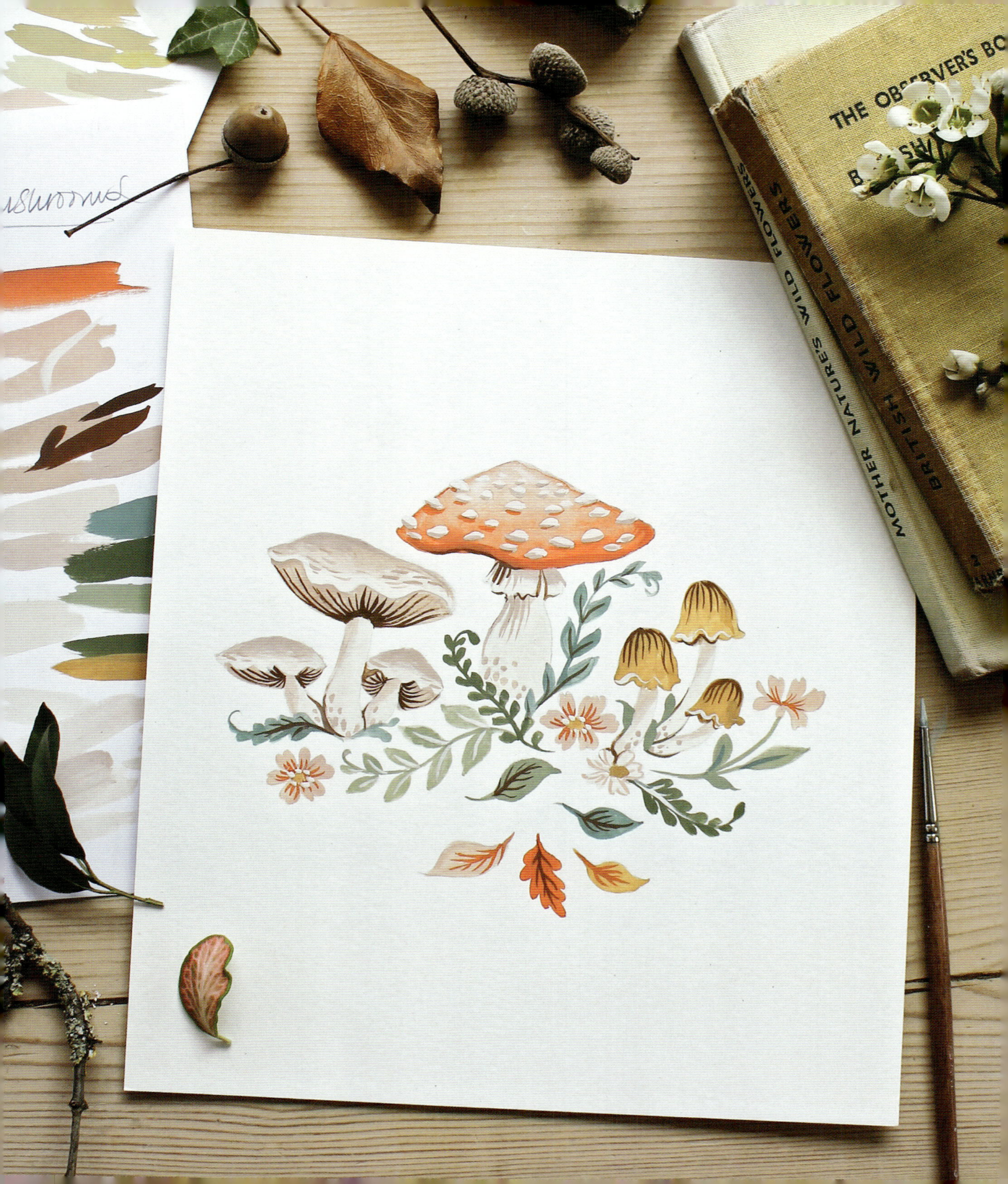
THE OBSERVER'S
BRITISH WILD FLOWERS
MOTHER NATURE'S WILD FLOWERS

Woodland Mushrooms

No woodland scene would be complete without a mushroom or two! The classic red spotty one here is called the Fly Agaric and adds a bright pop of color to this woodland floor border. Up to this point, most of the areas in our designs have been created by simply leaving them unpainted. However, it is really useful to sometimes paint with white over darker layers, which is called a light-on-dark technique.

COLOR MIXING

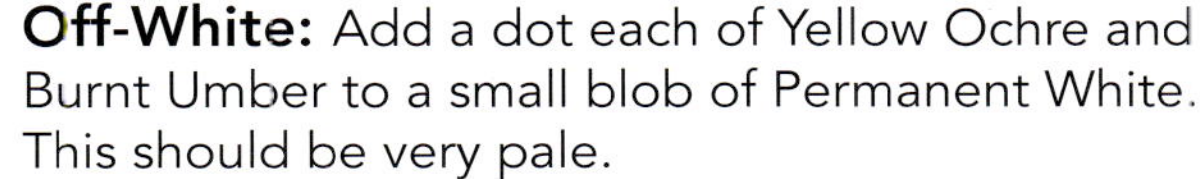

Off-White: Add a dot each of Yellow Ochre and Burnt Umber to a small blob of Permanent White. This should be very pale.

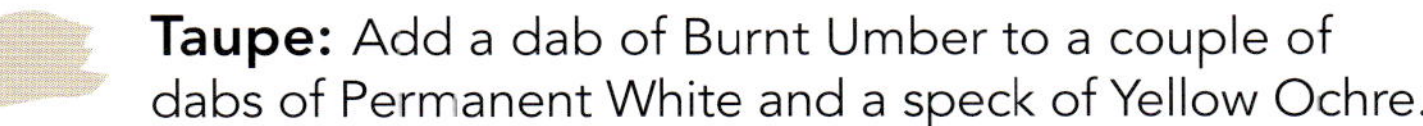

Taupe: Add a dab of Burnt Umber to a couple of dabs of Permanent White and a speck of Yellow Ochre.

Red: Add a dab each of Permanent White, Lemon Yellow and Burnt Umber to a small blob of Cadmium Red.

Light Ochre: Add a dab of Yellow Ochre to a small blob of Permanent White and a dot of Burnt Umber.

Light Pink: Mix a dot each of Cadmium Red, Lemon Yellow and an even tinier speck of Burnt Umber together with a small blob of Permanent White.

Bluey Green: Mix a dot of Lemon Yellow and dabs each of Phthalo Blue, Burnt Umber and Permanent White together.

Moss Green: Mix a dab each of Yellow Ochre, Phthalo Blue and Permanent White together.

Dark Moss Green: Set aside a dab of moss green and mix with a small dab of Burnt Umber to create a darker shade.

Dark Brown: Add a dab of Burnt Umber to a dot each of Permanent White, Phthalo Blue and Yellow Ochre.

SUPPLIES

Brushes: Fine round, small round

Paint Colors: Burnt Umber, Cadmium Red, Lemon Yellow, Permanent White, Phthalo Blue, Yellow Ochre

Other Supplies: Pencil and eraser, scratch paper

1a

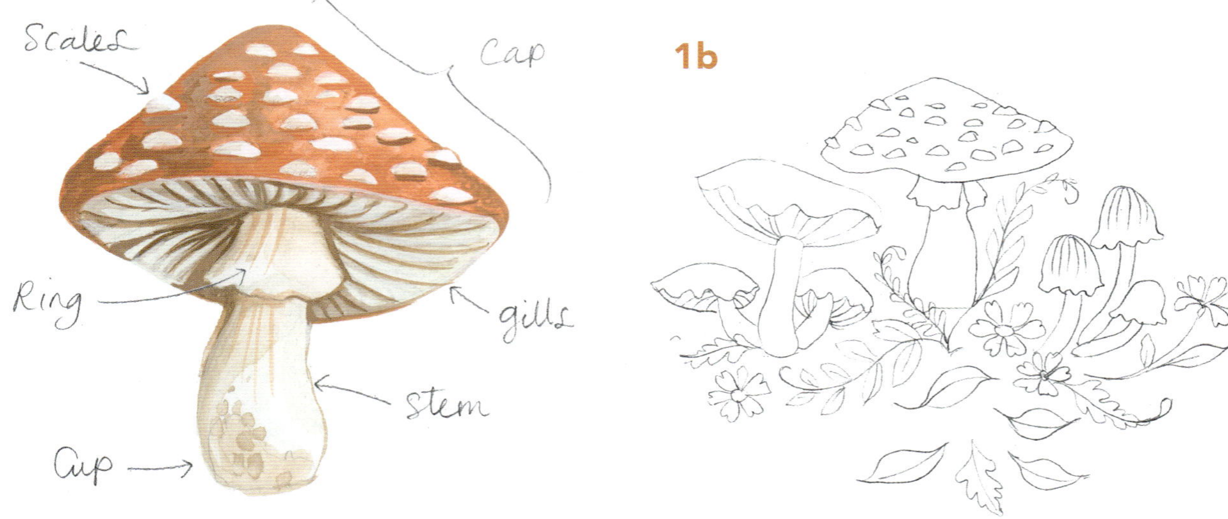

Step 1: Drawing the Scene

This little labeled mushroom diagram may help you to easily follow my steps:

Using a graphite pencil and my design as a reference, the first element to draw is your large red spotty mushroom. Place this on the middle of the page by outlining the cap. Follow the line around to make a soft triangular shape and then cover in small triangular scales. As we are viewing our mushroom from slightly above, we will only see the ring—the little frill below—poking out so draw it in using a wavy line followed by the stalk below.

To the left and offset slightly forward and below, we draw in the little clump of three mushrooms with flatter caps and visible gills. Begin with the wavy lines for the edges of the caps, with fan-like lines for the gills and tall thin stalks.

Draw in the bell-shaped caps of the clump on the right, with three curved stalks supporting them.

Now we can draw in the smaller elements. Start with the few little flowers, then move onto the ferns and leaves.

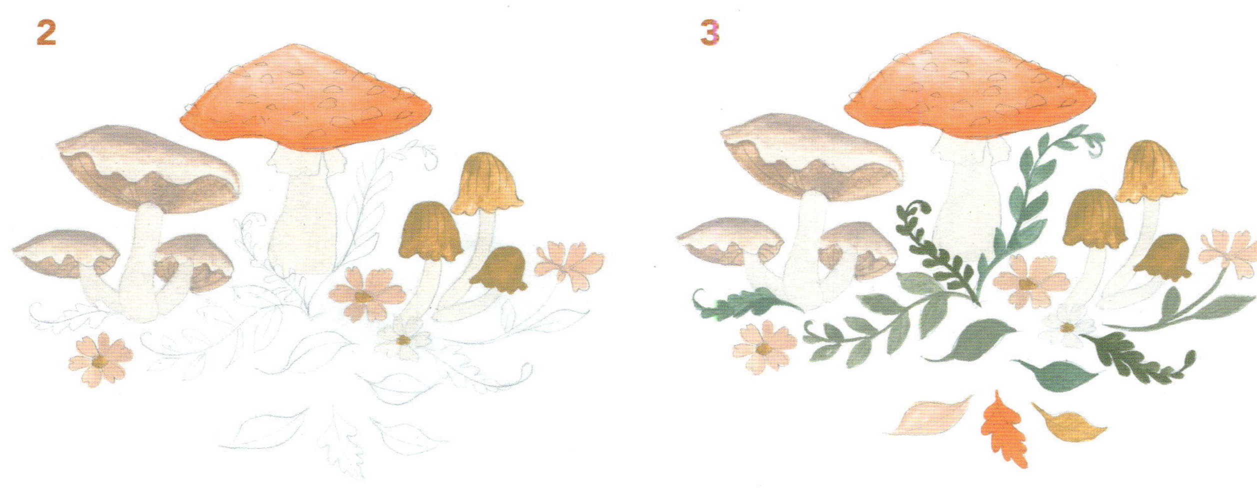

Step 2: First Wash of Colors

We will build the design up lightly, trying to retain a slightly washy feel. Using a small round brush and some off-white color, paint in the stems of all the mushrooms.

Turn now to the clump of mushrooms on the left. On all three, add a semi-opaque wash of off-white paint around the wavy rim and extending up toward the top of the cap. While this is still wet, get a little of the taupe and paint down from the top of the caps, blending together where the two colors meet. Paint in the gills with a light taupe opaque wash.

Load the brush with opaque red and paint along the rim of the central mushroom, extending this coverage up over about a quarter of the cap. Add a little water to the brush and use this to blend the color up into the top so there is a light gradient of color.

Use a little light ochre to paint in the caps of the mushroom clump to the right and the center of three of the flowers. Paint the petals of the same three flowers in light pink.

Step 3: Green Stems & Leaves

In this step, we will use the three tones of green for the foliage and leaves. Start with a bluey green color and, using my painting for reference, paint in the curling stem to the right of the red mushroom and the curling leaf on the far left, as well as one of the leaves in the foreground.

Paint the stem that runs left from the base of the red mushroom with the moss green, as well as the stem and leaves of the far right flower.

Paint the remaining two ferny stems in the dark moss green. Fill in the foreground leaves with greens, pink, red and light ochre.

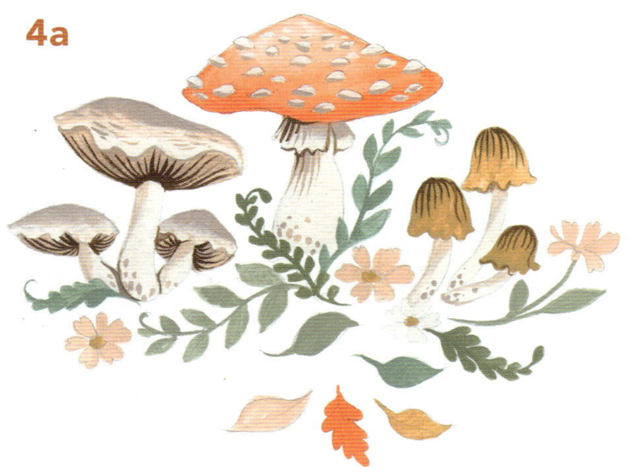
4a

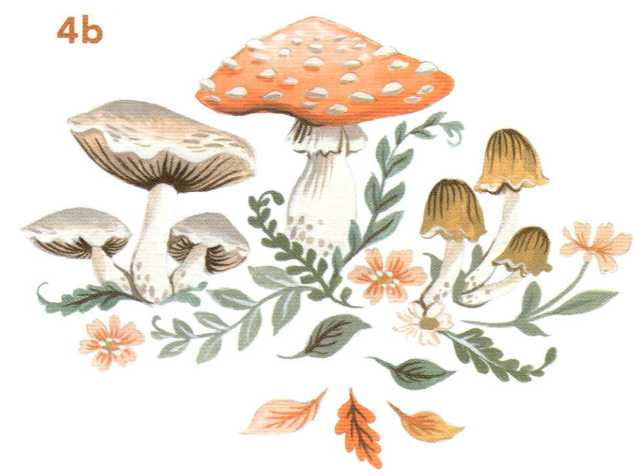
4b

Step 4: Scales & Details

In this next step, we will be adding a range of details across all the mushroom caps and stems. Load a fine round brush with a little watered-down taupe color so you can make semi-opaque marks. Working from left to right, add a few dots at the base of each mushroom stalk to indicate the cup and a little line of shadow down the left-hand sides of the stalks. On the caps of the mushrooms, paint in little curved horizontal patterned marks.

On the ring—the frill—of the central mushroom, paint in some taupe shadow and some tiny vertical lines coming down from the top and then do the same on the cups of the mushrooms on the right.

Use a little dark brown to add detailed lines to the gills of the clump on the left, the ring of the central mushroom and on the caps of the ochre mushrooms.

Paint the central mushroom's scales in off-white. In a fluid but completely opaque consistency, add small, almost semi-circular dots, making them very slightly smaller as they go up to the top of the cap. Use a little taupe to add a shadow to the bottom of each scale.

To finish the design, we will add a little light detailing to the leaves, stems and flowers in off-white, red and dark brown.

Take stock of the design and, if you feel like it, add a few leaves or details here and there.

TAKING THE PROJECT FURTHER:

There are so many strange and curiously shaped fungi out there, so it would be a shame to only draw a couple! Using references from books or online picture galleries, make a simple spot pattern with a variety of different mushroom types and a neutral, natural palette. Angle each one in a slightly different direction to give your design fluidity and movement. If you are feeling adventurous, paint a bright background of teal or warm red to make the earthy colors pop!

Hedgehog & Birdie

This whimsical little project is a great one to bring together different techniques and try a couple that you may not have before—scraping and wet-on-wet blending. We will be creating a lightly textured painting by using slightly thicker wet paint and then scraping some prickly texture for the hedgehog's spines. Set aside a little more time for this one as some of the thicker layers take a while to dry. Drawing together a range of techniques in one piece will help you find your own style and give you the confidence to create your own scenes.

COLOR MIXING

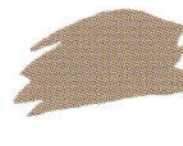

Pale Brown: Mix a couple of dabs of Burnt Umber, a small dab of Cadmium Yellow and a large blob of Permanent White.

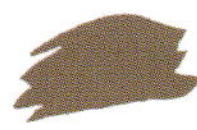

Dark Brown: Add three large dabs of Permanent White and a dab of Ultramarine to a blob of Burnt Umber.

Light Taupe: Mix a dot of Burnt Umber, a teeny dot of Cadmium Yellow and a blob of Permanent White. Mix plenty of each shade of brown so you can apply generously.

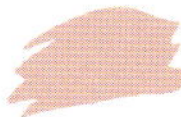

Pink: Add a large dab each of Opera Pink and Permanent White to a dab of Burnt Umber.

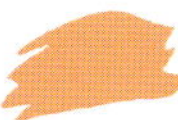

Burnt Orange: Mix two dabs of Cadmium Yellow and one each of pink, dark brown and Permanent White.

Dark Yellow: Add a couple of dabs each of Cadmium Yellow and Permanent White to a small dab of Burnt Umber.

Dark Green: Mix three dabs of Ultramarine, one small dab of Cadmium Yellow and a big dab of Permanent White.

Pale Green: Set aside a couple of dabs of dark green and create a lighter tint by mixing with a dab of Permanent White.

Blue: Add a large dab of Ultramarine, a dot of Cadmium Yellow and a small dab of Burnt Umber to a blob of Permanent White, mixing thoroughly. We need plenty of this color.

Pale Blue: Take two dabs of the blue color and mix with a dab of Permanent White.

SUPPLIES

Brushes: Fine round, small round

Paint Colors: Burnt Umber, Cadmium Yellow, Opera Pink, Permanent White, Ultramarine

Other Supplies: Pencil and eraser, scratch paper, fine tool for scraping—a blunted cocktail stick would work!

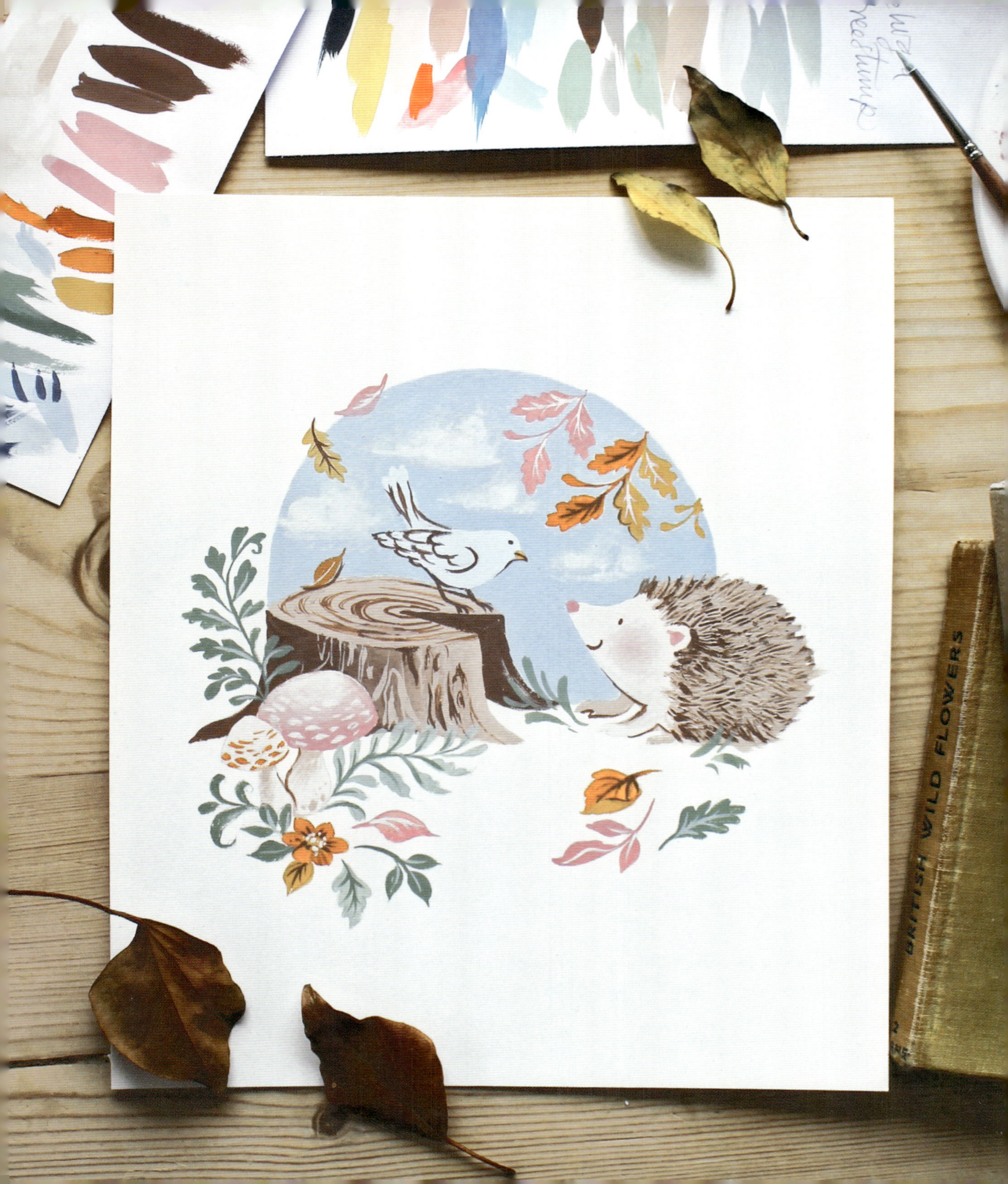
BRITISH WILD FLOWERS

Step 1: Drawing the Scene

1

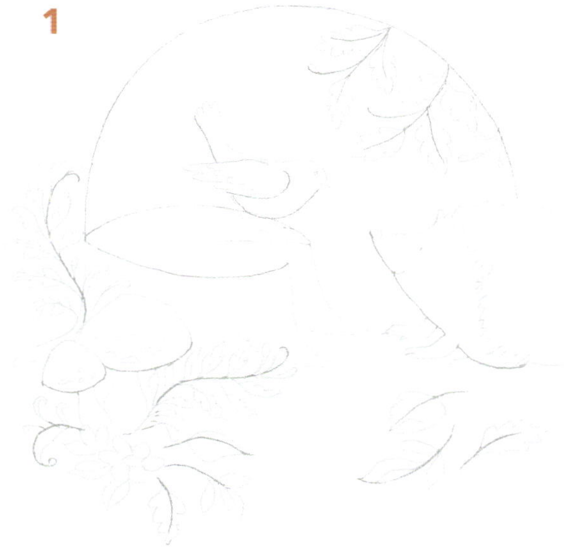

I suggest using sturdy watercolor paper for this one as we will be loading and scraping the paint. Using my image as a reference, begin by drawing the flattened ellipse of the tree trunk top. Take a slice out as you might from a pie, erasing the gap. From each of the three appropriate points, draw a line going down toward the ground and then curving out, suggesting roots.

Draw in the curve of the hedgehog's chest, his little pointed face and a big semicircle for the prickles on his back and then fill in details such as ear, nose, eyes, mouth and little feet. Perched lightly atop the trunk, draw in a little curve for the birdie's chest and fill in the details.

From the left side of the trunk to the middle of the hedgehog's back, draw in a semicircular dome. Add a few oak leaves hanging from the underside of this dome, just above the hedgehog to suggest the branches of a tree.

In the foreground, draw in the mushrooms, from which curl two ferns and scatter a few little flowers and leaves on the ground. Take a picture of the drawing and keep it handy as it will be a useful reference when painting in some of the thicker layers.

2a

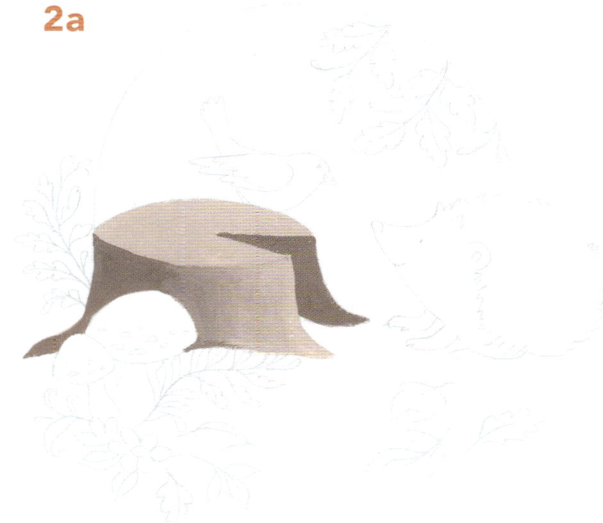

Step 2: The Tree Stump

Using only a little water and paint of an opaque, dryish consistency, use a small round brush to paint in the top of the tree stump with the pale brown color, using circular strokes. Again, with the pale brown, paint in half of the trunk from the right side in vertical strokes and, while the paint is still wet, paint the dark brown from the left, the two colors meeting and blending in the middle. Paint the 'v' area behind in the dark brown.

Paint both the mushroom stalks and the cap of the smaller one in the light taupe. Paint the bottom of the larger cap in the pink and the top in light taupe, blending as they meet.

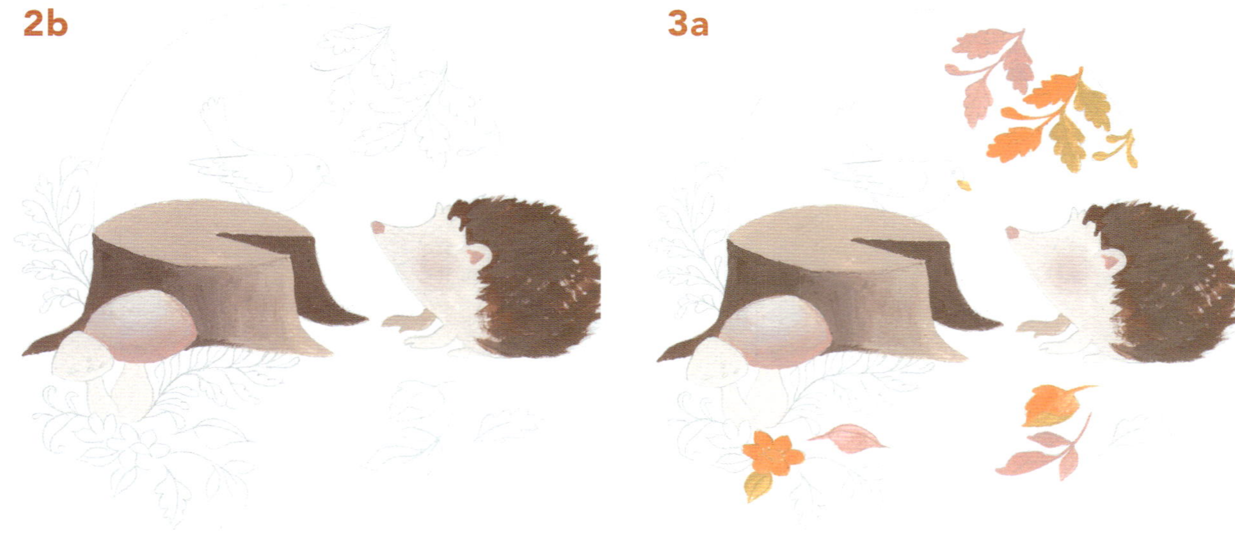

Turn your attention to our little hedgehog and paint his face, front paw and ear an opaque light taupe and, while his face is still wet, use a tiny touch of the pink to blend a little circular blush on his cheek. His nose and inside ear are also pink and his rear paw is pale brown. Cover all his spines in the dark brown color with scratchy spiky short strokes.

Step 3: Leaves & Flowers

For this step, we will be painting in the hanging oak leaves, leaving some to rest on the ground.

Working from left to right, paint the first hanging sprig pink, the left half of the second in the burnt orange and the other half and remaining sprig in the dark yellow. Paint the center of the flowers and the birdie's beak also in dark yellow. Paint a few of the leaves on the ground in a variety of colors and paint the flower in the burnt orange color.

The consistency of the dark green should be fluid and yet completely opaque. Paint in the large curling fern to the left of the trunk, overlapping the trunk so that the lines will no longer be visible and add a few curling leaves on the ground.

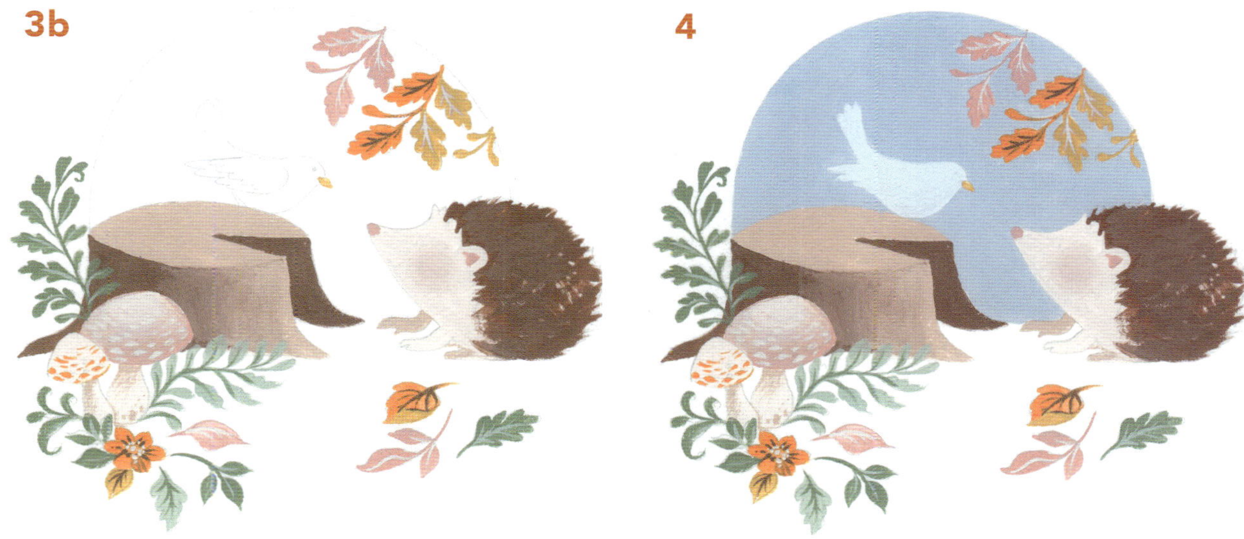

Paint in the other large fern and remaining leaf in pale green. When dry and using my image for reference, use a fine round brush to add contrasting color details for the leaf veins—pale-on-dark and dark-on-pale.

Add little spotty details on the mushroom caps in burnt orange and light taupe. Paint the veins of the pink, burnt orange and dark yellow leaves in a contrasting mix of light taupe and dark brown. Leave everything to dry thoroughly!

Step 4: The Blue Sky & Birdie

In this step, we will paint the blue of the sky and the birdie. Add plenty of water to form a fluid yet opaque consistency and with a steady hand and a small round brush, carefully paint around the inside edge of the dome and around all the little painted details it contains, such as the leaves, the birdie and the hedgehog. The paint should dry in a matte, even layer with no texture.

Using a touch of water, paint the birdie in the pale blue color.

5

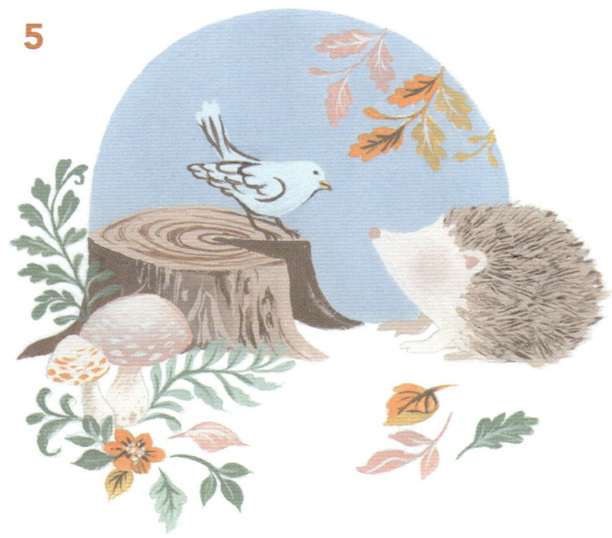

6

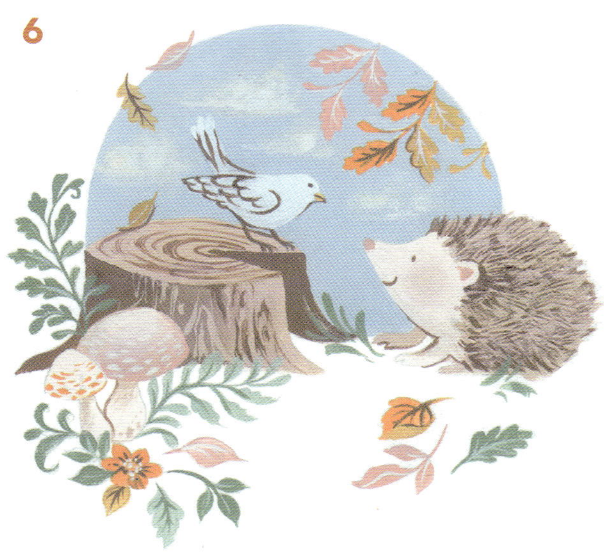

Step 5: Hedgehog Prickles & Dark Brown Details

Here we go with the scratching technique—have your tool handy as you will be moving fast! Make sure you have plenty of the pale brown color mixed and that it is still thick and wet. Using a small round brush and with rough spiky strokes, cover the hedgehog's whole back with a thick layer of pale brown, obscuring the dark brown underneath. When you meet his face, add little strokes overlapping the lighter taupe. While the paint is still wet, cover his back in short, scratched prickles, using your scratching tool and my design as a reference. Leave to dry, which will take longer than normal because the paint is thick.

In the meantime, using a dry fine round brush and a little dark brown, add in the concentric rings of the tree. Using a mix of the light taupe and dark brown colors, paint in short wiggly lines for the bark texture so that they contrast on the trunk.

For the birdie detailing, use more of the dark brown. Refreshing your memory with your drawing image, paint the eye and wing details on the little bird.

Step 6: Fine Details

With the dark brown, add a few 'v'-shaped strokes on the hedgehog's back to give it real depth and a feel of 'prickliness!' Don't forget a dot for his eyes and a tiny curved smiling mouth.

With a small round brush and no water, mix a small dab of the light taupe with a dab of white to lighten and paint a couple of strokes on scratch paper to remove excess paint. With the remaining color and in a light circular motion, paint in some fluffy-textured billowy clouds.

Use a touch of the mixed dark green to add a few light upward strokes suggesting grass on the ground around the hedgehog.

To finish the piece, use your creative intuition and add some pink, yellow and orange-colored freehand swirling leaves to add movement, as if there is a gust of wind on a blowy fall day!

TAKING THE PROJECT FURTHER:

Choose three of your favorite creatures and draw them seated on a blanket on the woodland floor with a teapot, little teacups and maybe even a plate of cake.

Songbird Nest

This project gives us an opportunity to be a little more spontaneous and imaginative. We will be improvising with a dry-brush technique to create a variety of twigs, leaves and flowers. Nests are a subject I go back to time after time and are infinitely variable, full of natural treasures. Think about how you might be able to personalize your design by entwining extra feathers, flowers, leaves or berries into the twigs.

COLOR MIXING

Medium Brown: Add several dabs of Burnt Umber and one dab of Yellow Ochre to a medium sized blob of Permanent White.

Off-White: Add a touch of Burnt Umber and an even smaller amount of Yellow Ochre to a little blob of Permanent White.

Turquoise: Mix equal amounts of Cobalt Turquoise Light and Permanent White together and then add in a speck each of Burnt Sienna and Burnt Umber.

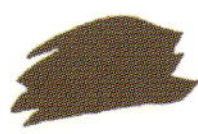

Dark Brown: Add a touch each of Yellow Ochre and Permanent White to a small blob of Burnt Umber.

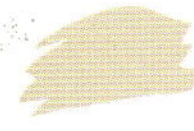

Light Ochre: Add a dab of Yellow Ochre to a larger dab of Permanent White, mixing carefully.

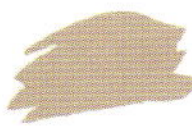

Warm Brown: Add a dab each of Burnt Sienna, Burnt Umber and Yellow Ochre to a couple of dabs of Permanent White.

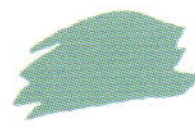

Bluey Green: Mix the color by adding a dab each of Ultramarine and Yellow Ochre to a couple of dabs of Cobalt Turquoise Light and three dabs of Permanent White.

Pale Green: Set aside a little bluey green and mix with a dab of Permanent White.

SUPPLIES

Brushes: Fine round, small round, small flat

Paint Colors: Burnt Sienna, Burnt Umber, Cobalt Turquoise Light, Permanent White, Yellow Ochre, Ultramarine

Other Supplies: Brown watercolor pencil and eraser, scratch paper

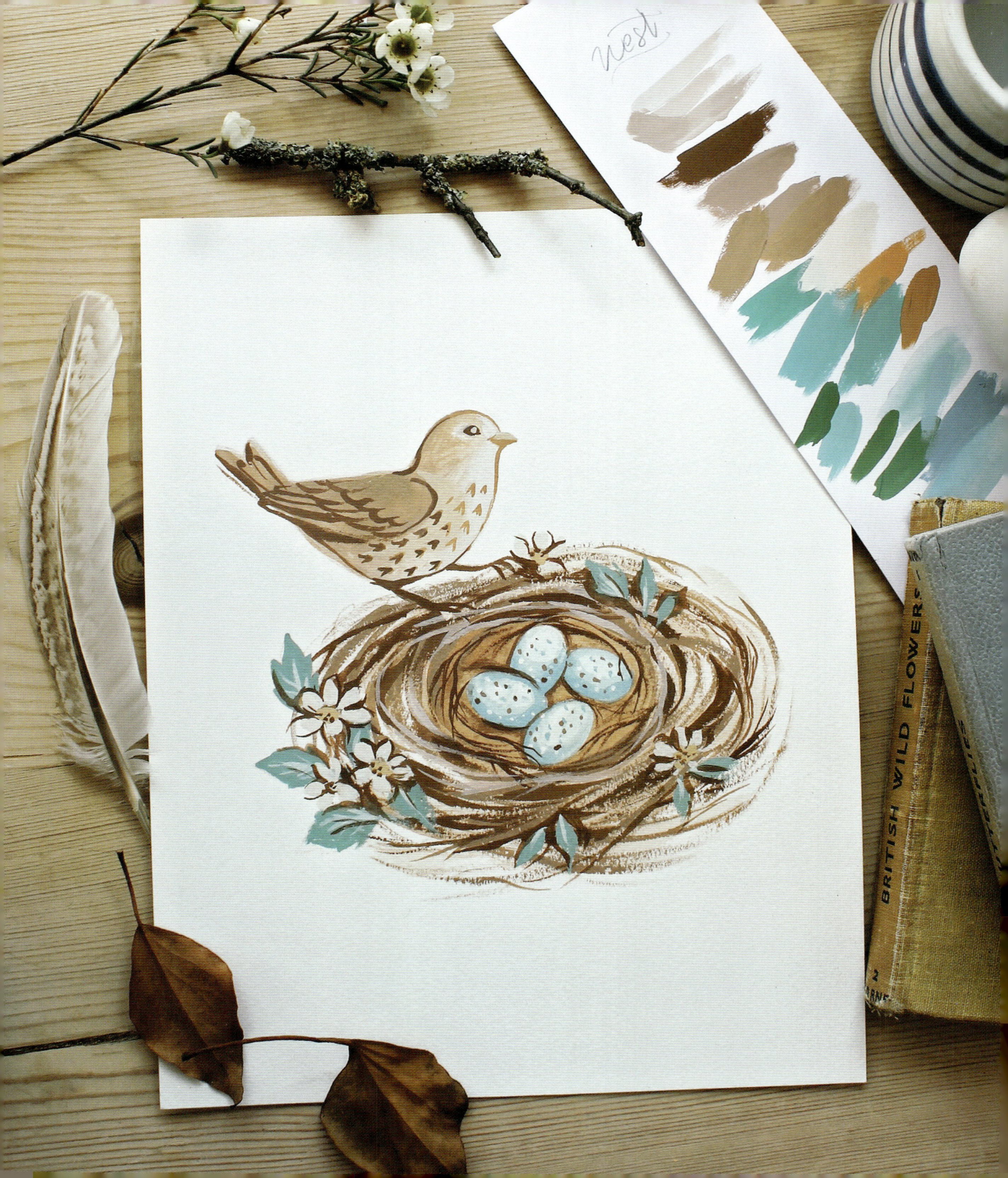
nest
BRITISH WILD FLOWERS

1

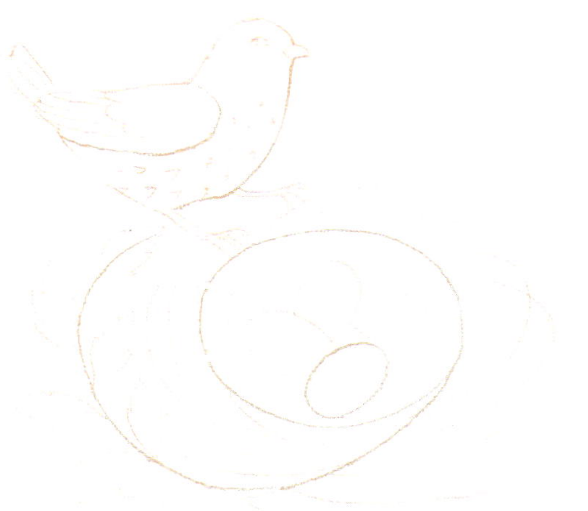

2

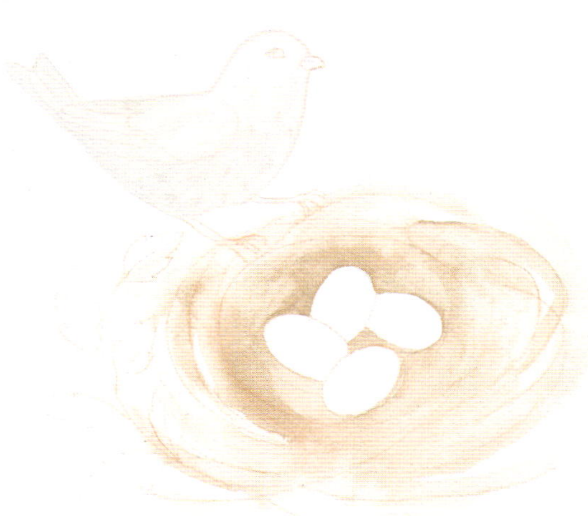

Step 1: Drawing the Nest & Bird

Using a brown watercolor pencil and, if you like, my darker guidelines as a reference, draw a smallish oval shape to suggest the rim of the nest placed slightly to the right of the center of the page. Draw lots of loosely spiraling lines radiating out from the center of this oval, which will represent twigs. Draw in the leaves up and down the edges of one curling twig on the left.

In the center of the nest, begin with the nearest egg, placing the others behind each other, working in a clockwise fashion.

Next, move on to our little songbird, again using my slightly darker guidelines as a reference. Draw a large, curved semicircle from under where the beak will be round to below the tail feathers. Draw in the beak and then continue up, over and down along his back, fanning out at an angle for the tail feathers. Draw in the pointed wing tip and the details across his body—the eye, wing, tail feathers and speckled triangular-shaped patterns on his breast.

Step 2: Washy Underpainting

The colors in this piece will be applied using a mix of both washy and dry textured paint to give a dense twiggy feel. Use a little of the medium brown color for the first washy layer. Using a small flat brush, dab a little of the color in a well with a couple of dabs of water to create a semi-transparent consistency. In the center of the nest, using the narrower and wider edges of the edge of the brush as necessary, carefully paint around the eggs, leaving them white. Following the swirly lines of the nest, paint outward without worrying too much about leaving a messy edge.

While this is drying we will paint in the bird with off-white. Add a touch of water so that the consistency is slightly opaque and paint the whole body with even coverage, leaving the drawn lines just about visible through the paint.

3a

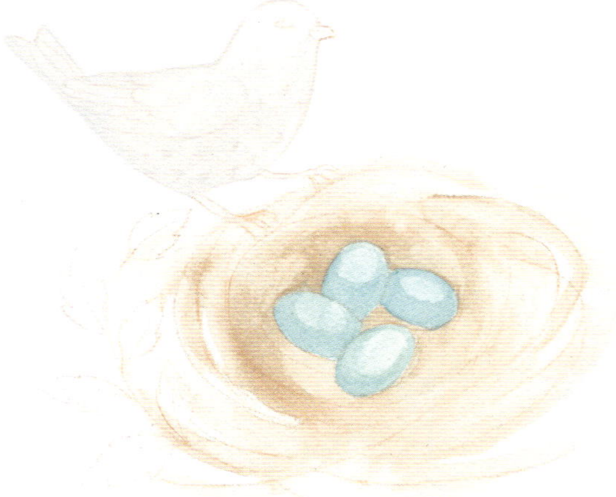

3b

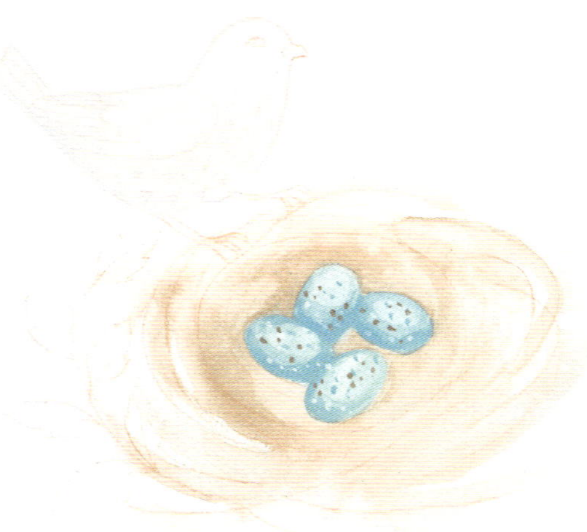

Step 3: The Eggs

Water down a little of the turquoise paint to create a very transparent consistency and cover the eggs lightly, leaving to dry. We will be imagining that the light source is streaming down onto the nest from above, so we will add a little shadow to the eggs to give the sense of volume and the idea that they are nestled close together. Using a touch of the semi-opaque color, shade around the bottom half of the eggs, leaving an oval area unpainted and blending lightly into the first layer.

With a slightly smaller brush so that you have better control, repeat the turquoise shading again to give even more pronounced shading. Finish the eggs by adding some tiny speckles of opaque turquoise, medium brown and off-white over the top.

4a

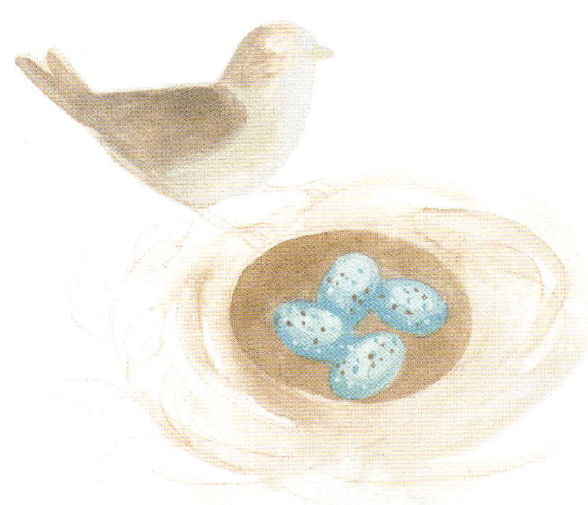

4b

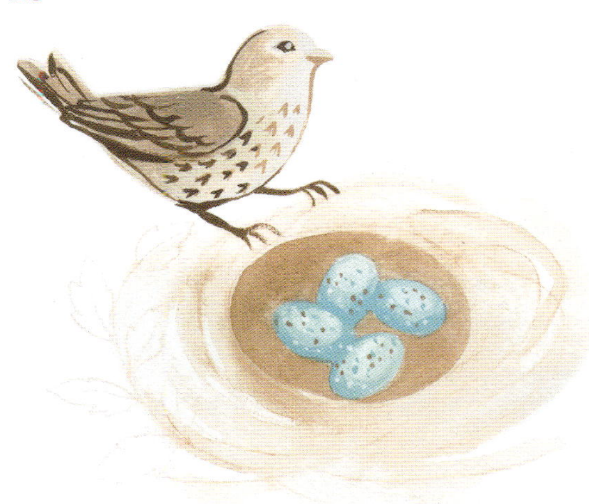

Step 4: The Birdie

Return your attention to the nest and use some watered-down dark brown to paint in an oval suggesting the shadowed center of the nest behind the eggs.

Now for the bird! Use a little light ochre to paint over some of the breast around the front of the wing and the beak.

Dabbing a touch of fluid yet opaque medium brown color on a small round brush, paint the wing, tail and the back of the head, leaving around the eye and all down the right side of the breast unpainted. Use a little of the off-white and a touch of water to blend the dry the medium brown into an ombré across his body. Leave it to dry.

We will use a little warm brown for the bird's detailing. Add speckles like upside down 'v's all over his breast and to paint the bottom of the beak, add a line from the beak both down the front of his chest and over his head to his back.

Paint in the eye with a little dark brown and add an off-white highlighted dot.

Again, using dark brown, paint the details on the wing and tail feathers using narrow linear strokes, as well as a few chest details. Paint in the little legs and three claws on each leg.

Step 5: The Twiggy Nest

In this stage, we will really be going to town with all the lovely twiggy details. Return to the medium brown you mixed originally and load your small round brush with some of the color and only the slightest touch of water so that it is dry and opaque.

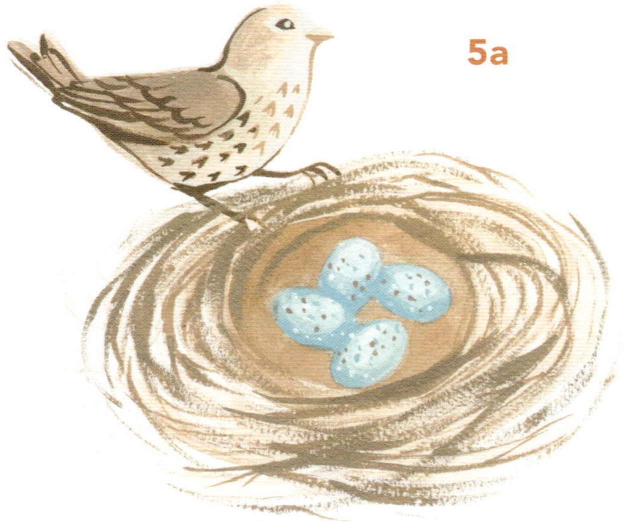

Tip: *Try practicing a couple of twiggy strokes on some scratch paper before you begin, varying the weight of the line so that it alternates between thick and thin while also curving to follow the contours of the nest. We are aiming for a dry-brush technique where the bristle marks are still visible.*

From the nest's circular rim and progressing out, paint in the twigs to form 'Y'-shaped pointy-ended twigs. To create dynamic movement, follow the contours of the nest in an uneven circular motion, with extra little twiglets poking in and out of the other branches. When you reach the edge of the nest, make them slightly sparser, covering up some but not all of the original wash.

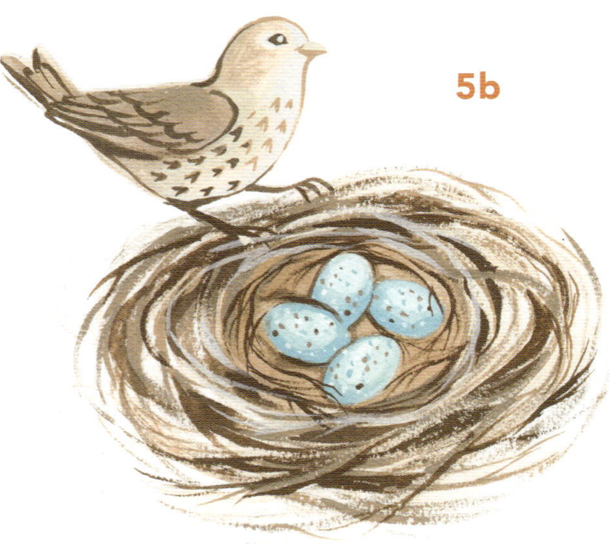

Using a little dark brown, roughly outline the eggs and add a few dark speckles. Paint in some of the gaps between the branches with this color, following the lighter lines as if you are creating shadows on the underside of some of the twigs. Add a few new twigs here and there to give variety and contrast.

Using a little of the opaque dark brown color on your fine round brush, paint in a few 'Y'-shaped twiggy lines over the shadowed center of the nest, some lightly overlapping the eggs.

Using a tiny bit of the off-white, paint some highlights over the twigs at the rim of the nest as if they are catching some of the light.

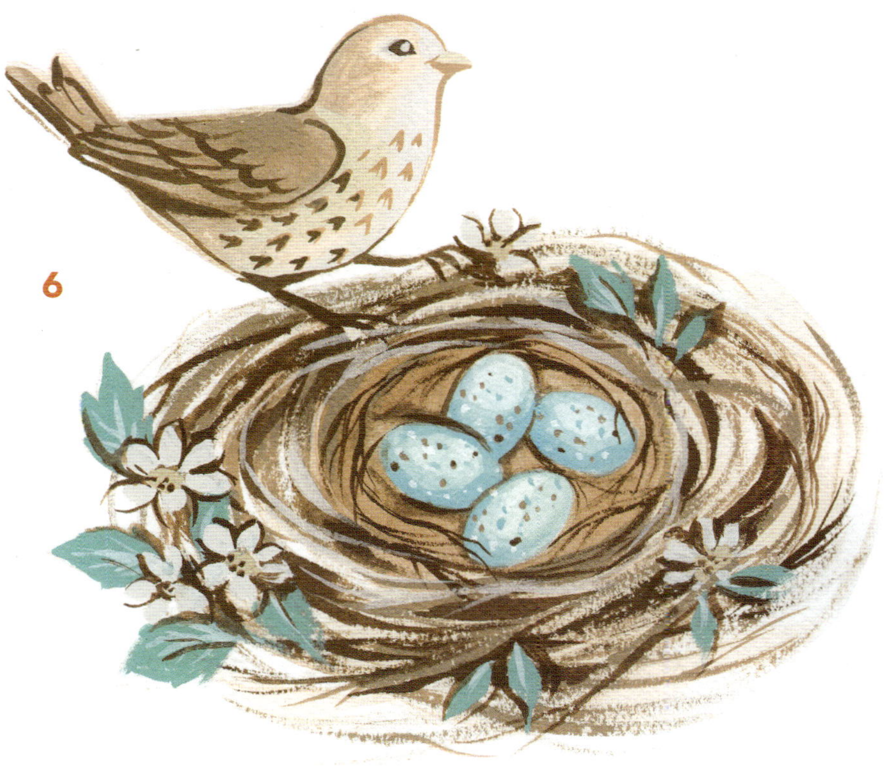

Step 6: Leaves & Flowers

To finish the piece, we will use the bluey green for the leaves that will be entwined in the twiggy branches. Keep a completely opaque consistency by adding barely any water and paint in the drawn leaves, adding a few extra leaves freehand here and there.

Use a tiny amount of the pale green tint to draw in the leaves' vein details with a fine round (spot if you have one) brush. Using a small round brush, improvise a few little off-white and light ochre flowers nestling in the branches and leaves.

Use the dark brown to paint a little shadow behind the flowers and leaves so that they don't look like they are floating on the nest.

TAKING THE PROJECT FURTHER:

Nests are essentially tiny natural homes and are therefore infinitely and wonderfully variable. You could choose to paint whole birdie families from the adults down to the chicks, fledglings, hatchlings and eggs!

Think about what season your nest suits. Is it a spring nest surrounded by soft blossoms? A verdant green nest using the bright fresh colors of summer flowers? Or a leafy fall nest with the gorgeous palette of leaves and fruits turning rusty? You could try a Scandinavian minimal winter nest with bare branches and the tiniest pop of red or pink berries.

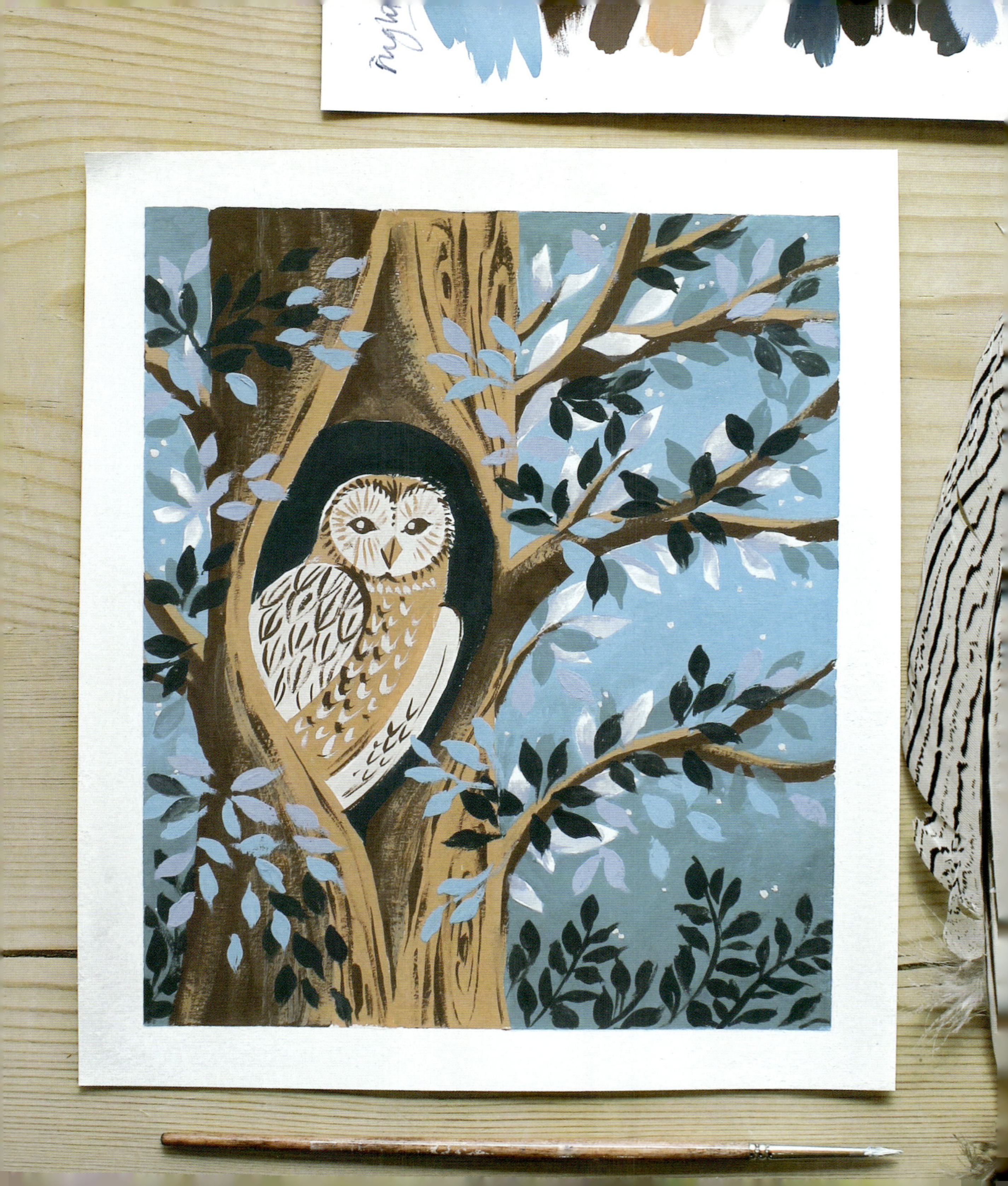

Twilight Owl

The final project in this chapter is a fully painted scene using a few techniques to evoke the sense of twilight in the forest. Owls are such textured and characterful creatures to paint and this scene aims to create a strong sense of his presence. It's also a deceptively simple technique of layering light on dark and dark on light, which we will unpack step by step. The shades of blue and brown here are just a wonderfully harmonious color combination and it is the color that brings this piece to life.

COLOR MIXING

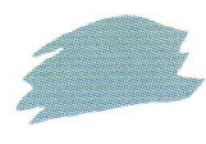

Light Turquoise: Add a small blob each of Permanent White and Phthalo Blue to two dabs each of Yellow Ochre and Burnt Umber.

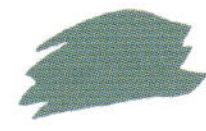

Dark Turquoise: Add two dabs each of Burnt Umber and Permanent White, one dab of Yellow Ochre and a small blob of Phthalo Blue and mix together.

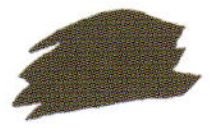

Dark Brown: Combine a medium sized blob of Burnt Umber, two large dabs of Ivory Black and four large dabs of Permanent White.

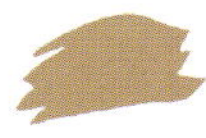

Warm Brown: Mix a small blob each of Burnt Sienna and Burnt Umber with a slightly larger blob of Permanent White.

Light Taupe: Add a dab of Burnt Umber to a small blob of Permanent White and mix thoroughly.

Blueish Gray: Mix a small blob each of Permanent White and Ultramarine with a dab each of Burnt Umber and Ivory Black.

Dark Charcoal: Mix a small blob of Phthalo Blue and a slightly smaller blob of Burnt Umber together with a dab of Permanent White.

SUPPLIES

Brushes: Fine round, small flat, small round

Paint Colors: Burnt Sienna, Burnt Umber, Ivory Black, Permanent White, Phthalo Blue, Ultramarine, Yellow Ochre

Other Supplies: Ruler, pencil and eraser, scratch paper

1

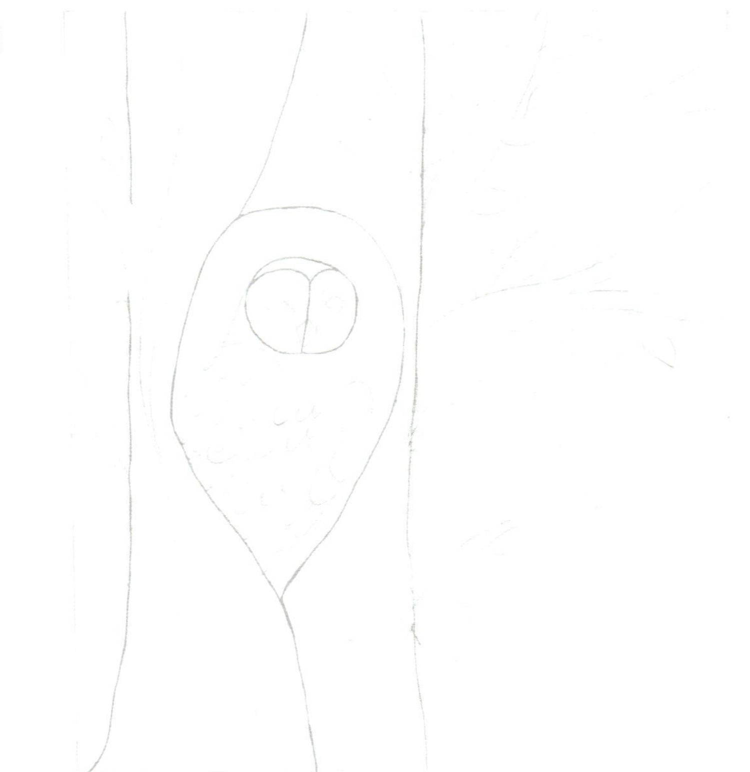

Step 1: Drawing the Scene

As this is a fully painted scene, we will contain the design and give it crisp edges by measuring out a rectangle with a ruler and then applying masking tape to form a frame.

Draw one vertical line down the length of the page, just a smidge to the right of the center, for one side of the trunk and another a finger width in from the left edge of the frame. From almost the center of the page, draw two close parallel lines to form a branch curving up to the right, branching out in a 'v' when halfway to the edge of the page. Draw in branches above and below, also ending in tapered 'v's and three curving upward on the left of the trunk.

Using the darker lines in my design as a reference, draw in the shape for the owl's hole. This is really two shapes, the pointed oval of the actual hole, then the rough triangle above and the other lines sweeping down alongside the hole and continuing below to the bottom of the page.

The owl nestles in his hole, so draw a flattened oval for the owl's head and divide his face with a line down the middle and a curved 'v'-shaped hairline. He has two roundish almond-shaped eyes with circles in the centers and a narrow diamond-shaped beak. Next, draw in two lines for the sides of his body. The wing on the left is a simple semicircle shape, with another peeping from the right side.

We will be painting over the leaves, so take a quick photo as a reference for later steps.

2

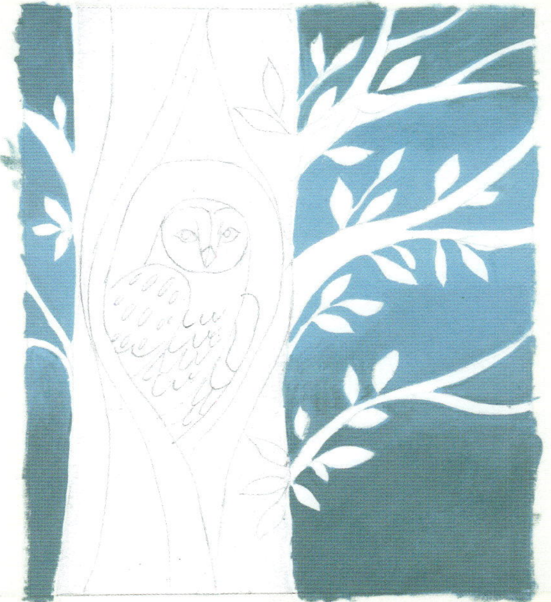

3a

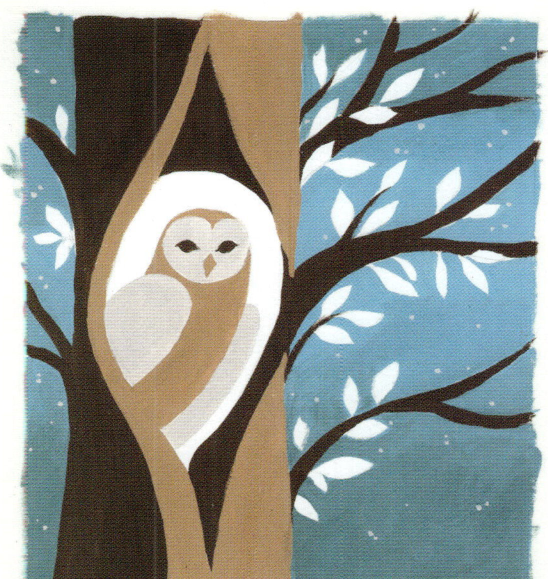

Step 2: The Sky

First, we will blend the light and dark turquoise blue into an ombré for the sky. The branches and leaves are a bit of a pain as they are in the way but have patience! Work around them, leaving them unpainted until the next step. Using a small flat brush and a thick opaque consistency, begin below the central branch on the right, painting in the light turquoise down to the bottom of the page. Working quickly while the paint is still wet, load your brush with the dark turquoise shade and work from the bottom of the page to about a third of the way up, blending as you go with light strokes. Repeat this above the middle branch, but this time with the dark turquoise shade coming down from the top. Repeat on the little sliver of sky on the left of the tree trunk. The end result should be a dark-light-dark turquoise sandwich!

Step 3: Block Color on Tree & Owl

We will be using several shades of brown for the tree and our friendly owl. Using a small flat brush, paint in the majority of the tree with dark brown, excluding the following areas—the owl's hole, the thin strip that runs to the left of the owl's hole and the top and bottom right-hand section of the tree.

The next layer is a warm brown. This color will form the base of the owl's chest and some of the tree trunk and branches. Paint in the remaining unpainted areas of the trunk. Using a small round brush, add highlights to the top of the narrower branches. Turn to the owl and paint in his body and the little 'v' above his face.

Use the light taupe to paint in the owl's face and both wings. Swapping to a fine round brush, add little stippled dots across the sky areas to suggest a starry night. Use a little of the dark brown to paint in the owl's eyes.

3b

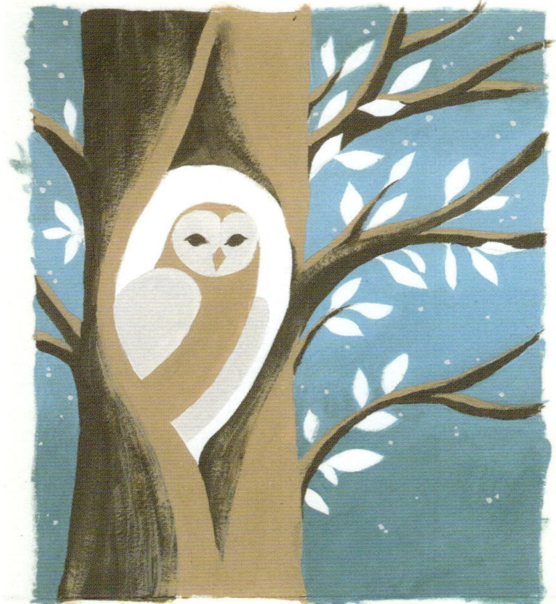

3c

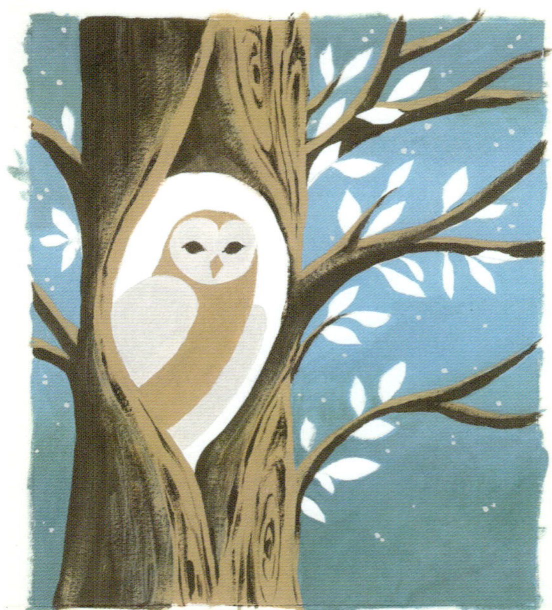

Using the thin edge of the flat brush, paint a little warm brown in single strokes as highlights along the top edge of each of the branches.

Next, load a little of the color on the brush and then remove most of it on some scratch paper, using the resulting dry brush to paint some textured strokes on the dark brown areas of the trunk.

Next, we will be adding line details to the tree to build texture and three-dimensionality. Return to the fine round brush and load with dark brown paint and no water to again create a dry textured line. Painting only on the warm brown areas and with several short strokes, roughly outline the pointy almond shape of the owl's hole. Up and down the warm brown, paint in a rough bark pattern, starting with little round knots and then radiating out in long concentric ovals and lines as you might see in the rings of a tree.

4

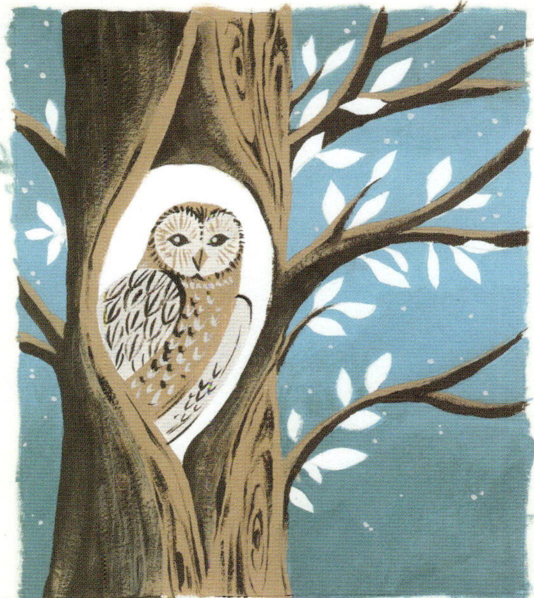

5a

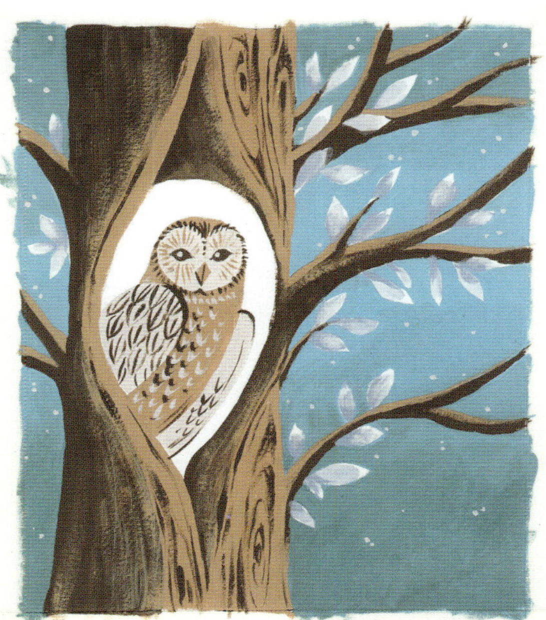

Step 4: Owl Details

Turn your attention to bringing the owl to life in his tree. Using a fine round brush and the warm brown, add tiny line details radiating out from each of the eyes. Use a little of the light taupe to paint in tiny 'u'-shaped feathers on the chest, a dotty collar on his neck and round dots on the eyes—these dots are slightly offset to the left of the center of each eye.

Add tiny dark brown radiating lines to outline the face and shadow of the beak. Paint in detailed feathers on the wings and over some of the lighter feathers from left to right on the chest.

Step 5: The Leaves

In this step, we will be playing with a variety of light and dark colors to create a silhouetted leafy shelter for our owl. The shape of the leaves will be traditional pointed oval almond-shaped leaves, but you can slightly vary these by making some flat, some curled, some on their side or foreshortened. Vary the pressure you apply to the brush to create variety.

The first step is to add color to the unpainted white leaves by adding a watery wash of blueish gray to suggest dappled moonlight. Using a small round brush, paint in the unpainted leaf shapes with a semi-opaque wash, being careful not to bleed into the sky.

5b

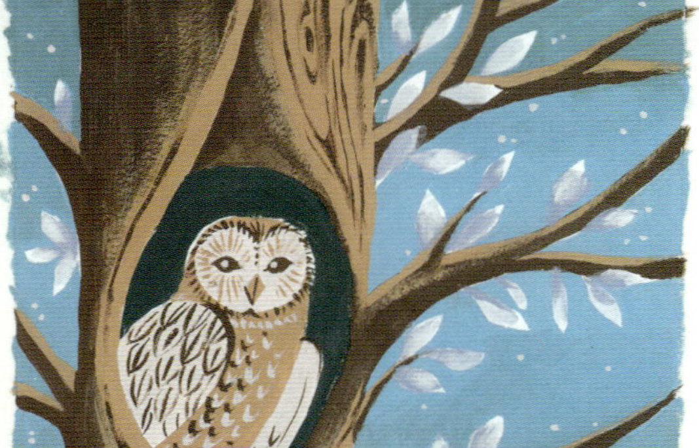

5c

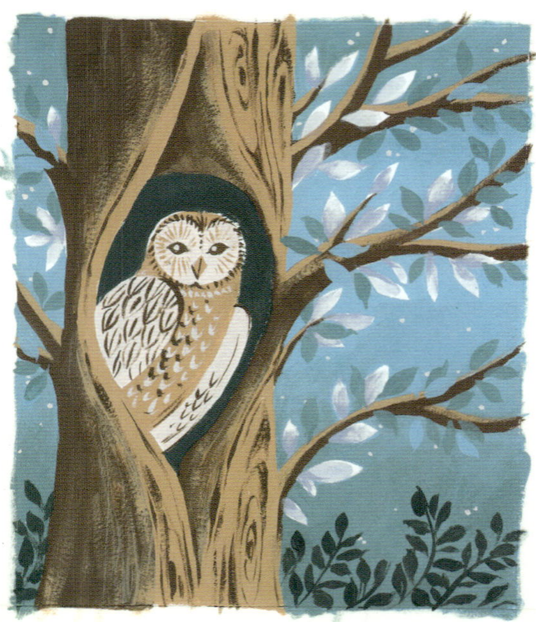

Next, we will start to add dark details to create the atmosphere of a night scene. Use your dark charcoal to paint in the hole behind the owl.

Paint in four little curved stems coming up from the bottom of the piece and add traditional almond-shaped leaves up and down each line, to suggest the silhouette of branches below.

Now we will paint some light-on-dark details, so make the consistency of the paint fluid but opaque, using very little water. Reactivate the light and dark turquoise colors used for the night sky. Working up and down the branches on the tree, paint in some light-on-dark and dark-on-light leaves with the two colors. Think of the trunk, branches and sky as the background and this layer of leaves as the midground, before we add the foreground leafy details.

5d

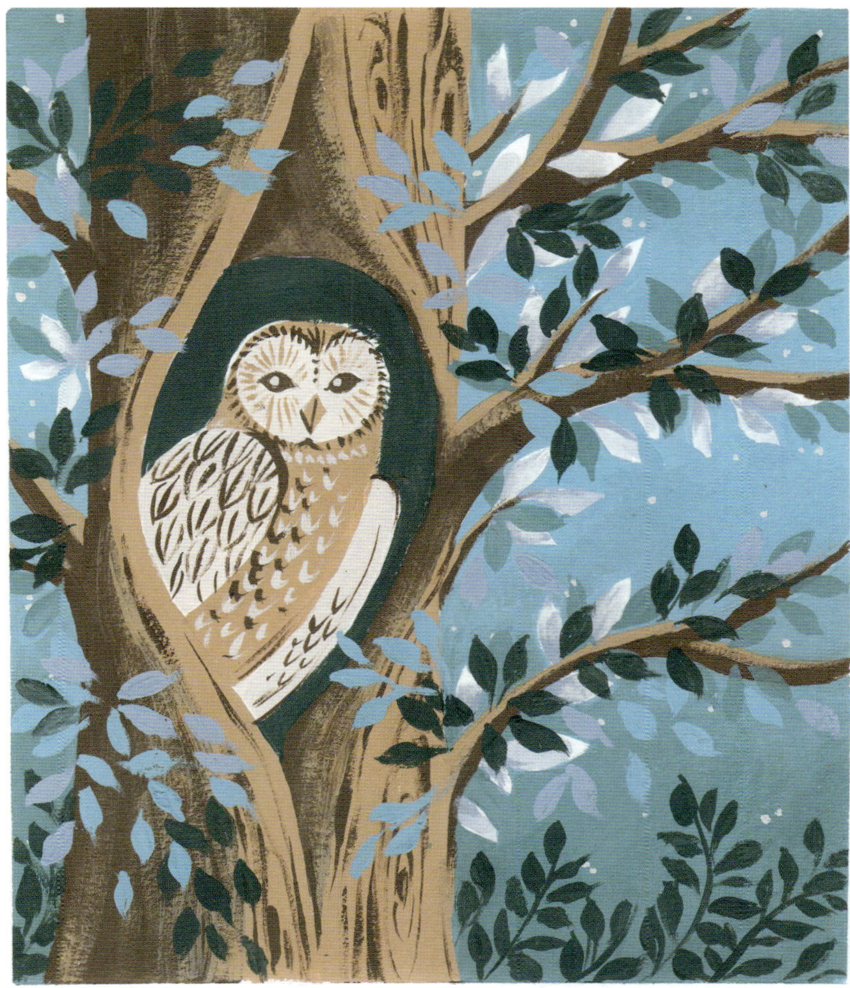

Next, focus on layering some darker leaves using the mixed dark charcoal. Work up and down the branches, varying the direction that the leaves are pointing, including a few overlapping onto the tree trunk. In the bottom left of the trunk, paint in a little cluster of leaves as if they are blowing right across.

Next, turn to the light turquoise and add a few leaves above as well as several up and down, all over the painted trunk.

Lastly, add several opaque blueish gray leaves here and there to tie the piece together. Peel the tape off carefully, leaving a lovely crisp edge.

Acknowledgments & Thanks

My heartfelt love and thanks to my lovely husband Tom for walking with me each step of this journey, for meticulously reading every single page several times and removing hundreds of commas—I couldn't have done any of this without you.

My dear friend Camilla for her unfailing support and positivity, as well as the care she took to paint samples and read my proofs.

My wonderfully supportive family and friends, in particular my parents Peter and Jean and my patient little babas Rose, Theo and Toby. Our lovely Oma Rosi for her thorough proofing of my final manuscript. Also Dominic, Rachel, Clare and Hannah for cheering and chivvying me along!

The marvelous team at Page Street, particularly my editors Lauren Knowles and Sarah Monroe. Thanks also to my copyeditor Colleen Smith and Creative Director Meg Baskis.

Winsor & Newton for supplying all the paints.

Lastly, thanks to the wonderful gang of creative folk who have supported me so very much over the past few years in my business and personal creative journey, especially on Instagram—you inspired this book and I so hope you enjoy it.

About the Author

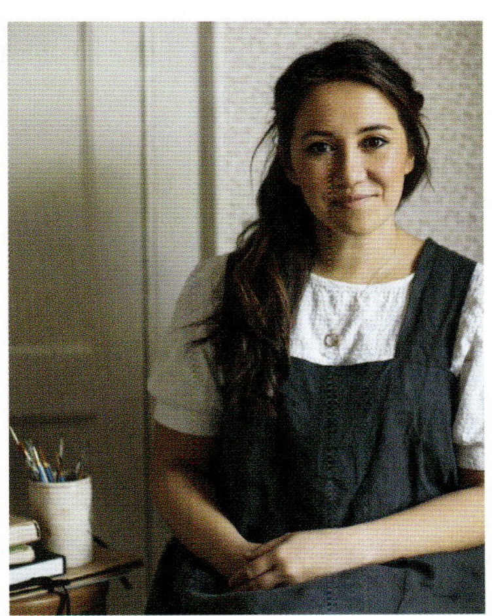

Clare is a surface pattern designer and illustrator inspired by the natural environment of her rural Hampshire surroundings, where she lives and works on a farm with her husband and young family. After studying Painting at Art School in Norwich, she went on to the Drawing Year at the Royal Drawing School where she focused on imaginative and observational drawing & printmaking. She then went on to develop design skills in London pattern design studios before launching a freelance career.

Clare creates surface pattern designs and illustrations for textiles, papercraft collections, packaging and homewares. Aside from pattern designs, she takes on project-based collaborations with like-minded companies.

She has a passion for lino printing on paper and fabric and loves spending time in galleries drawing ceramics and paintings. Otherwise, she can often be found enjoying the English countryside with her family, growing and collecting flowers to dry and, of course, drawing and painting every single day.

You'll find a glimpse of her studio life almost daily on Instagram @claretheresegray. Connect with your own artwork using the hashtag #paintwithclare.

Index